ALSO BY BETHENNY FRANKEL

Naturally Thin

The Skinnygirl Dish

A Place of Yes

10 Rules for Getting Everything You Want Out of Life

❧

Bethenny Frankel

with Eve Adamson

A TOUCHSTONE BOOK

Published by Simon & Schuster

New York London Toronto Sydney New Delhi

Touchstone

A Division of Simon & Schuster, Inc.

1230 Avenue of the Americas

New York, NY 10020

First Touchstone trade paperback edition December 2011

TOUCHSTONE and colophon are registered trademarks of Simon & Schuster, Inc.

For information about special discounts for bulk purchases,
please contact Simon & Schuster Special Sales at
1-866-506-1949 or business@simonandschuster.com.

The Simon & Schuster Speakers Bureau can bring authors to your live event.
For more information or to book an event contact the Simon & Schuster Speakers
Bureau at 1-866-248-3049 or visit our website at www.simonspeakers.com.

Designed Joy O'Meara

Manufactured in the United States of America

1   3   5   7   9   10   8   6   4   2

Library of Congress has cataloged the hardcover edition as follows:
Frankel, Bethenny.
A place of yes : 10 rules for getting everything you want out of life /
by Bethenny Frankel, with Eve Adamson.
p. cm.
1. Self-actualization (Psychology).   2. Self-realization.
3. Self-defeating behavior.   4. Success.   5. Frankel, Bethenny.
I. Adamson, Eve.   II. Title.
BF637.S4F723 2011
646.7—dc22   2010050090

ISBN 978-1-4391-8690-9
ISBN 978-1-4391-8691-6 (pbk)
ISBN 978-1-4391-8692-3 (ebook)

This book is dedicated to you:

my passionate, fearless, inappropriate,
supportive, caring, hilarious fans.

You go for it, you want more, you believe in yourselves
and in the fight and you know that good enough
simply isn't good enough.

You have come into my life and allowed me to come into yours.
Everything I do is to show you that anything and everything
is possible, and we will get there together.

Trust this book, love yourself,
and allow yourself to live the life
you always dreamed of.

Contents

Contents

Introduction

Who I Am, What This Book Is About, and What You Need to Know Before You Begin

*M*y parents make me crazy. I'll be stuck in this job for the rest of my life. I can't stop spending money. I'll never find the perfect guy so I might as well just settle. I don't care if I end up single, I'd rather be alone. Why do I get so irritated at my husband? I can't stop eating. I'll never get in shape, so why bother? I don't spend enough time with my kids, am I a bad mother? Why can't I get organized? I can't sleep. I have no self-control. Did I sell out? My life is not what I once thought it could be. Maybe I should just accept that I can't have it all.

Does any of this sound familiar? If you have any of these thoughts, if you look at your life and you think, "Is this as good as it gets?" or even if you don't really want to look under your hood because you're afraid of letting thoughts like this come out, then this book is for you.

A Place of Yes is about how to stop saying no and start saying yes to your own life. It's about how to get unstuck and start moving forward with vision and a plan and the guts to tackle any obstacles that get in your way. It's about looking, really looking at your life, then rolling up your sleeves and getting your hands dirty and making it into the life you really want.

It's easy to say no, to say "I can't," to expect the worst, and doubt yourself. Expecting the worst feels safer because when you fail, you won't be disappointed.

But your life can be better than "just good enough." It can be amazing. You can be more successful, more fulfilled, healthier, and happier than you are right now.

I know what it's like to think some of these negative thoughts and worse. Believe me, it has been a long road to where I am today. I've cried, pounded the pavement, picked myself up and brushed myself off time and again. I know what it's like to doubt myself and feel out of control. I know what it's like to go for weeks without a good night's sleep. Many times, I've just wanted to give up. But I have also figured out how to conquer the noise in my head that holds me back and tells me I don't deserve everything good in my life. I've learned to listen to the voice inside that shows me the path forward and gives me a push. I've learned how to come from a place of yes, and it continues to be a worthwhile struggle every day of my life. Make no mistake—it is hard, but it makes my life better. It has made my life what it is today.

Fear, doubt, and defaulting to *no* are the reasons why so few people end up where they really want to be. Life is easier when you settle for less than your dreams, but "good enough" is not good enough for me. Is it really good enough for you? Most people don't bother trying to go all the way with their lives. They are afraid, or they just don't believe they can have anything better than they have now.

But you are reading this book, so I already know you want to come from a place of yes. I already know you want something more than settling for just okay.

A Place of Yes is your road map to changing the way you do things and to taking action when "good enough" isn't good enough. Coming from a place of yes can color everything else you do. No matter who you are and what you do in life, it will transform you. It's like upgraded software for your life. It will change your world.

My name is Bethenny Frankel, and you might know me from my first book, *Naturally Thin,* or from my second book, *The Skinnygirl Dish.* You might know me from *The Real Housewives of New York City,* or from *Martha Stewart: Apprentice,* or from my own shows, *Bethenny's Getting Married?* and *Bethenny Ever After.* Maybe you've seen me on *Skating with the Stars,* or tried my Skinnygirl cocktails, or seen my column in *Health* magazine, or seen me on the cover of a magazine.

Or maybe you've never heard of me at all but picked up this book because the title intrigued you and your interest was piqued by the promise on the cover. Frankly, it doesn't matter whether you've heard of me or not. You're here, and I'm here, and if you are reading this, we're in this journey together. We may not have started in the same place, but we can walk together for a while, and I bet we'll all be better for the company.

This book isn't a memoir. I'm not Barbara Walters. I haven't lived long enough to write my autobiography. I can't yet look back on my life with that kind of wisdom because my life is, in many ways, just getting started. I've still got a lot to do, and I'm the first to admit that I am still very flawed.

This is just my story so far, coupled with my advice to you, because while my life isn't over yet, I've come a long way, and I've learned a lot, and I hope to inspire you and help save you from some of the mistakes I've made in the past. So, while I will share my story with you, I do so with the knowledge that my story isn't nearly finished.

Not only is my story not finished, but it keeps changing, right out from under my nose, just as yours will. I wrote this book not once, not twice, but three times. I threw one version into the BBQ because it wasn't me. It didn't reflect me anymore. My life had changed so drastically, *as I was writing it,* that I needed to start all over again.

But that's also exactly in keeping with my story, and with the rules I've developed for getting what you want out of your own life. Sometimes you do have to start again, and you can do it over and over. When you find you are off track or your actions aren't in line with your true nature, you change course. You start again. It's never wrong. It's just what is.

I started this book again, and this is the new result. I wrote this book for all of you, as a way to thank you for all the love and support you've given me over the years. I've come a long way, in my forty-something years, but you've helped me to be a better wife, a better mother, a better *person*. You've inspired me in ways I never could have imagined, so I feel humbled and grateful to have this opportunity to share my experiences with you.

You've showed me yours. Now I'll show you mine.

I believe that some of what I've learned can help you. I have some issues you probably don't have, and you probably have issues I don't have, but the ten rules I give you here can help anyone with whatever issues they face. Life evolves, and I keep learning and changing. I'm always in flux, and you are, too. There is no final resting place. Life is vibrant and in motion, always changing, throwing you off or clearing the way. Sometimes life will be difficult, and sometimes life will be easy, and at every moment, you have a choice. Which way do you want to go? Where are you going? How do you want to get there? Who are you becoming? Those are the questions you can answer best if you come from a place of yes.

I've gone through a lot of pain and climbed over a mountain of obstacles. Today I'm married to a man I adore, I'm a new mom head over heels in love with her baby girl, I'm a bestselling author and a television personality, and most important, I feel better—physically and mentally healthier—than I ever have in my life. I'm calm, centered, energized, and *happy*. Ten years ago, I never would have believed I would be here now.

And it came from a place of yes. One by one, goal by goal, I've managed to achieve the things I wanted to achieve to the best of my ability. It's been one step at a time, one goal to focus on and reach before setting my sights on the next one. It's been a process of closing doors and then opening new ones.

You can do this, too. To show you how, I have put together ten rules that describe what I do every day to keep moving forward. These rules have helped me break the cycle of self-defeating behavior and that inner noise that tries to hold me back. They apply to everything—health, money, work, friends, family, love, eating, dieting, and anything else we all struggle with in life. You can use these rules to break the cycles that limit you and stop the noise in your head that tells you *no*. Each chapter in this book will tackle one rule, showing you how I've used it in my life, and how you can use it in your life. The rules are:

1. Break the Chain
2. Find Your Truth
3. Act on It
4. Everything's Your Business
5. All Roads Lead to Rome
6. Go for Yours
7. Separate from the Pack
8. Own It
9. Come Together
10. Celebrate!

No matter who you are, these rules can work for you. Anyone can practice them, at any stage of life. Your dreams don't have to be out of reach, no matter what has happened to you before. You can move forward, one step at a time, if you focus on the next step and just go. I didn't always think I'd be able to do it. Sometimes I wanted to give up, but I didn't. I always kept coming back to myself and moving myself forward, and I believe that my success so far in life has been because of that internal drive to say yes instead of no.

I get many letters, emails, Facebook messages, and tweets from fans, and you ask me a lot of questions. You say that you relate to me, and I am here to tell you that I relate to you, too. We all have our obstacles, our pain, and our challenges. I've dated all sorts, run from happiness, endured bad jobs, suffered from bad friends, tortured myself with bad diets, all of it. We all get in our own way sometimes trying to move forward and get what we want.

I hear you. I read your messages and I know that many of you struggle with the same things that have plagued me—issues with body image and weight, relationships and family, money and career, beauty and self-esteem. Some of you are single and searching, some are newly married and struggling, some have new babies and are navigating those waters, some are struggling to get a better job, more supportive friends, a better *life*.

I get it. I'm right there with you, and that's why I'm sharing my story and the lessons I've learned so far. Whoever you are, no matter your circumstances, no matter your age or status or plans for your own life, I welcome you to *A Place of Yes*. This is the story of how I climbed out of a bad place (many times) and back into my own life, where I could finally achieve everything I had ever dreamed of. Sometimes it got worse before it got better, but it always got better, and it keeps on getting better every day. Because of a place of yes, I know it always will.

This is also a guide for your life, a guide that will show you how to do the same thing I have done: Say yes. With the ten rules in this book, you can take back control of your life and make it into whatever you want it to be. Use them to figure out where you are now, *who* you are now, where you are going, and how to get there from here. These are "point-A-to-point-B" rules that clear your path for your bigger, better, brighter future.

Unpacking a Place of Yes

Before I get into the ten rules that will teach you how to come from a place of yes in your life, let's define a few terms that will be integral to understanding the rules. First, let's talk about what a place of yes *isn't*.

Coming from a place of yes isn't just having a positive attitude, being an optimist, or being cheerful all the time. You don't have to see the glass as half full every second of the day. You don't even have to consider yourself an agreeable person. Hell, I'm in a crappy mood half the time, I'm a pain in the ass, and nobody would describe me as cheerful or agreeable.

And don't worry, it doesn't mean being a "yes man," agreeing to everything when you don't really agree, or saying yes to everything, like in the Jim Carrey movie *Yes Man*. In fact, sometimes, you have to say "No!" to come from a place of yes.

I'm not the kind of person who goes along with the crowd, nods and smiles, or compromises to avoid conflict. In fact, I try not to go along with crowd, I don't always see the silver lining, and I consider myself a realist. I'm definitely not a glass-half-full kind of person. Actually, I can sometimes be a shattered-glass kind of person. I guess I'm known for the occasional sharp or snarky comment (and that's an understatement), or taking the cynical perspective, and that's something I continue to work on in my life. However, I often walk the line between appropriate and inappropriate (my husband, Jason, says I dive right over it!). Oddly, that is a place of yes for me. It is my particular sense of humor, and also usually a reflection of what I really think.

The point is, the Optimist Club is not calling me to become an honorary member anytime soon. And that's fine. Coming from a place of yes is not the same as being an optimist.

Everybody has issues, problems, doubts, fears—and some people are just naturally more positive than other people. That has nothing to do with *this*. Even if you tend to be shy or abrasive or insecure or overly cautious or people often tell you to quit being so negative, you can learn to come from a place of yes.

A place of yes is an "It-will-happen-because-I'll-make-it-happen" kind of an attitude. And this is an "It-will-happen-because-you'll-make-it-happen" kind of a book. You won't always be in a place of yes. Bad things will happen. You'll get angry or depressed or negative. You'll doubt yourself and you'll sometimes be afraid. Occasionally, I utter the words, "I hate _____" (fill in the blank). Don't tell me there aren't days when you wake up and you just want to smack someone, and it would give you real joy to do it. I will not take the joy of thinking about it away from you.

I know what it feels like when your husband or your boyfriend leaves you all weekend to play golf or lies there like a corpse on the couch, his lazy ass watching football while you are cleaning the whole house. Does he sit in bed eating and farting, or flip the channels for twenty minutes, only to stop at the Victoria's Secret commercial as you sit next to him, eight months pregnant with hairy armpits? (Hmm, that sounds awfully familiar . . .) I've been annoyed by the loud breathing from someone behind me in a checkout line, by the instrumental music in a department store, by nosy people, rude waiters, or a coworker's mere existence. Frankly, sometimes I come from a place of go-screw-yourself.

This book isn't about being perfect, or even about being nice. It's about getting through your life in the best possible way for you, and learning how to stop getting in your own way. It's about making your life better, no matter *what* kind of person you are naturally.

It's about learning how to have and do and be anything you want.

It's important to understand that a place of yes isn't somewhere you are all the time. It's somewhere you always *go back to*. It's your home. It's the real you. The negativity you sometimes hide behind is just a protective shell you've built around yourself—a digression and a distraction from what you really want to be doing. Self-doubt is a bad habit. Fear is an excuse and a shield. Irritation is a sign of stress. Those things that keep you from saying yes and getting things done are habits you've learned, and habits can be broken.

It's Not a Secret

A few more things a place of yes is *not:* A place of yes is not the power of positive thinking or the law of attraction. It's not a "secret." I understand the power of positive thinking and the law of attraction, and I believe in what those things are about. I agree that being positive and focusing your energy does attract good things to you, but not because of a mystical process involving some conscious universe that doles out the good and the bad according to who has the best attitude.

Thinking more positively changes how you relate to the world, but a place of yes is not some kind of mystical magical spiritual process where you just think something and it comes true. If you're not the type to meditate or chant or visualize yourself richer and thinner for three hours every day, don't sweat it. That's just more pressure. It's just one more thing you don't have time to do. Coming from a place of yes is about getting right down to business. It's active, not passive. *Yes* gives you something to do: a mission, a purpose, a goal.

If you don't have an athletic bone in your body, coming from a place of yes is not going to make you an Olympian, just because you will it to be so. You are not going to turn into an Elle Macpherson look-alike just because you wish to be a supermodel. You aren't going to become an astronaut if you aren't willing to go through the training, if you have vertigo or bad vision. Coming from a place of yes is not going to give you naturally supple 34C breasts or your husband a twelve-inch penis. It's definitely not going to bring Prince Charming on a white horse holding a sack of cash to your front door, just because you imagine it happening.

If you are a size 12, it's not going to transform you into a size 0 by tomorrow (or ever, necessarily). But it can help you love your size 12 self, or inspire you to get down to a size that is more healthy for you. It's not going to raise your IQ, fire your obnoxious boss, solve global warming, or "fix" your parents, but it can help ease your anxiety and obsession and self-destructive behavior that may stem from your feelings about any of those things. Coming from a place of yes will not make your crazy best friend suddenly see the light and stop choosing the wrong men—but it can help *you* stop choosing the wrong men. A place of yes has nothing to do with anybody else. It's only about you.

When you choose *yes*, your whole attitude will change, no matter who you are. You can be a born optimist, pessimist, realist, anarchist, whatever, and still come from a place of yes. You can be a meditator, a yogi, a kick boxer, a triathlete, a couch potato, and still come from a place of yes. You can be sixteen or sixty-six years old and come from a place of yes. No matter what you've done or haven't done or hate to admit you've done, you can come from a place of yes.

A place of yes is a way to get through things when you feel it is impossible to do so.

Your mind creates the landscape of your life. Your perceptions about everything that you've ever done and every thing that has ever happened to you all come from your mind. Change your mind, and things change. However, coming from a place of yes goes a step further. You change your mind, and then *you act on it*. You don't wait for someone or something else to do it for you. No excuses. No luck. No passing the buck.

A place of yes is about taking responsibility for moving forward, even if you have to climb over a mountain of obstacles. You are in charge, nobody else. A place of yes is your engine. Your energy changes, and people around you sense it. They want it to rub off on them, and it does. Incredible opportunities start happening and people start reacting differently to you. The world around you changes, not because the universe suddenly decides you are worthy, but because *you change it*. You stop being a victim and you start being the ruler of your own destiny. And that, my friend, is the point and purpose of coming from a place of yes.

The bottom line is that when you come from a place of yes, you don't wish something to happen. You *make it happen*. You are driving. You don't daydream in the passenger seat of life; you don't hand over the work you need to do to somebody else and then sit back, waiting to reap rewards that never come. You don't wait.

Instead, think about the things that you wish would happen to you in your life. Are you waiting for them to happen? Deep down, do you think they won't happen? This can apply to anything—getting a job, finding love, losing weight, making more money, getting organized, making more time for family, whatever it is. How proactive are you being in reaching that desire?

Coming from a place of yes is hard work, but it's the work of a lifetime, *your* lifetime.

Your Noise, Your Voice

Another important concept to understand is the difference between *noise* and *voice*.

I first heard the term "noise" years ago, from Breck Costin, a life coach who teaches a course called Absolute Freedom, about how to clarify what you are doing with your life. He used the term in a different way, but it resonated for me. I've thought about it over the years since then, and developed the idea into something that works for me.

To me, noise is what gets in your way. It's a self-generated obstacle, the negative talk inside your head that keeps you down, too afraid to go for what you want.

There are many types of noise, and in each chapter of this book, with each new rule, I'll also talk about a specific kind of noise that tends to crop up along with that rule. Noise can come in many forms—food noise, money noise, beauty noise, relationship noise, family noise, call it what you will—each person develops personalized noise, but in general, noise is that feeling you get that you aren't good enough, or you don't deserve what you want, or you'll never be able to be the person you wish you could be. Noise holds you back. It psychs you out. It distracts you and blocks you and makes you believe there are insurmountable obstacles in your path.

Most of us have noise about something, but knowing this doesn't mean you'll automatically be able to make it stop. If you have noise that you don't recognize and can't control, and I say to you, "All you have to do is come from a place of yes," what you hear is, "All you have to do is quit your job and get a new one" or "All you have to do is eat less and exercise more" or "All you have to do is leave him" or "All you have to do is push this two-ton boulder up this mountain." We all know that doesn't work. It's too hard. Noise *makes* it too hard.

You can't do it because you don't know how. You're too overwhelmed. The noise in your own head is too loud. As much as you want to change things, noise is the elephant in the room that makes something achievable into something seemingly impossible.

Noise tells you to eat a bag of cookies when you are trying to lose weight. It tells you not to ask for a raise because your boss will laugh at you or tell you that you don't deserve it. It tells you that you won't ever be in shape enough to be seen at the gym so you might as well not bother exercising at all. It tells you that nobody good will ever fall in love with you. It convinces you that you are predetermined to live the life your parents are leading or led, or that you will never live up to what they expect, or that you can't really be who *you* want to be.

Noise convinces you that you don't really deserve love, that you will never make enough money to stop worrying, or that you are just one of those people who can't be happy. Noise bullies you until it gets its way. In fact, if you feel bullied by *other people,* you are probably actually being bullied by your own noise, which can make you feel like a victim.

I'll never forget the night I was lying in bed with Jason discussing our future. We didn't agree about everything we wanted in our lives, so I immediately thought that meant we had no future. I hadn't yet learned that two people can build goals together, and that our desires can evolve.

Before I met him, I had almost given up—I had assumed that I could have *some* of the things I wanted, but not *all* of the things I wanted. I had come to terms with the idea that my career came first so that was what I would get—a great career. Maybe I would find a way to have a baby and raise it myself. I was resigned. Even after meeting him, I didn't think I could have it all.

So even when Jason told me that he wanted a commitment and a family, I didn't consider that as a real option for me. It seemed impossible. I couldn't believe it.

My noise was wrong—as noise always is.

Noise comes out of past experiences where you were hurt or scared or just didn't learn how to believe in yourself. It can start from one comment someone made to you years ago that you believed, or it can come out of years of abuse or neglect. Noise makes you give up, settle, accept less than you wanted, or never try for the thing you want the most.

Without recognizing your noise, you won't be able to come from a place of yes. Noise is strong and has power. Your noise might be in a different category than my noise, or you might have noise in all the same places. There is childhood noise—the noise that repeats all those stories that you have learned about yourself based on what your family told you, that holds you back from growing up. There is career noise—the noise that tells you that you don't deserve to get ahead, that you aren't qualified to be where you are, or that you'll never be able to have the job that makes you happy. There is food noise—the noise that urges you to binge or starve or beat yourself up if you were "bad." There is exercise noise that keeps you on the couch because what's the point. There is beauty noise that tells you that you won't ever be beautiful because of this or that feature. Imagine if Lauren Hutton, with the gap in her teeth, or Cindy Crawford, with her beauty mark, or Barbra Streisand, with an imperfect nose, had listened to beauty noise? Thank goodness they didn't change a thing about their beautiful faces.

There is money noise—the noise that tells you that you might as well charge your credit card to the limit because you are so far in the hole that it doesn't matter, or that you better not dare spend anything on yourself because you are scared to death that you might not have enough money for something else. There is relationship noise—the noise that encourages you to endure horrible relationships, or attracts you to the wrong men, or tells you that you should get married now or you might never get another chance, or tells you to run whenever a relationship gets serious.

Your noise will change as your life changes. Now that I have a baby, I have parenting noise and sleep noise and breast-feeding noise. Sometimes I lie awake and wonder, am I doing it right? What if I mess up my daughter? This noise is totally new for me but there it is—noise can come and go according to what is happening to you right now.

You might have other kinds of noise, too. Friendship noise, sibling noise, sex noise, clutter noise, body noise, cooking noise—whatever your issues are, whatever holds you back or stresses you out, that's where your noise is.

Fortunately, like the devil on one shoulder and the angel on the other, your noise has a counterpart: it is your voice. Your voice knows what's good for you and right for you and what is authentic to who you really are. It tells you what to do, why you are good, and why you deserve the best. It shows you the map for reaching your dreams, and when you learn to hear it and ignore the noise, the noise gets quieter and the voice gets louder. This is the key to unlocking the best parts of yourself.

When you are used to your loud, rude, clamoring noise, your voice can be hard to hear. But it's in there. *A Place of Yes* is about how I found mine, and how finding your voice and learning to listen to it can allow great things to start happening to *you*. Because you'll stop getting in the way.

Sometimes your noise will be louder than other times. Sometimes you'll listen to it and go the wrong way. You'll make mistakes. That's life. Part of coming from a place of yes is to accept that you screwed up and move on. Forgive yourself and don't dwell in the past. It's okay because it has to be okay. It's what happened. If you can make something good out of a mistake or learn something from it, you are coming from a place of yes. If you keep moving forward, despite your mistakes, and if you keep trying, even when you fail, your voice will lead the way and you can always find your way back to your path forward.

If you have read my books or watched my shows, you know I'm not perfect and I don't have life totally figured out and under control. I will never pretend to have all the answers. I'm just someone who has learned how to stop getting in my own way more often than not. I'm on a path just like you are, but I'm managing my noise and I've learned how to make things happen in my life. I've finally found my voice.

My Story and Yours

I've put my experiences into a framework of rules, to make my personal lessons relatable and to help encourage you to go for yours. I show you how I climbed out of an unhappy childhood, dealt with the aftershocks of a dysfunctional family, built my business despite the obstacles, and got healthy and fit. I say what I mean and honesty matters to me, so don't expect me to dress it up for you or make it look pretty—it isn't always easy to go for your dreams, and life can get messy sometimes. It can even break your heart. I have given up a lot to get where I am today. I've worked harder than I ever thought possible, practically killing myself to achieve my dreams. I've taken on too much, broken down in tears—it has not been easy. But I got through the bad parts and so can you. There will always be more challenges ahead—but now you have the tools to tackle them.

No matter how hard your life gets, you can put yourself back together and come out stronger than you were before, if you learn how to come from a place of yes. Part of me has always said *yes* to my own life, even when the yes was nearly drowned out by my noise. That *yes* inside me was the part of me that recognized when something was a career opportunity or a *life* opportunity. That was the part of me that recognized Jason and the part of me that recognized that I didn't have to settle or give up *anything* I really wanted. Thank goodness I listened. Are you listening to your voice?

Because I learned to listen to my voice instead of my noise, I have gone from unemployed actress to sometimes-successful entrepreneur to personal celebrity chef to television personality to best-selling author, and that's just a partial job history. I've also gone from food-obsessed to healthy, money-challenged to comfortable, commitment-phobic to blissfully newlywed. I still struggle with noise, I don't always make good decisions about what to eat and drink, Jason and I get in fights just like any other couple, and I still have anxiety about money. I've suffered a lot, worried a lot, wasted a lot of time, stressed myself to the point of breaking, endured tragedy, but I've finally found some peace . . . even, dare I say, happiness.

Take It or Leave It

The last concept I'd like you to understand before we start with the rules is one I'll refer to often throughout this book. I call it *take it or leave it*. You can apply this to relationships, family, career, money, or any other aspect of your life—even cooking. In fact, I first came up with the concept in the kitchen while renovating recipes.

Here's how it works. If, for example, I'm creating a healthier cookie recipe, I might find that the cookies are not just healthier but taste better when I replace white flour with oat flour and white sugar with raw sugar. I'll take it—those are changes that work, so I carry them forward into my next cookie experiment. If, however, it doesn't work to remove all the fat—maybe the cookies are too dry or tasteless—then I'll leave it. I'll discard that idea and bring some of the fat back next time. Take it or leave it—you take the good and build on it; you leave the bad, in favor of a new idea. Most important, you keep moving forward, never settling for what doesn't work.

This applies to any area of your life, and it represents how you can learn from your own experiences. Successes are victories that teach you how to get what you want. Mistakes are opportunities to do something different next time. What worked and didn't work in your last relationship, job, diet, financial endeavor? You can always choose to take it or leave it.

Unfortunately or fortunately, life is an obstacle course. You succeed at one thing and then you move on to the next. When an obstacle is tough, you try harder. When an obstacle is insurmountable, you change course. But you never sit down and refuse to finish. And when you do get over each hurdle, it's the best feeling—you're stronger and wiser than before you tried it, and you're even more ready to tackle the next one. The fact that there always *is* another obstacle can seem overwhelming sometimes, but then again, that's the good news. Life never gives up on you, either—it always has a new challenge, something more that you can succeed at achieving. And if you fail? One more lesson learned.

So stop waiting for someone else to fix things. It's time to step up to the plate. It's your career, your body, your health, your relationship, your money, your path . . . *your life*. You can be everything you ever wanted to be. You can have it all. Everything is about to change. All you have to do is begin at the beginning. We'll do it together.

....

Break the Chain
Surviving Childhood

You gain strength, courage, and confidence by every experience in which you really stop to look fear in the face. You are able to say to yourself, "I lived through this horror. I can take the next thing that comes along."

—Eleanor Roosevelt, former First Lady

Life is full of noise, and the noise begins in childhood.

Everyone has childhood noise. Everyone. It doesn't matter how good or bad, idyllic or dysfunctional your childhood seems to you now. We all grow up believing things about ourselves, good and bad. We get yelled at or ignored or coddled or left to our own devices before we have any idea of what we are doing in the world. We see the adults in our lives doing things and we hear them saying things and we try to figure out what it means, or we mimic those things or rebel against them.

No matter how beautiful or terrible or uneventful you think your childhood was, every childhood has its periods of suffering and every family enacts its beliefs about you on you, and, of course, in many cases, you believe them. That's where the noise begins, when you start telling yourself stories about who you are based on your childhood instead of your inner voice. As you get older, this noise can keep you entrenched in patterns and habits, unable to get out.

This can happen to you no matter how your childhood went. For example, my husband, Jason, had what he feels was an idyllic childhood, completely unlike my perception of mine. His parents are still together—but when he lost his brother the whole family dynamic changed. He became an only child and he has noise about that. I'm sure his parents also have noise because of what happened to their family. Your situation might not be so dramatic, but there are so many ways a child can take on noise—big and small ways— that will have an impact for years to come. Regardless of how perfect someone's family seems, everyone has issues that can affect the future.

This is why the first step in coming from a place of yes involves breaking the link between what your family thinks of you, and what you think of yourself. The first link of my chain began in childhood, so that's where I'll start. Understanding where you came from will help you take it or leave it—breaking the bad links in your chain, but keeping the solid ones intact. Because who you are now doesn't have to be a product of your past. You don't have to keep re-creating your past. You can start creating your future.

Break the Chain

When you carry your childhood with you, you never become older.

—Tom Stoppard, British playwright

The first rule in *A Place of Yes* can help you climb out of your child-hood noise into a new place, and from there, you can head in any direction you desire. It's the first rule to work on when you want to change your life and break out of the old patterns that hold you back. Tackle this rule first and you'll free yourself to grow up (no matter how old you are) and be who you really are.

At my wedding, my high school friend Natalie told me that she felt I would have a baby girl. When I asked her how she knew, she said, "Because you're going to break the chain." She might not have meant it to be a life-changing statement, but it was. Having my daughter has motivated me to live this rule. It's rule #1 for coming from a place of yes: *Break the chain.*

Break the chain means recognizing the patterns you are carrying forward in your life, patterns that belonged to your past, and choosing to go a different way when those patterns are destructive.

People often ask me how I got out of my childhood alive. They ask if I'm a survivor, what my secret was. My secret is simply to practice rule #1 as an adult. On my show, *Bethenny Getting Married?*, I've said I was raised in a cave, by animals. I said it to be funny, in a way, but the truth is that the damage my childhood inflicted on me emerged later in my life. My childhood is more traumatic in retrospect than it was to me at the time.

When I was in it, as a child, my life was all I knew. I loved my parents because they were my parents. Sometimes I wanted things I couldn't have—a normal name, siblings, to stay in one place for a while, to have parents who didn't fight, to have my father and mother back together—but I also accepted that my life was just my life and there wasn't really anything I could do to change it. You know what you know. When you grow up, that's when you get to decide how much you are going to let it all shape who you are. That's when you can change things.

It doesn't do me any good to get mired in where I came from. It isn't going to help anything to spend my days steeping in regret and anger. I'd rather come from a place of yes and go in a different

direction today. I'd rather break that chain than carry it throughout my life, no matter how hard that is. And it *is* hard, because it's
breaking away from what you know, from what's comfortable even
when it's destructive.

To do this for yourself, first you have to look back and figure out
just where your childhood is holding you back and where it can
help you. No matter how dark your childhood, there will be parts
that will help you now—for me, it was learning to endure, to be
flexible, and to be strong. I've benefited from those qualities all my
life. I didn't feel like a victim as a child, and I don't feel like one
now. Sometimes my childhood was colorful, exciting, stimulating,
even dangerous. But there were other parts that have stuck with me
in a negative way. My childhood was often lonely, frustrating, and
sad. I never felt very safe, and I never felt like I could just trust that
someone else was in control of the situation. Everyone's childhood
contains its elements of destruction, and those are what you have to
dig out of your own past so you can break your attachment to them.
You have to decide what to take, and what to leave behind.

· ·

THE MYTH OF "NORMAL"

Don't get fixated on whether or not your childhood was normal.
I can say this because I often used to bemoan the fact that my
childhood wasn't normal. I'd think about all the things that
"should" have been. I hated that I couldn't look back and recall
all those typical childhood things—but then again, what typical
things was I looking for? What you think you missed might not
really exist at all, because what's normal? There is no normal.
People and families are who they are, and each one is unique.
Your childhood was what it was, and your life now can be whatever you want it to be. Don't seek out normal. Seek out *func-
tional*. Seek out *successful*. Seek out *happy*. To do that, you have
to find what works for you, never what you think is supposed

to work for people in general. Don't look to others to show you what you are supposed to be. There are no people "in general." It doesn't matter what anybody else thinks of your life. All that matters is what *you* think of it, and what you decide to make of it.

. . . .

Breaking the chain is a gradual process, but it's one of those things you have to do for yourself if you ever want to get somewhere better. Having my baby girl brought this dramatically to the forefront of my life: I've been breaking the chains that bound me to my childhood noise for years, but having Bryn taught me how important it is to break them in earnest and break them for good, so she never has to grow up bearing the weight of mistakes committed by the generations before her.

So, go back with me into my childhood. Maybe you'll find some similarities to your own, maybe you won't, but I know from the letters I receive that many of you experienced similar situations in your own childhoods. As you go through this chapter, use it as a vehicle for deconstructing your own younger self, to see where your patterns lie, what stories you tell yourself about yourself, what habits you've taken on, what behaviors from your parents you mimic today without realizing it. Then you can begin breaking the chain that binds *you*.

My Mother

Biology is the least of what makes someone a mother.

—Oprah Winfrey, actress and host

I had my first drink when I was seven years old. I was betting at the track by the age of eight. Before I was in grade school, I was calling the police to stop my mother and stepfather from fighting—they would haul him away, and the next day, my mother and I would scan the ads for apartments. But we never left, and I never understood why.

I attended multiple schools because my parents couldn't stay in one place. I was partying at clubs in the city when I was fourteen and crashing expensive cars before I had a driver's license. This was my "normal."

Sometimes I wonder how my mother could have allowed me to do the things I did growing up, but my mother came out of her own bad situation, and she didn't know how to control many aspects of her own life let alone mine. She chose men who, in my opinion, were obviously not good for her. She was married maybe four times, all told—at some point I lost track. She has denied it publicly, but in my memory, from what I saw, she had issues with alcohol and food. She lived in fear and she hid things from me all the time. She had a terrible temper, maybe because she was so angry at what her life had become. She loved me, but she didn't know how to raise me.

Few relationships are as basic and influential as the relationship between mother and child. Maybe your relationship with your mother wasn't as dramatic and chaotic and tumultuous as mine, but because no mother is perfect, no mother-child relationship is perfect, either. Maybe you were loved but didn't get everything you needed. Maybe you had everything handed to you and you never learned how to make it on your own. Maybe you were a lonely only child, or had middle-child syndrome, or were babied or had to be a mother to your mother. Maybe you know your mother did the best she could, but you've inherited some of her bad habits, poor self-esteem, anger issues, insecurities, weakness, addictions, or something else. Maybe she was *great*, and you want to be just like her . . . except for that *one thing*. . . .

For me, my mom was a wild card. One minute she was my best friend. The next minute she was screaming and seemed completely out of control. She didn't understand me, but I don't think she understood herself, either. When I look back at my relationship with my mother from my perspective as an adult, I can see the big picture—her issues with men became my issues with men. Her issues with money became my issues with money. Her wild partying lifestyle threatened to become mine. Her issues with food also threatened to become mine. She became a mother before she became an adult, and that may have been why she never really seemed to understand what children need.

I vowed to wait to become an adult before I became a mother—one more link in the chain I was able to break.

But let me go back to the beginning. I was born in 1970, on my mother's twentieth birthday, in Queens, New York. My mom was a baby having a baby. She was a tiny, thin, beautiful blonde who looked like Michelle Pfeiffer. Men fell at her feet. She smoked Virginia Slims and she looked like one herself. She had green eyes, a wide jaw like mine, a tiny nose, and straight hair.

My mother was just five feet four inches, but she would take on anyone, anytime. She had a habit of putting her fist through windows when she lost her temper, which was often. She was smart, sassy, talented, sarcastic, ballsy, opinionated, and a fighter—in many ways I take after her. She was funny, too—but also angry, frustrated, and incredibly insecure. She had so much potential, but in my view, she was never able to realize it, or to find peace.

In season three of *The Real Housewives of New York City*, you might remember the scene when Ramona and I were taking a walk across the Brooklyn Bridge. In typical Ramona fashion, she blurted out a mean comment. She said I had screwed up all my relationships and I would probably screw up my relationship with Jason, too. That really hurt me, it cut me to the core, because it has always been my greatest fear and the thing I've tried hardest not to do: be like my mother. My mother's string of failed relationships and her multiple marriages have haunted me, the ghost of what I hoped would never be me. She never broke the chain to her own past, and

Ramona's comment brought my worst fears to light: Could I break what she couldn't? Could I make a relationship last? Could I ever be happy?

My mother did give me some gifts. Despite her selfish nature and her inability to act like a responsible parent, she truly adored me, and knowing that was worth a lot to me. In many ways, I think I baffled and amazed her. She used to say that she wanted to come back in her next life as me, and that I was special. She convinced me that I had a star above my head. Something about that image stuck with me—it was the most important thing she ever gave me.

But adoring your child isn't parenting. You can't just love your child when you feel like it, when things are going well, and then forget about her when times are tough or you want to go out and party or go to war with whatever man currently supports you. My mother was so tough but also so vulnerable. The bottom line is that she didn't protect me, and to this day, she won't admit it. She refuses to see it. She still says she has no guilt about anything.

I'm not a person who believes that there is anything beneficial about guilt or regret. If something happened, it happened. I believe in owning it, as I'll talk about later, but not in denying or torturing yourself about it. Admit it and move on. What I can't understand is how she still doesn't see what really happened. And I don't understand why she still can't tell me she is sorry.

Having Bryn makes this even more incomprehensible to me. She's already taught me a lot because she has made me see my childhood in a whole new light. I look at her, and I think: I was like this, in my mother's arms. How did our relationship ever get the way it is now? I vow every day that such a breakdown will never happen between Bryn and me. I'm breaking the chain, for me, and most of all, for her.

Kids take on the responsibilities the adults won't acknowledge, and that's something I never want to do to my daughter. It serves as an inspiration for me to build a secure home for her. I don't ever want her to feel responsible for me or my issues.

At the same time, I understand why my mother had so many issues—so much of her own childhood noise. Her father was a dictator type who forced her and her sister to conform to his idea of how women were supposed to be—quiet and submissive, beautiful and thin. Long hair was required and being fat was not an option. My mother said she ran away when she was sixteen, but the damage was already done. I think her food issues must have begun in her own childhood, and she was just trying to survive. I understand how she might have felt. I certainly understand having father issues.

I think a lot of women's issues and self-esteem come from their fathers, and I'll talk about my own father in a minute. My mother's father certainly did a number on her from her account. He was cold and mean-spirited the way she tells it. He was also hyperconscious of appearance. He told my mother, before she married my father, that if she was going to marry a Jew, she would have to take responsibility for what her children would look like.

My mom used to tell me the most heartbreaking story, and it always made me want to cry when I heard it. One Christmas morning when they were little, my mother and her siblings all ran to the Christmas tree to open their presents. All her brother could find for himself was a single broken toy. My grandfather apparently thought this would be funny. He had presents hidden for his son, but he was being cruel and wanted to see what would happen if his son thought he wasn't getting anything. The saddest part is that the little boy was simply defeated. My mother remembers him saying, "I guess Santa didn't think I was good this year." My grandfather thought it was hilarious.

The truth of the matter is that perhaps my mother and her siblings never really believed they deserved anything better than ridicule and disdain. I wasn't there, but I imagine that they must have had lives built on disapproval and disappointment.

My grandfather was a horse trainer, and like everyone on the track, he had a wild lifestyle. My mother grew up on the track, so that's what she knew. My mother, at just five foot four inches, wanted to be a model, but that dream was thwarted by her biology, so she worked at the track as an exercise rider, working out the horses in the morning. And yet, there's so much I don't know about her early life. It's funny, you spend your whole life with people and when you think back, it's surprising what you realize you don't know. I do know that the track was in her blood, and not surprisingly, she ended up marrying two different horse trainers—first my father, Robert Frankel, and later, my stepfather John Parisella. Although neither one of them was like her father in personality—they each had their own issues—they all came from that same racetrack world of shady characters, sketchy situations, and living on the edge.

When I think back on her life, I have a lot of compassion for my mother. Her life was never easy, and she made it even harder for herself. She wasn't exactly easy to get along with. Like me, she can be difficult to deal with, but she's also a person who can sit in a bar and talk to anyone she meets. I remember her as mercurial and gregarious, but also sporadic—if she wasn't in the mood to get along with someone, she wouldn't pretend to be nice, and at any moment she could snap. You could never be sure which side of her you were going to get.

Unfortunately, I identify with this quality. It's one of the things I've really had to look at in myself and try to change—one more way I am breaking the chain. I can still be difficult, but I decided long ago to work on it, and I'm getting better at controlling my own mood shifts and behavior when I'm not in the mood to be social. I've also learned something I feel that she never learned: When I do cross the line, I've learned how to say I'm sorry.

Her default mode was "fight" and she could fight hard, but at the same time, she always seemed to be helpless. In that way, my mother was a barrage of mixed messages. She would tell me one thing but then do the opposite. I never knew quite what to believe. She would say *be strong,* but then she would be weak. She'd fight as if her life depended on it, and then give up and never do anything about her situation. She would act as if she needed a man to save her, but she kept choosing men who abused her. She would tell me, "Never be dependent on a man," but when I look back on it, she was always dependent on a man. She would tell me I had to make it on my own, and then she would tell me that she was forced to be with men because of me.

Was I supposed to make it on my own, or find a man with money so I wouldn't have to make it on my own? I really didn't know what to invest in, what to believe. It became a major source of noise for me, and I fought that noise for years.

Now that I've gotten some distance from it, I think she was probably trying, in the only way she knew how, to save me from her fate. She was telling me to do what she said, not what she did, but that never works. At the time, I only saw what she did, and that was confusing. She was volatile and she always seemed unhappy. I was always terrified that she would lose it and humiliate me in front of my friends or in public. She was the mom who always said, "Do I have to drive you *both ways*? Can't somebody else's mother drive?" She would say it in front of everyone. I never knew what might set her off.

I also felt like there was so much I didn't know about my family. We rarely talked about our heritage or religion or things like that. People often ask me about my religion or nationality. The truth is, I never really knew what I was. I was a little of everything. Supposedly, my mother converted to Judaism to marry my father, even though she claimed to be an atheist. My stepfather was Catholic, so later I went to Catholic school. My stepfather wanted me to be Catholic, like him, so I would go to church and take communion, but I never really felt as if it was my religion. It makes me a little sad—who the hell knows what I am? I wish I would at least have had a little more guidance, or at least been told more about my heritage.

It wouldn't be honest of me to deny there were good times, too.

Despite the volatility, life with my mother wasn't all bad. I believe that at her core, she isn't a bad person. She is just a tortured person who could never seem to get her life together the way she wanted it. I have some great memories from my childhood—many of those memories are about food, and maybe that's why food is still so important to me. I think everyone in my family used food to comfort themselves, to feel secure.

For instance, when I was about seven years old, my mother and I had dinner at a fast-food restaurant, Hardee's, on many nights, and I thought those dinners were the greatest thing. When I was a little older, she used to drive me to the roller rink on weekends. She'd pick me up and we would go to McDonald's. She also took me to get Slurpees in the summer. I still love Slurpees, although now I sometimes like to put vodka or tequila in them. When my stepfather was involved, food was even more of an event, like when we would all get dressed up to go to Nathan's at Coney Island.

But my food experiences with my mother also had a dark side. She was obsessed with being thin but she would tell me to eat things like tempura in a Japanese restaurant because she said tempura was clean, even though it was fried, because of the way the Japanese made it. She never wanted me to be on a diet; she was like one of those girls who is always trying to get their friends to eat fattening things. She would eat them, too, but then she would go into the bathroom and I knew she was tossing it all back up, which would infuriate me. Sometimes it felt as if she was sabotaging me, because I was obsessed with being thin, too. Because of course, I wanted to be like my mother.

She also exposed me to some amazing experiences. I remember our trip to Mexico when she took me into the kitchen to meet the chef at a restaurant, and when we took hula lessons together in Hawaii, and made leis on the upper deck of a 747. When I was five, I was watching a children's show on television, and they made a recipe I wanted to make. I needed maraschino cherries, but we didn't have any, so my mother gave me money and sent me off to the store. I think she watched me until I turned the corner, and most people would probably wonder what kind of mother would send her five-year-old daughter to the store alone in Manhattan, but for me, it was freedom and independence.

At the same time, I was often lonely because I was usually the only child around. I used to make up imaginary friends. I had an imaginary sister named Annabelle and an imaginary brother named Kevin. I love being an only child now, but I was a lonely child. I got used to being lonely, though. Maybe that's why I've always been more comfortable by myself.

When I was thirteen and other kids were going to summer camp, my mother took me to Europe. I feel melancholy when I think how young she was during these times, younger than I am now—just thirty-four—and she chose to travel with her teenage daughter.

On that trip we went to Greece, Egypt, Italy, France, England, and Turkey. I had the best calamari I've ever had when we were in Greece. We took a cruise down the Nile in Egypt. We shopped all over Paris and London. So much was fun, in such a highly charged way. My mother was fun, and funny—the life of the party. But then, so much was also volatile—it was all or nothing, extreme ups and downs. We would be having a great time, and the day would end, and I wanted to go to sleep, and she would suddenly get so angry at me and tell me I was boring when I didn't want to go out dancing and drinking in the discos all night.

Another source of stress on that trip was my secret plan. I knew my mother had some food issues, even though I didn't have a word for what she was doing. There was no Internet back then but I was a sleuth about it. I noticed the large number of laxatives in the bathroom, containers and shelves full of laxatives (I've suffered from constipation most of my adult life, so maybe that was part of it—what are we holding on to?). When we'd drive to the city, she'd often have to stop to go to the bathroom. After meals, she would

usually go into the bathroom and run the water for forty-fi
utes. Sometimes I would hear her hurling, or see the remna.
the toilet, or smell it when I went in the bathroom after her. It m.
me angry and I wanted to catch her in the act of something so
could confront her about it.

During that trip, I decided this was my chance—I thought that
if I could actually see her throwing up her food, she would have to
admit to me what she was doing, explain it, get help, *something*. I
became obsessed and I followed her everywhere after meals so she
wouldn't be able to go into the bathroom alone. That would put her
in a bad mood, so for much of the trip, she was angry and grouchy
and secretive, and we were both walking on eggshells. She always
denied anything was going on—she still does.

Not that I think my mother could necessarily control what she
was doing. It was her noise, her way of trying to be in charge, I suppose. She probably wasn't able to just stop, but she didn't want or
know how to explain it or even acknowledge it to herself, let alone
to me. What I think my mother didn't realize was that although parents try to hide things, children are smart. They always know something's wrong, even if they don't know what it is, and sometimes,
not knowing is worse and makes kids worry more than if their parents just told them the truth.

My mother's obsession with hiding food issues rubbed off on
me as an addiction to dieting and, in another way, an addiction to
getting rid of things—my own personal brand of purging, but I do
it with stuff, not food. Having too much stuff gives me anxiety, so I
am constantly throwing things away. As a teenager, I was definitely
influenced by her behavior for a while. I used to steal her laxatives
and use them because I wanted to be thin. Through my whole
childhood, I was obsessed with trying one diet after another. Fortunately, later I decided to go in the opposite direction—I learned all
about health, and portion control, and sensible eating. I broke the
chain, choosing not to let myself become ensnared in an eating dis-

l. I vowed never to diet again, and even built
le concept of balanced, healthy eating and

. . . .

THE STRESS OF LIVING A LIE

Sometimes I try to imagine what it would do to a person to live
a lie—to keep a secret, like an eating disorder, and never be
able to confess it to anyone. When a big portion of your life is
a secret, what happens to you? What breaks down, what falls
apart, what hardens and keeps others out?

Maybe one way I've broken that chain is to make myself an
open book and put my life out there for everyone to see. Maybe
that's one of the reasons why I gravitated toward reality television. It was scary at first, to live in front of a camera, and also
scary to write my first book and put myself out there. However,
being brave paid off—things I thought would be humiliating
and terrifying turned out to be blessings. I learned how to love
being open and honest because of how it helps people who are
struggling with the same things that I struggle with. So many
people have come forward and said, "I've had this happen, too!"
or "You deserve better!" I think showing my vulnerable moments
to the world really helped a lot of people. And it helped me be
more honest with myself—when things happen on camera, on
television, you can't deny them.

During the filming of *Real Housewives,* my boyfriend at the
time used to say, "Don't use the show as therapy," but now I say,
"Why not?" My fans have taught me more than any therapist
ever could about everything—relationships, business, recipes,
even being a wife and mother. My willingness to be vulnerable
on television has yielded amazing things, not just for me but, according to the letters I receive, for many of my fans.

You don't have to be on TV to refuse to live a lie. Owning up to your vulnerabilities doesn't have to hurt, or hurt for long. It can build a bridge between people, and change your life for the better. For me, it's my own strange kind of therapy, to help me break the chain of secrecy and lies I could have inherited from my mother, but chose instead to leave behind.

• •

A lot of what went on in my household was right there in the open, too—in ways it shouldn't have been. There were no prohibitions for children. My parents were taking me to rated-R horror movies when I was six years old because they wanted to see them— I saw *Halloween* and *Friday the 13th* when they first came out. Clubs, casinos, wherever my mother and stepfather went, I went, too, if they could get away with it.

I ate almost every meal in a restaurant because even though my mother was a great cook, my stepfather and I knew the price we would have to pay for the meal—her cooking at home inevitably turned into huge, stressful, angry productions that more often than not resulted in broken dishes and screaming. On the other hand, eating out with her was also frequently humiliating. If her food wasn't done right—if the spinach salad wasn't absolutely drowning in warm bacon dressing or the bacon cheeseburger wasn't practically raw or the eggs weren't running all over the plate or the steak wasn't charred enough on the outside and bloody enough on the inside, she would torture and humiliate the waitstaff.

I remember dreading what was to come, every time she would order eggs Benedict. She would poke at the yolks to test them. If they didn't ooze, she would scream at the waiter. She happened to be right about the proper way to cook eggs Benedict, but her reaction was so embarrassing. She loved to make a big deal about how much she ate. She wanted the attention, and she wanted everyone to know if the food wasn't up to her high standards.

Maybe it's ironic (or no coincidence at all) that I'm the first one to say something if I'm served subpar food in a restaurant, but as a child, I wanted to crawl under the table when she started yelling and everyone at the other tables would turn to look at us. I'm still traumatized by eggs Benedict.

On the other hand, one thing I've taken with me into adulthood is the idea that children should eat what the adults eat. Bryn will not order off the kid's menu! I think my palate is more refined because of my early experiences with adult food.

My mother gave me the occasional pearl of wisdom. When I was a freshman in high school, I came home drunk one night, and my mother told me that it never looks good to be the one person who gets too drunk at the party or to be the one who is out of control. She never said, "Don't drink." Instead, she told me *how* to drink (says the girl who went into the booze business with her own line of cocktails).

She was also incredibly permissive with me. She never made me do things I didn't want to do, and so I spent most of my childhood doing what I wanted, when I wanted. If I didn't want to go to school, I wouldn't go. If I wanted to take gymnastics or baton twirling or violin lessons and quit after one day, she let me. If I wanted to go out to a club, long before I was old enough to get into a club, I went out to a club. She even helped me find an ID to use to get in.

I think that she thought that she was being supportive, but letting me do whatever I wanted never taught me follow-through or discipline, or the notion that sometimes you have to wait for or work for or earn the things you want. I had to learn that on my own, later in life. I definitely had to grow up fast and figure out a lot of things by myself because I wasn't getting much guidance. My mother and stepfather knew how to have fun, and how to be angry, but there wasn't much structure or discipline or guidance going on in my home. So I took the independence and resourcefulness I learned—and I left behind the refusal to take responsibility or follow through with what I start.

I can adjust to almost anything, anywhere, anytime, because I learned at such a young age how to deal with being thrown into extraordinary situations. I'm not saying you should do this to your child, and I certainly don't intend to do it to my child. Seeing my experience in this light is my way of coming from a place of yes when I think about it.

When I think of my mother now, I can see her more objectively than I could as a child. She was stuck. She couldn't get out. She didn't know how to break her own chain, how to escape her own noise, and I feel compassion for her, not anger.

My impression of her has always been that she saw herself as a victim and her problems were always someone else's fault. The few times I have spoken to her over the last sixteen years, she has always been full of complaints, especially about having no money. She never tells me about anything great she's doing. It's always some version of how the world has wronged her. It's very "place of no," very "glass half empty." For years, she told me, "I gave up my life for you" as if her unhappiness was my fault. She also blamed the men she was with—she often told me, even in her twenties, how she gave up this opportunity for that man, that opportunity for this man as if she had already wasted her life.

Now I wonder: How is any life wasted in your twenties? What can't you change in your thirties? I'm forty and I'm still changing my life every day. On the other hand, I remember being that younger age. I know how that feels. It's common and even normal to feel as if it's too late, like you're too old even if you look back later and realize that "too old" is relative. When I was twenty-six, I felt this immense pressure to have my life all figured out. That's why I quit pursuing an acting career and got married. (I'll tell you that story soon.) Now I see that I was following in her footsteps. My first marriage didn't last—just like my mother's marriages never lasted. At the time, I panicked because I felt doomed to repeat her pattern. Yet I also realized that I couldn't possibly settle for something that wasn't right for me, so in that way it was actually a step in the right direction, a way to break another link.

I just wish she could have stepped outside herself and been

more objective. I wish she could have learned how to take responsibility for her own actions and her own life. But it was her life, not mine. All I can do is live my own life.

Recently my mother talked to several tabloid magazines and websites about me. She called me a liar. Then she provided the press with my baby pictures. People have asked me if I'm angry that she did this, and honestly, I'm not. I'm sad and frustrated. I know she must feel exposed and vulnerable, to have the world know things about her that she was never even able to admit to herself, things she never wanted people to know. I'm sure she never imagined that I would end up where I am now, and I struggled with whether I should tell my story, but how can I talk about where I came from without talking about my mother? How could I urge others to be honest about the past if I can't be honest about mine?

What I've recognized as I look back on her life and our life together is that I can't fix my mother, but I can decide whether I want to be like her, or whether I would rather be someone else. I can break the cycle and turn it around and come from a place of yes. I can be *me*, not another version of her.

If you look back on your family, you may be able to see your own examples of how the actions of the mother are visited on the daughter, down through the generations. You may have someone who played a crucial role in your upbringing who was full of excuses and pain, blame and sadness. That person probably inherited those behaviors from someone else.

It can stop with you. No matter what your age, if you feel that you are trapped in repeating a pattern, you can instead commit to breaking out of it. It won't necessarily be easy. It might even be excruciating. But the pain is momentary compared to the freedom it will bring.

I've decided it has to stop with me because it's no longer only about me. I won't pass on the dysfunction. I refuse to do it. Instead, I'll take it or leave it—I'll say *yes* to all that is good in me, and leave the rest behind.

My life now is so different than my mother's life used to be. Every week, I try to reserve Mommy Monday for Bryn. We go out to lunch together, or stay home and snuggle. It's our time. Sometimes it's difficult—trying to coordinate peeing and zipping up my pants and changing the baby's diaper and finding a place to put my purse and the diaper bag can be as challenging as an ice-skating routine! I have so much respect for women who are mothers. Most of you are underestimated, but you just keep going. You find a way.

But you have to find ways to deal with your stress too, if you don't want to take it out on your innocent child—and of course you don't. Being a mother is a lot of work, but it's the work of your life, and you chose it. You don't have to keep dragging around your own mother's mistakes. You can turn it around and focus on what kind of mother *you* will be, even when it's difficult, even when you want to break down and cry. That's coming from a place of yes.

My relationship with Bryn and our little family is so pure, it makes everything else seem dirty, and I have this huge, powerful force in me that wants to protect her from everything and never, ever make her suffer because of *me*. When I look at her, all I see is this sweet, beautiful, pure little soul, and all Jason and I want in our lives now is for her to be happy. How is it ever any different in any family?

Sometimes it is—don't I know it—but that doesn't mean you have to carry it forward. Coming from a place of yes means turning your childhood noise into a voice that shows you what kind of mother *you* want to be, what kind of *human being* you want to be. At forty, I still remember so many little things, painful memories and precious ones, so I think, *she'll remember, too.* Bryn will remember little things that don't seem important at the time, and she'll remember them for her whole life. When *she* writes a book, her book will be different. It will be a happier story.

My story is happy, too, now that I've broken the chain and found a career I love, a husband I love, and a daughter I live for. If I hadn't been coming from a place of yes, I might never have gotten to this point and been able to find my way to a better life. Now that I'm here, breaking the chain will help my daughter come from a place of yes as well.

Break the chain. You are not your mother. Do it for your own children. Do it for yourself.

My Real Father

It doesn't matter who my father was. It matters who I remember he was.

—Anne Sexton, poet

Who influences a girl more than her mother? Arguably, her father. My issues with my mother pale in comparison to my issues with my father, maybe because he was not actually in my life for so much of it. His absence and all the things I didn't know but imagined about him tormented me, becoming a gigantic emotional presence in my life. I hung all my hopes and dreams on him because he wasn't there. He became almost mythical in my imagination, but it was a role he would never actually step in to fill.

Where do I begin with my daddy issues? The funny thing is that of all my parents—my father, my mother, and my stepfather—I was with my father the least, but I just might be the most like him. I've also been the most tortured by him and he's had the biggest impact on me. I suppose it's not fair—my mother and my stepfather spent so much more time with me and I spend so much time talking about my real father, but that's the truth, that's my reality.

It's a shame that my father and I were never able to connect, considering our similarities. I inherited his ambition and single-minded drive to succeed, along with his abrasiveness and tendency to push people away. Maybe that's why we always clashed. We were too much alike. Like him, I shy away from intimacy. Like him, I define myself by my work. Like him, I failed at a long string of relationships over the course of my life. Like him, I'm very comfortable spending time alone.

My father was a tanned, dark-haired, hot shot lady's man and Hall of Fame horse trainer who will go down in history as one of the best in his field. He had a gift and an incredible drive. Over the course of his career, people learned to admire and fear him. He was an intimidating presence and people rarely lived up to his expectations. He put most of his efforts and care into his horses. The press described him as having a "tight inner circle," but what I saw was a man who cared about his horses and his dogs more than the people in his life. At least, that's the impression he seemed to want to project. I don't know anything about my father's parents, so I can't even begin to imagine what his childhood noise was about, but I do think that he was simply incapable of being vulnerable or opening himself up to other people.

Everyone who ever tried to love my father became a casualty to the track. Life on the racetrack is full of gambling and drugs, hustlers and vagabonds. Robert Frankel was a character and he surrounded himself with characters—men of questionable ethics and women who didn't have a clue about anything but horses and the racetrack life. I remember that after he and my mother divorced, he always had young, sexy girls on his arm who were very green and impressionable and frankly, not the sharpest tools in the shed. After I turned eighteen, his girlfriends were rarely older than I was, but they knew horses so they were enthralled with my father and his talent, and that's what he liked. He had a sleazy streak—maybe that sounds bad to say about him, but I always had my radar up about that, and it has become something I notice, that makes me uncomfortable, in certain men.

My mother fit my father's pattern at first glance, but there was something more about her. She was a tough cookie—a knockout but not dumb, and she wasn't about to just shut up and idolize him. Maybe that's why he really loved her—I believe he did, and when they divorced, he never got over it. I was too young to remember much about them together, but from what I can recall, it was a relationship full of pain and heartbreak. After the divorce, I was the rope in a tug-of-war. Long after their war was over, and even now that my father is gone, I still feel the pain of being pulled between them.

But in the beginning, even before I can remember, it was different. I have baby pictures of me with my father, and I have looked at those pictures over and over through the years—pictures of him holding me up at Disneyland, playing with me and holding me on his lap. I've obsessed about them. From the way he looked at me, I could see what it meant to him to have a daughter. I wish I could remember more from that time, because most of my memories about my father are unhappy ones, and I have only little glimpses of wonderful, seemingly perfect times with him.

When I was four, my parents moved to California, but my mom didn't last very long out there. She left my father and moved back to New York. I was just a baby, I had no idea what was going on between them and, of course, I couldn't have done anything about it, but my mother told me there was a lot of fighting. It makes me feel helpless to think about it. All I really know is that they didn't stay together, and that was my first real taste of bitterness and abandonment. My mother couldn't afford to support me, so she left me with my father. As a successful horse trainer, my father could afford to support me, but he refused to pay unless I lived with him. So I stayed in California and said good-bye to my mother.

I think my father played it like this to get back at my mother, but I also think at the time that he wanted me around. He took me to the track every day and it was exciting and fun. Still, he was constantly working, so he didn't have much time for me. He ran with a hard-partying crowd and I was always left with someone—usually a housekeeper or whichever nineteen-year-old hottie he was sleeping with at the moment. I spent a lot of time alone.

I have just a few vague memories of my father. I remember sitting in IHOP and giggling when he would put a whole fried egg in his mouth, just to amuse me. I get emotional remembering that day. Looking back, I can see how it might have been just one part of a long and wonderful relationship that was never to be.

My few early memories of my father carry with them this intense feeling, this whole inner, romanticized world. Whether it was real or not, I'm not sure, but I think it was at the time. For years afterward, I created and sustained an extensive, imagined father-daughter relationship with him based on a handful of vague memories.

Instead, what I have more of are bad memories associated with the string of babysitters who took care of me when I lived with him. I think they were often so young that they just didn't think about feeding me properly or on time, or they got irritated when I didn't want to eat what they were eating. I remember one girl giving me a sandwich of avocado on whole wheat—but I didn't like the look of it. I was four, and the sandwich was green. I refused to eat it. She forced it into my mouth. For a very long time, I hated avocados because of that experience.

Sometimes, my father left me with a friend, another successful trainer who sadly committed suicide later in his life. He had twin daughters who became my only friends because we were close in age. Brooke and Esme were adorable little blond girls with a nasty nanny named Beatrice. I remember the nanny forcing us to eat a disgusting dish of pasta with raisins. It made me sick. That nanny hit us when she thought we were bad. Those little blond girls would bawl and I was the smug, belligerent one, smiling through it all, pretending with every ounce of courage I could summon that it didn't bother me. I bit my lip and refused to show the pain. I still react to adversity this way.

My high threshold for physical and emotional pain helps me get through some situations, but it's been one of my greatest stumbling blocks in trying to maintain intimate relationships because it still feels risky to me to show weakness. I hardly used any pain medication after my C-section—I always just plow right through things. It's funny, I'll cry over spilled milk—I'll sweat the small stuff—but barrel through something really big. I think my childhood desensitized me. It also gave me resolve: I will never spank my own child, and I don't understand how anybody could ever do this to a child. I set Jason straight on that one—he'll be spanking me, or I'll be spanking him, before we ever spank our daughter.

Those long hours and days with babysitters were torture. I was a little girl and I missed my mommy. I didn't understand (and still don't) how she could have moved across the country without me. I called her on the phone so many times, crying and begging her to come and get me. It all just seemed wrong.

I don't know how much my father knew about what was going on while he wasn't around. To him, his work was everything—the horses, the track, that was life. I get that, because I can be that way, too. But . . . I was his daughter. How could he not know how much I needed something more than a string of careless babysitters who ignored me? How could he not know that I needed at least *one* parent? The occasional roller-coaster ride with Daddy does not a relationship make. And another link is added to the chain.

When I finally saw my mother for the first time after I had been living with my father, she was startled at how thin I had become. Years later, whenever she would tell me what a bad person my father was, she would always reference this. They both used to talk badly about the other to me; it took me years to realize you don't do this to kids. I would never say anything bad about Jason to Bryn— the idea is horrific to me! So much of this period I don't remember well, so I only know what my mother told me, but from what I can determine, my apparent lack of care prompted her to find a way to get me back.

During this time, my mother was in a relationship with an East Coast horse trainer named John Parisella. Because my mother grew up around the track, all the trainers knew who she was. Like most men, John always had a thing for my mother, and the story on the racetrack was that they had been having an affair even before my mother was divorced, but who knows what was really true? I later learned that John and my father had been former friends, and I know there were bad feelings between them because my mother was now with John. Thinking back, it makes sense when I remember the animosity between John and my father. John eventually became my stepfather.

John was influential in my coming back to New York because my mother couldn't afford to bring me back and support me. I had no idea (considering that I was only four) how much this would impact my relationship with my father. My mother took me away, and I think it broke his heart. He never forgave her for that—and somehow, I got tied up in the blame. I had no idea how much it would change the course of my life. I didn't hear from him for years.

Finally, a few years later, my father reached out to me when we were living in Queens, New York. He wanted me to come see him. I was so excited! I didn't remember him very well but I was intrigued by the storybook idea of him. I used to think to myself, "Somewhere out there, I have a *real father*." I was seven years old and had already begun to idealize his vague memory.

He made arrangements for me to fly out to see him a few days after New Year's. My mother and my stepfather were against it, but I wanted to go so badly that they said they would allow it.

That New Year's Eve with my mother, I drank champagne and banged pots and pans in the street barefoot and got a terrible fever. It reached 105 degrees. A few days later, I was supposed to be on that plane to visit my father. At the airport, my mother was checking me in, and realized that he had bought me a coach ticket. She threw a fit.

Why hadn't he bought me a first-class ticket? She said he was *rich*, and she knew he could afford it. I was sick, I had a fever, and she wasn't going to have me travel coach. She said it was unacceptable.

I specifically remember money being used as a weapon during this incident. Maybe my money noise began on that day.

I think she was just angry and wanted to hurt him. I don't know exactly how the conversation went, but my mother didn't put me on the plane. When my father went to the airport to pick me up, I wasn't there.

I think he shut down to me that day and it was never the same between us. This always hung in the air between us, this event over which I had no control.

All of this over first class? It's never about what it's about, is it?

I found out, decades later, at my father's funeral, from some of his friends, how crushed he was when I didn't get off that plane. His friends told me he had been so excited about my visit. He had fixed up the house and planned a whole schedule for us. It breaks my heart to think about it.

If I could go back in time, I would change that moment—I would somehow convince my mother to put me on that plane, just to see how it would have played out. Given my father's limitations, it probably wouldn't have changed a thing.

Still, the way she handled every situation throughout my life when I had any contact with him built up roadblock after roadblock, and that may have been what permanently damaged our relationship.

After that incident, my mother told me that my father said he was washing his hands of the whole situation, and I didn't hear from him again for years. But I can't help wondering: What if he had told me how brokenhearted he was? He could have saved himself years of misery, and me years of anguish. But he didn't, or couldn't. He let me go. He didn't fight for me.

I think my father did the best he could, but it's sad—for all of us. Every decision we make has a consequence, even when we don't think anyone will notice or it doesn't matter or the consequence doesn't happen for years. He gave up on me, and the consequences rumbled on for decades, affecting us both, irreversibly. If we ever had a shot at a relationship, that killed it. Although my father made brief attempts to reach out to me later, I think that was the last time he ever let himself be so vulnerable.

I understand how easy it can be to make this mistake, and not realize the damage you've done until it's too late. Whether with friendships or family, the bottom line is that actions have effects. A throwaway comment or a spur-of-the-moment decision made in anger or thoughtlessness could still have an impact thirty years later. After that, our interactions were few and far between. On my seventh birthday, he said he sent me an ID bracelet for my birthday. I watched the mail for weeks, and finally gave up. It never arrived.

When I was thirteen, my father saw a picture of me in the newspaper, in the winner's circle after a horse race, with my stepfather. He was known for being jealous and competitive, and I believe his ego made him call me. All those years my stepfather was struggling, we never heard a word from my father, but as soon as John started to do well and win a lot of races, that's when he called. He didn't like to lose.

He was coming to New York and he wanted to have lunch with me. I was nervous and excited, but I also felt guilty about wanting to see him because my mother kept telling me that he abandoned us. I felt like it would be disloyal to her and my stepfather if I wanted to see him. Yet, I began to have these fantasies that I would meet him and everything would be perfect. I wanted to be an actress when I grew up, so I imagined moving to Los Angeles with him. It would be this beautiful movie ending, or a tearful climactic moment on *The Oprah Winfrey Show*.

However, I didn't know him at all, so I convinced my mother to go along, which was a mistake. There I was, stuck at a table between two of the most negative, miserable people in the world. My mother spent the whole lunch berating him, and it was not anything like the reunion I imagined in my head. The next day, I agreed to go shopping with him alone, and he bought me a $365 Louis Vuitton purse. I held on to that memory and the purse for years, as if one contained the other—that purse represented a lost past and a future that was never to be, the father who would buy me whatever I wanted and make all my dreams come true.

Sometime after that ill-fated lunch date, my father took me on a weekend ski trip to Lake Tahoe, but the weekend was short, and then it was over. I received a few halfhearted phone calls or requests to get together after that, but that is pretty much the sum of our relationship. I can count the times he called me on one hand.

Maybe having a relationship with me was just too much for him. Maybe I reminded him too much of my mother. Although I still kept the fantasy of a reunion in the back of my mind, I learned not to believe in it anymore. My father would never be there for me in any regular way. He was in and out of my life at his own whim, or according to his own reasons that I would never know, and there was nothing I could do about it.

After that our very rare communications became defined by money.

When I was a teenager in New York, I took the Mercedes out one night with my friends, to show off, when my parents weren't home. I didn't know how to drive very well yet, and as I was pulling up to a bar, I crashed into some guy's new Corvette, just as he was walking out of the bar to show a friend his car. I managed to convince the owner not to call the police if I would pay the damages, and I went home and called my father in Los Angeles, asking him to help me. I felt like he owed me that, at least. He sent me the money, out of guilt, or just because he didn't know how else to relate to me.

As I got older, there was a battle between my father and stepfather about who would pay for college, for my car, for my rent. I always felt helpless, like I had to make it work even though I was completely dependent on both of them to finance me. Once when I was in college in Boston, my father came to visit me after another long stretch with no contact and he said he would take me and my friends out for dinner, so I invited a bunch of my friends. I wanted everyone to see him, so they would think I had a normal, even an *impressive* father, to see how lucky I was. It was my delusional way of pretending we had a relationship even though we'd only seen each other four times in fifteen years.

Ironically, even though he was rich and successful, my father was one of those people who always wanted what he couldn't have. He used to covet other people's wives, possessions, successes. I think more than anything else in the world, he wanted to win the Kentucky Derby. He would have given up anything to have that success, and I can't help thinking that karma kept it from him. He died never knowing that victory. It's too bad the Triple Crown was more important to him than being a father.

A few years ago, before my father died, I was on the *Today Show*, on Father's Day. When the subject inevitably came up, I said, very casually, as if the holiday didn't apply to me at all, "I don't have a father."

My father was watching, and I heard later that he was infuriated by that comment. I'm sure that when I said it, I was angry, but I had also finally realized that my own success and independence had liberated me from having to be dependent on him, financially or emotionally. He couldn't hurt me anymore. I had to do a lot of work to get from that place with my father to a place where I could regain control of my own life, stand on my own two feet, find Jason, and be a mother. But I did it. I made it, without him.

Now that Jason and I have a daughter, memories of my father make me realize just how precious Jason is. Our daughter is his world and I know that he would never cut himself off from her because of anything I did or she did. He does funny, cute, endearing, loving things with her every day and she will never have to obsess about the few good times with her father—there will be so many, she won't possibly be able to remember them all. He doesn't have to force himself to be great with her. It's innate, it's just who he is: open-hearted and loving.

I understand that my father had his own noise and his own reasons for everything he did. It was his life to do with what he chose.

But I can control whom I marry and who will be the father of my child, and this time, I chose well. Maybe because of my father, I know what I need in a relationship. I know what kind of father my daughter needs—one who loves her unconditionally and without ceasing. So I guess I can thank my father for teaching me those things, even if the lessons were painful. That's how I can come from a place of yes.

My father died recently, and that was life-changing for me. When I first heard he was sick, I got very upset. I was already having a lot of stress in my life, I was right in the middle of filming the third season of *Real Housewives*, I was pregnant but didn't know it yet, and then I found out he was doing pretty badly.

I fell apart. It's hard to describe how I felt. My childhood noise became very loud. It brought out a lot of the anger I had buried because I didn't know what to do with it. I was also confused. I was sad, but not because I was losing him—maybe because it made me realize I was never going to find him. I wasn't sure what to do. Should I forgive him? Should I tell him I'm okay? Did he even want to know? Did he even care?

I flew out to Los Angeles to see him. I didn't really want to see him, but I knew it might be my last chance, and I thought it was the right thing to do. And he refused to see me. What a kick in the head that was. So I turned around and went back to New York and wrote him a letter. I wrote down everything I wanted to say to him in person. Maybe this was the best way I could have communicated with him, because I had time to think and revise and make sure I said what I really wanted to say.

I told him that I had found love and that maybe I had a real shot at being happy now. I said that no amount of money or fame or success or races won was ever going to make him happy, and maybe if he pulled out of this, he might recognize that and in some small way start over. I didn't say I loved him. That was not a word that could be applied to our relationship. There was too much breakage there, and no structure on which to hang anything resembling love. But I did tell him that I forgave him.

Not long after that, his ex-wife (not my mother) called to tell me that he was getting worse and that it looked as if this really was the end. She was taking care of him, and she said he asked her to call. Would he see me this time? She said yes, I should come.

So I sucked it up, and I went. Jason and I weren't married yet, but he came with me. We went to the hospital and we saw him.

It had been years since I'd seen him in person—I don't even know how many years. He looked very old and pathetic in that hospital bed, not able to do anything for himself anymore. He'd always been slick and powerful and in control of every situation, running the show. Not anymore. It made me sad to see him, as it would make me sad to see any human being in pain and suffering. But it wasn't sad like the end of a relationship. Seeing him in person made me realize with even more force that ours was a relationship that might have been, but never was.

There was still part of me, somewhere in the back of my mind— the little-girl part—that hoped for a reconciliation, in the same way I had dreamed at the age of seven that we would finally be father and daughter again, the way fathers and daughters *should* be (whatever that means). I thought maybe he would tell me he was sorry for how he treated me, that he regretted refusing a relationship with me, that somehow he would make it all right again. I thought maybe, just maybe there at the end, he'd pull out of it.

He didn't. He had some words for me, though, that sounded a little bit like regret. He told Jason and me that we should fight for our relationship. He never could fight for any of his in his life. He wasn't capable of it. Somehow he recognized, I think, that this was something I could do that he never could do. And that was something.

But we didn't get it all out in the open and make up, or anything remotely like it. I remember at one point, Jason and I were standing by my father's bed with his brother and one of his employees, and my father said something like, "We were all so lucky to have such wonderful childhoods." And he smiled.

I felt as if I was falling into a black hole. Who was he talking to? What wonderful childhoods? I guess he really wasn't there for mine, so how could he know? He didn't look at me, and even to the end, he was dismissive and rude to me. I wondered why he had asked for me at all.

He died without ever saying he was sorry. There were no tears. I don't know if he loved me or not, but he did die with my forgiveness. I forgave him, not for him, but because I had to do it for myself. I had to let it go. I was tired of living with that noise. I realized that even if he never loved me at all, I could move on. This is how I broke the chain.

I went through such a range of emotions that day. I kept expecting something. I see now that I was never going to get whatever it was. My father died alone. He spent his life alone. I heard that when he wasn't at the track, all he did was sit in his club chair and watch TV. In the end, all he had were the emotional walls he built—or, that's what I guess. I really wasn't allowed to know.

Sometimes family issues *don't* get resolved. Sometimes you don't get a tear-jerker, Hollywood ending. Sometimes it's just over, and you're left to deal with the aftermath, but it doesn't have to define you.

All I can say is thank goodness I had Jason there at my side through it all. I don't know if I could have done it without him. He was such a rock, so calm and reassuring and a constant reminder that what my father did, he would not do. Looking at my father dying made me realize what I had next to me—someone who is strong, who is always there, who never wavers. Someone who has inspired me to intervene in my own destructive behavior—as much as any human can. Jason isn't like my father at all, and when my father died, my childhood noise crawled back into its cage and shut up for a while.

So much of a woman's relationship with the men in her life comes, obviously or not obviously, from her relationship with her father. One doesn't have to be a psychiatrist to see this truth. When you look back at your own life and your own father (or lack of a father), what kind of links do you see to the men you choose? Some will be strong and good and true, if you had a father who was all those things and shared them with you. Some won't be. Not all links in your chain will require breaking, but take it or leave it—find the ones that set you free to find a relationship that works for who you are, and let the others fall away.

All I ask of you is to look back and *see*. Seeing is the first step. When you see what didn't work, even what hurt and harmed you, that's when you can break the chain. Your childhood noise tries to hold you in a pattern. Be your own woman. Coming from a place of yes helps you step into something new.

My Stepfather

Action is the antidote to despair.

—Joan Baez, folk singer

In many ways, John Parisella was the only real father I've ever had. At the same time, he was even more dysfunctional, unpredictable, unstable, and psychotic than my father ever was. Bobby was cold and callous. John was absolutely crazy, but he loved me, even though I wasn't his child. He would have done anything for me, and that's what I choose to take away and remember about him.

I loved John, and for many years, I thought of him as my father. I will always want him to know this. But he was as volatile as my mother was. Life with the two of them was completely insane—full of spectacular high points and abysmal lows.

John was always stressed out, and it seemed to me that much of this stress was about money. I remember that it seemed like he was always borrowing from Peter to pay Paul. He lived the life of the racetrack, just as my father had, but he was more social, more erratic, more on the edge—not the caliber of a trainer my father was, but a warmer and more passionate man. John was always in some mad rush to make something happen. Jason has a saying: "Everybody's a big-timer." That was John.

Our house in Queens, New York, was always full of nervous, rebellious, frenetic energy, and life was a string of altercations, screaming, fighting, embarrassment in front of the neighbors, and police intervention. My mother loved to party and she would often stay out all night doing who knows what, then come home at five in the morning and if my stepfather had locked the door, she used all of her ninety-eight pounds to punch her tiny arm through the glass window. Then they would fight.

It was like living in a house full of land mines. Nobody ever said, "Wait, this isn't appropriate, let's take this in the other room. Let's not do this now." I'm still piecing together what really happened during those years with my mother and John, but sometimes it was truly scary and nobody ever explained anything to me. Every so often, I'll think about something that happened and I'll have an a-ha moment, but I wish someone would have made it all more clear to me. I might have felt safer

But life was exciting. John was an action junkie, a gambler, and always seemed to be involved with questionable characters. My mother and I never knew all the details, but we often had to move, sometimes suddenly, and often away from a home I loved. John never told us why.

One day we would have six luxury cars in the driveway. The next day, we'd have just one. Where did they go? Were they ours? Were they rented? I never knew. We'd live in a nice house with little furniture in it, except in my bedroom, which they always made sure was perfect. But we'd eat dinner on a card table.

It was an unbalanced life. We'd take a limo into the city, and then we would be broke. To see it in a more positive way, I did learn how to survive, be flexible, and go with whatever was happening, and I still have those qualities. I had to learn how to deal with this crazy life, do or die. Because of those days, I can be just as happy shopping at a ninety-nine-cent store as at Bloomingdales.

I spent a lot of time away from home, or so I remember, when my parents left me with other people. I remember a lot of my stepfather's buddies who had to take care of me. Bruce was the nerdy accountant, Sneakers was the jockey agent, Jules was the bookmaker. They were all shady racetrack characters, usually men. Some of them were inappropriate with me, although I only remember bits and pieces. Maybe someday I'll remember more.

One of my favorites was Wilson, one of my father's grooms, who was always sweet and kind to me. Wilson often took me to stay with his mother, Pat, in Ozone Park, Queens. Those were good times. Pat was Irish, and like a mother to me, in many ways more than my own mother. She was nurturing, and I felt safe around her. I thought of her house as my second home. I played stickball and hung out on the street with the other kids. It all seemed so normal. Pat taught me how to play gin rummy, and I hung out with her and her friends and watched her smoke cigarettes. She used to say to me, "Cool your pits," by which she meant "calm down." It still makes me giggle to think of that.

Pat contacted me recently, after the success of my show. She says that she remembers that my mother was always dropping me off at her house, like she wanted to get rid of me. To me, Pat's house was a relief, and I'm still grateful to her for taking me into her home.

Despite the insanity, I really am glad that I had John around growing up. I think he was a damaged person, but as volatile and inconsistent as he was, he was also there for me, more than either of my real parents. Of the three of them, I think he was the only one who tried to come from a place of yes. He always had hope and he always aimed high. He could be manipulative and mean sometimes, but I also think that in some ways, he knew what was important.

Even when my mother would take off on long trips without us, he was there for me. I remember that he didn't want me to go to summer camp or off to private school because he would miss me too much. He always tried to give me what I wanted, when he could. When he had money, I always had a couple hundred dollars in my wallet. He used to tell me that I would never have to worry about money because everything would always be taken care of. Sometimes it was true—and at other times he had nothing, and we were on the move again—or our furniture was.

I'll never forget the day that he asked me to break open my piggy bank for him. He always remembered that I agreed to do it, and for years he talked about the time I saved him with my piggy bank. I don't know what he needed it for, but I was willing to give it to him out of loyalty. He was my father—the father who was trying to be there for me.

For many years, I used the last name Parisella. I remember standing in the school office with him, registering for yet another school, when they asked me my name. Suddenly it seemed inappropriate to say "Frankel." I went by Bethenny Parisella for years afterward, even though John never actually adopted me. I called him Dad.

I have some really good memories from this time, even if now, thinking back, they seem unsavory, things that I would never let my daughter do! When I was thirteen, John got me into a U2 concert in Vegas and showed me how to gamble at the craps table in Caesar's Palace. His uncle was Don Rickles's manager, and he knew a lot of other high-profile people in Vegas. We walked around as if we owned the place, and I felt so proud to be with him. I felt like we could do anything we wanted to do. That's how it was with John, no matter where we went. It was the racetrack mentality—a high-roller lifestyle. He was mercurial and tumultuous and full of pride, and I loved that about him.

Food was a common theme in those days, too. My stepfather considered good food the highest priority, and he loved to find the very best of whatever he wanted. We would go all the way to Spumoni Gardens in Brooklyn to get the best pizza and Italian ices; we'd go to Queens for the best cannoli; we drove to Coney Island

and my mother would get a lobster roll and I would get a hot dog at Nathan's. Every Sunday, we'd have fresh bagels and lox. Food was an event, and it was always worth a long trip and a lot of trouble to get food that was really worth eating. I still feel that way. I go on food crawls through the city or whenever I travel. It's part of what I've taken from my childhood and carried on—Jason and I eat dim sum or go to Little Italy or Brooklyn for pizza, and we love to seek out the best of the best whenever we travel. I'll pass this down to Bryn. John made that important to me.

My very favorite thing about my childhood was spending every August in Saratoga. Those were the proverbial "good old days." On the road trip there, in the middle of the night, my mother and I would go to a rest stop and get popcorn. Once we arrived, the race-track living began.

People see horse races on TV and they think of well-dressed ladies with big hats, but I saw the seamier side. I spent mornings in the barn and afternoons with the jockeys. I was a "hot walker," walking horses around the track to cool them down after their work-out. At the end of the day, everybody would go to the Wishing Well, a restaurant, to eat and drink and brag and yell and act like a big family. I loved going there with all the adults, talking to them, eating what they ate. It made me feel important. I was truly comfortable around those crazy, hustling, gambling racetrack people. It helped shape me, for better or for worse. I was always very proud to be at the track—when you are the daughter of the trainer, everybody knows who you are.

Rituals were so rare in my crazy life that I remember the few I had as the highlights of my childhood. Every morning, I went to the track with John. We frequented Dunkin' Donuts, or found this guy named Red who sold chocolate cake in the mornings at the track. I can still taste that moist chocolate cake, the best I've ever had. We would buy one and share it. I can also taste the fresh tomatoes and corn we bought at the farm stands. Every day, we saw the same people at the track, in the paddock, hanging out in the winner's circle. It felt so *reliable*.

Sometimes my mother and stepfather and I drove from Saratoga to Lake George. We ate hand-dipped ice cream with the hard chocolate shell that they used to call "chocolate honey dip," and played skee ball. It really felt as if we were a family during those times, and that was because of John. He was crazy, but he had a big heart and he shared it, and his life, with me. Maybe he would put me in the middle of things, and maybe he would pit me against my mother sometimes, but he always seemed loyal to me. I certainly can't say that about my real father.

In the press, my mother has said that my horrible childhood is a myth, and that we had a lot of good times. She's wrong and she's right. There was a lot of bad, but there was good, too. Saratoga was good. There were still fights, drama, all of that—I leave those. I take warm memories from that time, and I keep them with me now.

When I was a teenager, John started to enjoy some real success, and he always said it was because of me. That's because of one particular event. My mother had gone off to Wales for several months, leaving me with John. Her family is from Wales—very poor people who lived in shacks and raised pigeons. I used to spend the summer there sometimes. On this occasion she went alone.

I was thirteen years old. John had to entertain a potential business partner and he needed help. He wasn't sure what to do, but he needed to make a big impression. It was a morning meeting and he asked if I could help him. I said yes.

I guess my domestic side came out—I made breakfast for them both, and served them, and acted as charming and grown-up as I could. I was the consummate hostess, and it worked. I made a good impression, and so did John. The meeting went off without a hitch, the deal went through, and John's career was launched. He always thanked me for that, saying he couldn't have done it without me, that it took him to the next level. I felt so proud and important for helping him. I also discovered that I had a special talent for cooking and entertaining and even organizing a social event. I could pull it together and make things happen.

Then, my mother divorced John.

At first, John said he would continue to support me because he considered me to be his daughter. But then my mother took up with someone else, and when John found out I was still speaking to her, he went ballistic. She had betrayed him, so my association with her meant I had betrayed him, too. It was the one and only time he got physical with me—and just like that, as if our entire past had never happened, he cut me out of his life.

That's when I reached out to my father again. What a broken record I was. I thought, John's gone crazy, I'll start using the name Frankel again and now my real father can sweep in and become a father to me, after all these years. I won't have to worry anymore. Everything will be the way I imagined it so many times in my life. You would think I would have learned my lesson by then. In fact, this became my pattern with men—if this man is done, the next one will save me.

Predictably, however, when I called my father, and asked him to help me, he wanted nothing to do with me. It reminded me of when a guy is courting a woman he can't have, and when he finally wins her over, he doesn't want her anymore. I remember crying and saying, "Why won't you be my father?"

He told me it was because he had cancer.

I remember thinking, *You have cancer. Isn't that when you want to be close to your family?* Not for him. A few years later, his cancer went into remission. This didn't make him want to reach out to me. I'd reach out to him every few years after that, but he never responded. He was always cool and dismissive. Ultimately, his cancer would return.

All of them always had conditions for their love, and I spent so much of my life feeling guilty for wanting to love any of them, because of those conditions. When John was with my mother, they didn't want me to speak to my father. When my mother left him, I couldn't speak to her. It was all about control, with every one of them failing to recognize that I was a child and they shouldn't be using me this way.

I didn't choose to marry my father, or my stepfather. My mother did. I was the only one who didn't have a choice about being in this family. So why was I punished when it all fell apart?

Now that I'm an adult, I realize how complicated life is, and what a huge and difficult and beautiful responsibility it is to have a child. But could I have done it at age twenty? Or twenty-five? Or even thirty? I don't know. All I know is that I lost both my fathers, in different ways, and walked away feeling like I never had a father at all. It became a theme: men would come in, take care of me, and it would all be okay . . . until it wasn't.

The chain I inherited from John was the belief that men would always take care of me, and if they suddenly couldn't, I was simply out of luck. Powerless. The message I want to give you here is that you can't look to other people to take care of you financially, especially if that's not what you really want or need. Money can never stand in for a relationship. It will never fill the hole left by the withholding of love.

Broken, blended, extended—whatever you want to call a family like mine, I know I'm not unique. So many people have lived through divorce now that it's hardly unusual anymore, but that doesn't make it any less painful. However, if your parents divorced, I think it's worthwhile to contemplate whether the divorce itself affected you more or less than the way your parents behaved afterward. What insecurities have you internalized because of it? All kids want is security. If you didn't get it, where will you find it?

In your future.

My Daughter

I have enjoyed life a lot more by saying yes than by saying no.

—Sir Richard Branson, entrepreneur

Having Bryn changed everything. Suddenly, everything I ever thought or believed about my parents, I saw through a different lens. I could see how they were hurt, why they screwed up, where they came from, how their own noise got in their way. I got softer, less angry.

At the same time, I was baffled—how could they have behaved that way?

As I hold Bryn in my arms, she has already taught me more than I ever knew before—and she can't even talk or walk yet. Having a child is the most important reason to break the chain. If you were ever hurt by your parents in any way, and of course you were, then you need to stop the madness and turn in a new direction: toward a place of yes.

Looking back, I can see how easily in my life I could have gone in so many different directions, and a lot of them could have ended in disaster. But no matter what happened to me, no matter how much trouble I got in or how many times I was disappointed, something inside kept me moving forward.

I still beat myself up a lot. I usually default to the notion that if Jason and I argue, I must be wrong, I must be crazy, I must be the bad one because I had the messed-up childhood. I think a lot of people do that—beat themselves up, disqualify themselves, for whatever reason. One of my goals is to stop doing this—to leave it behind.

But I also acknowledge the good that I've brought out of my childhood—strength, flexibility, open-mindedness, resolve to do a better job. These qualities I take with me in order to break the chain. I think this is a crucial way to see your childhood—you have to sift the good from the bad, like putting vegetables in a colander and rinsing away the dirt.

I never wanted people to feel sorry for me. I never felt like a victim. I was analytical and I always figured out how to get to the next place. At my core, I always believed I was going to be something more than a troubled kid who never made anything of herself.

I recently received three emails, one from an old high school friend, another from a college roommate, the third from an old boyfriend. None of these people knew each other, but their emails were almost identical. They all said some version of: *Bethenny, you always talked about having it all. You worked hard for it, and despite everything you went through, you made it. I'm proud of you.*

They are describing a place of yes.

The thing about childhood noise is that if you let it take over, it can obliterate your true nature. The best qualities in you have always been there, but when you get stuck in the past and make your pain your identity, then that's what you become. After I was featured in *People* magazine, a lot of people called me and asked, "Are those things about your past true?" Yes, but I've moved on from the old story of my life.

To have a future, you have to let the past be past.

So, my message to you after sharing these difficult memories is just this: Instead of letting the negative parts of your childhood drag you down and suck you in and spit you out as some carbon copy of your dysfunctional parents or traumatic experiences, let them transform you. You have to decide who you want to be. Take it or leave it. You have to take the good and leave the bad. My mother taught me how to love—and she also taught me how *not* to love. Both lessons are valuable, and the second one might turn out to be the one that will help me the most.

We are all the products of our parents' actions but we can move on. It doesn't have to be my fate, and it doesn't have to be yours. Breaking the chain can be difficult, and it can take a few swings of the axe before you actually sever the links. You have to keep trying. Just when you think you've broken out of the dysfunctional patterns you learned from your family, something may trigger them again. You have to be motivated *not* to carry on a legacy of harm and pain. You have to be willing to start over, in every way, again and again. It took me most of my life so far to be able to do this, and if coming from a place of yes *today* can help keep some of you from having to repeat your mistakes as many times as I did, then it was all worth it to come clean.

Sometimes when I'm holding Bryn and we're having a moment, Jason will say to me, "She loves her mommy." It makes me happy when he says that, so happy I can't even put it into words. It makes me feel as if the chain is truly broken.

It's a tricky balance, to find the parts of you that have always been strong and true and good, and it's even trickier to go with those, while rejecting the parts of you that are drowning in the noise of your childhood stories. Cast off your story like a bad outfit that has gone out of fashion, and you'll be set free to look back at the parts of your childhood that contain glimmers of the real you.

It's time to change your outfit. Ask yourself: *What if I am none of those bad things I believe about myself? What if I can put on something else, something that actually makes me feel beautiful?*

Every childhood has sparkly parts. Dwell on what you loved, your own private discovery of your special talents and passions, what thrilled you and amazed you and made your eyes go wide. I dwell on the warm memories, the horses, Saratoga, Christmas and Thanksgiving. I dwell on the funny, clever Bethenny who never let a bad situation get her down—the one who wouldn't be bullied, who kept her chin up, who lay on the school bus seat alone making up songs and singing them to herself, who kept on reading her book report in front of the class, even when her wraparound skirt fell down around her ankles, the mischievous Bethenny who scooped snow off the ledge and threw it into the classroom when the teacher wasn't looking, and hung out with the boys and climbed trees and always took a dare and who sometimes felt triumphant and proud and even happy.

Let those glimmers stay. Let the rest of it fall away. When you focus on the bad, you risk becoming the bad, or getting pulled down by the bad. When you say yes to the good in you, then you become better and better, and you have the potential to go anywhere and do and be anything. So hold on to the best parts of you from the past, and let go of the parts that hurt. They aren't you. Take it or leave it. Your natural talents and dreams have been there all along, so look inside to find them, not to the world to fix you.

In other words, *you can fix yourself.* That was an incredible realization for me. *You can fix yourself.* Break the chain, come from a place of yes, and you'll torch the obstacles that are keeping you from seeing who you really are and what you can be. You'll break the chain and escape the bondage of your childhood noise.

What you need to succeed in your life you already have inside you. What you do, where you are going, those things will change, but the core of you that is true and real will always be there for you to find, if you can just dig down past your noise. So start listening.

Whether you want to be a better mother or a better CEO, to find the love of your life or make a million dollars, to finish a marathon or lose twenty pounds or get your degree or finally find your true passion in life, it doesn't matter. You can turn any piece of clay into a masterpiece, and you are the piece of clay. If your path is to get healthy or be a better citizen or love your family more or just gain a certain degree of self-awareness, come from a place of yes and you can do it.

In the coming chapters, I'll talk more about how to get to the next level, but for now, remember this one rule: *Break the chain.* It doesn't matter to me anymore that my parents came from a place of no. Maybe that's not totally true—it does matter to me, but it doesn't hold me back anymore. It doesn't hurt my soul anymore. Because I broke the chain.

You can look at your past, recognize the noise and how it is holding you back, and choose to go a different way. But you can't live your life looking in the rearview mirror to see who you are. Look yourself straight in the eye. That's the real you. You get to decide what comes next. Stop getting in your own way, and stop telling yourself you can't. Because you *can*.

Rule 2
· · · · · · · · · · · ·

Find Your Truth
How I Finally Met My Match

Accept no one's definition of your life; define yourself.

—Harvey Fierstein, actor

Who are you, and what do you want?

It's not an interrogation. It's a call to introspection. How often have you looked back at certain decisions and actions, and wondered what you were thinking? Maybe you weren't thinking. Or maybe you weren't thinking hard enough. People say they know who they are, and they think they know what they want, but they go through life making random decisions without thinking about the potential impact.

Let's talk about truth. If you want to come from a place of yes, to move forward in your life and become the best version of yourself, you have to seek truth. You have to ask yourself what's genuine and true for you—not for your parents (break the chain), not for your friends, not for your siblings or your school or your society, but for *you*. It's the question of a lifetime, and it can take a lifetime to really answer it, but you still have to keep asking.

Your truth will change as you keep changing. Who I was at twenty, and what I thought I wanted, is totally different from who I am and what I want now. I wasn't ready then for what I have now. And I wouldn't choose now what I chose then.

Still, you have to keep asking, "Who am I?" and "What do I really want?" It's the best way to cultivate integrity, make the right decisions, and save yourself from a lot of stupid mistakes.

That's what the next rule is all about—digging deep inside and figuring out what is authentic for you, based on who you are and what you want. It's rule #2, and it is the next rule to face after you've broken the chain from childhood and are setting out on your own: *Find your truth.*

Find Your Truth

Finding your truth is the key to finding your life. How can you pursue a dream if it isn't your dream? Do you even know what your dream is? This is your work, after you've broken the chain: Find what's true for you, based on who you are, and what you really want.

I call it "find your truth" rather than "know your truth" because truth is not something you pluck out of the air. It's not objective. You can't just know what it is without doing any work, and you can't rely on anyone else to know what it is. It doesn't exist apart from you. It's not who others think you are, it's not who you want to be, and it's not written in any book. It's not even, necessarily, who *you* think you are, if you aren't really digging deep to get the answer.

It's also not something you can fully know right this second. Finding your truth is like putting the pieces of a puzzle together. It takes some time and concentration and concerted effort. It evolves. You will have clarifying moments, like when someone makes some casual comment that exactly describes you and something inside of you says, "Yes!" Or it could be that a familiar pattern recurs— someone wrongs you or you make a mistake—and suddenly, maybe even right in the middle of your "woe-is-me" tantrum, you see why it happened.

Everything that happens to you, each experience, each stumble or achievement, is another piece, and the more the puzzle comes together, the more clearly you start to see where the next pieces should go. But nobody would blame you for not knowing where one puzzle piece out of a thousand is supposed to go, when you've only got one corner of the puzzle put together. Be patient. Your life is the puzzle, and it's fun and challenging to put it together, even if you sometimes spend too much time trying to shove a piece into the wrong space. At some point, you figure out that you're doing it wrong, and you try a different piece.

Your truth is a *process*, not an end. Your truth is the journey, not the destination. In this puzzle, the pieces are always changing, so it's a brainteaser like no other, but it's *your* brainteaser, and you'll be working it out for years to come. And that's *good*. That's *life*. Even better, that's *your* life.

When you are faced with a major decision, like whether to get married, change jobs, or move to another city, it is essential to seek what's true for you, rather than for the people around you. The people around you will always want you to do what they want. That's human nature. Unless you know what you want, you'll be making decisions and living your life on somebody else's terms.

Even when the decision is a small one, or even when you are sitting alone thinking about your life, finding your truth will make everything clearer. You won't get distracted, misled, or lose focus, because you know what's true.

When you know who you are and what you want, you'll be more confident, even if you don't always know exactly what the outcome of a decision will be. When your decisions, your actions, and your words come from your truth—even if it's only the truth of the moment—then you will be practicing authenticity. You'll know that you are moving in the right direction, and when you screw up, you'll be able to stand up and admit it. Truth will back you up every time.

It's not always easy to act out of truth, especially when you aren't sure exactly what your truth is. For example, religion is a tricky issue for Jason and me. Jason was raised Catholic, and he goes to church every Sunday. I was raised . . . well, you read chapter 1. Clearly I am religiously confused. I practice yoga.

Jason and I recently had an experience that helped us both to practice rule #2, find your truth.

Our baby nurse, Gina, asked us to come to church with her, and we thought this would be a nice way to experience an important part of her life. We all dressed up and brought Bryn, and the service was progressing as church services do, when suddenly, much to our surprise, people began to crowd around us. The bishop said he wanted to do a special blessing for Bryn, so Jason and I said that would be nice, but then Jason said, "Take the baby out of the carrier."

I said, "I don't want to take the baby out of the carrier!" But Gina said we should.

This was a moment—I had an instinct that I didn't want to do this, but we were both concerned about not disrespecting the service or the bishop, or Gina for that matter. So, I took Bryn out of the carrier, all the while thinking, and then saying to Jason, "This doesn't feel right. This doesn't feel right."

As the congregation began to move closer, I began to get more and more nervous. Then the bishop took Bryn for the blessing and handed her to another church officiant, who handed her to another woman. That's when I started to freak out. At one point, the person holding her turned away, and I couldn't see her for a minute. I felt so out of control, and then I took freaking out to a new level.

So did Jason—we were panicked. We saw an urn and a basin and the setup very much resembled a baptism—what were they going to do? Some part of us knew that nobody was going to hurt her, but suddenly, all our concerns for what others would think fell away. Disrespecting anybody was the least of our concern. Jason and I shared a truth: Protect the baby! It was pure instinct. I was a

mother, and someone had taken my baby out of my arms. That's all
I knew.

Frantically, I pushed through the crowd and grabbed Bryn back,
and Jason and I walked straight out of that church. Out on the
street, we were both very upset and we each had our moments of
tears. We decided we should just take the baby home. Then we
took it easy for a couple of hours. Jason went for a run. I tried to
calm down. Then we had a heart-to-heart talk.

Why hadn't we reacted more quickly? How had we let this happen? I felt frustrated that Jason hadn't taken control of the situation, but I realized how upset he was about this. He felt like he
had let us down. This was when we realized that we have become
different people now that we are parents, and we need to trust our
instincts. Maybe it was rude to walk out of the church when they
only had good intentions and thought they were doing something
nice for us, but we realized that none of that matters to us now. We
no longer care about what anyone thinks or how anything looks.
Our priorities have changed completely. Our number-one priority is
to protect Bryn.

Jason said to me, "You are the mother. If something doesn't feel
right to you for any reason, even if you don't know why, then we
both have to trust that. That's a good enough reason to step in and
stop whatever is happening."

It was a clarifying moment, a moment of truth neither of us will
forget. This is us now.

Gina had a few days off, but when she came back, we had a talk
with her and explained our point of view. We hope she understands,
but in the end, what matters is that we followed our gut instinct,
and that's a result of embracing rule #2. In spite of anything else
going on around you, you have to do what you think is right.

When you are faced with a clarifying moment, it might not be
as dramatic as this one, or it might be even more dramatic, but only
you can decide what action is authentic for you because only you
know who you are inside. Only you know what feels right. For some

people, the situation might have felt fine and nobody would have been upset. Every person, every situation is unique, so you have to stay in touch with your truth. Trust your instincts and learn from your mistakes, and you'll know exactly what to do.

Often, you will discover what's true after making a mistake. So that relationship didn't work? That job was a bust? You got in a fight with your friend? Instead of beating yourself up about it, figure out why it happened. What does it say about you? Every crisis is an opportunity for self-examination. When you figure out why you did what you did, you'll be less likely to make the same mistake again. And that's how you evolve into the person you are meant to be.

Finding your truth can help direct the entire course of your life. What are you going to do with your life? What's your purpose? What's your passion? Do you want to solve problems, make the world better in some unique way? Do you have a great idea and you just have to make it happen? What dictates your decisions? Figure that out, and you've got it made.

Still, figuring it all out can be hard without some kind of strategy. That's why I want to focus on one aspect of life that reveals quite a bit when it comes to questions like "Who am I?" and "What do I want?" It's the part of my life that began after I left home, and it's a part that continues to this day. It's the barometer for my truth, and it's likely a barometer for yours. It's instructive, enlightening, and the quintessential example of the importance of rule #2.

I'm talking about *relationships*.

· ·

FROM MY IN-BOX
∽◦∾

"Don't be who you're not."
—Kathy Griffin, actress and comedian

· ·

Defining Relationships

Our relationships are mirrors—who we choose, who we let choose us, how people treat us, how we allow ourselves to be treated, how we stay, how we leave, how we handle the hard patches and the good times—it's all a microcosm of our own personalities. Every relationship you've had says something about who you are and what you want, even if (especially if!) the relationship didn't work. Often, when a relationship fails, it's even more defining and instructive. Each relationship gets you to a new place and can help you see what you don't want as well as what you really do want.

Relationships can also reveal patterns and recurring themes in your life. You might always choose partners who are like you, because you are trying to figure yourself out, or you might choose partners who are completely unlike you, because you are looking for something. Maybe you choose people who are caretakers or abusers, or exactly like your father, or exactly the opposite of your father. Maybe you go for handsome or rich without paying attention to kind or supportive. Maybe the timing is wrong every time.

Your relationships aren't coincidences. They are telling opportunities for learning more about yourself. If you've been with at least three abusive or cold or codependent people, it's not because they found you. It's because you sought them out, whether you want to believe it or not. Believe it. This is where the growth begins.

Finding your truth by thoughtfully examining your past relationships is the only way to use your truth for better future relationships. What happened, and how does that clarify matters for you? What do you want? What are your deal breakers? Only you can answer these questions.

You have your own journey and priorities that will teach you your truth. Maybe you are religious and you've had relationships fall apart because your partner didn't share those values, and you need to realize that this is important to you. Maybe your family always had money issues, and finding someone who can provide financial security really matters and makes you feel safe and loved. Maybe you re-create an abusive past through your choice of partners, and you need to recognize that so you can go in a different direction. Maybe you seek something from someone else that you really need to find inside yourself, so you can be whole on your own.

Relationships are like recipes. When a recipe doesn't work, you have to do something differently the next time. Change the ingredients and you change the result. You take it or leave it—keep what worked in each relationship as you choose the next one, but learn to leave behind the dysfunctional parts. It takes some self-analysis, but you can do that. Anyone can.

And if your relationship does work, learn to leave it alone. Don't overthink what's good. Are you creating problems where none existed before? That says something about you, too.

My past relationships have consisted of what I sometimes think of as ill-conceived recipes. Each was missing something, or had too much of something else. My relationship now works, like a recipe that never fails, so my task now is to stop messing with it.

Whatever your story, take a magnifying glass to it and look to see if there's a flaw in your approach to relationships—how you started, how you communicated, where you've been, where you are now, and what it all means to you. What you find there can tell you everything you need to know about what you should do next—what you should take, what you should leave, who you want to be with, and even who you want to *be*.

Relationship Noise

If you can't live without me, why aren't you dead yet?

—Cynthia Heimel, humor writer

I've been through it. You've been through it. Crushes, love, lust, breakups, crying, getting over it (sooner or later), moving on, and then doing it all over again. He can't live without you, or you can't live without him, and yet somehow you both manage to move on eventually . . . because it wasn't right, for whatever reason. Whether you are single, actively dating or not, hopeful or disillusioned about relationships, engaged to be married, a newlywed, or in a committed relationship for decades, no matter your age or sexual preference, you have a relationship history and it is illuminating. All you have to do is look at it honestly, without pasting prefabricated stories and assumptions onto it.

Have you had dozens of boyfriends? I'm not going to judge you. I've had plenty myself. You can boyfriend-hop forever if you really want to, but at some point, you will probably want to settle down. You aren't going to find someone perfect. You just need to find someone perfect for you.

Have you had just a few relationships or no relationships yet? That's fine, too. It's where you are right now, but consider the reasons. Maybe you aren't ready, or too busy, or too scared. Be honest. Do you feel insecure? Do you fear you aren't good enough in some way, that you don't deserve someone who will really love you? Do you fear letting anyone get too close? I'm not going to judge you. I've only let myself get really close to a few people. Intimacy is hard, and vulnerability is scary.

This is about you and what your history means to you, so it's time to look frankly for the patterns, common themes, and threads, as well as how each relationship in your past grew out of or was a reaction to the one before it.

Maybe it's because I'm a "cook," but I like to think of relationships as a sandwich. This is a metaphor for the "take it or leave it" concept. That first relationship is like a trip to the store to get bread. But a sandwich with just bread is boring. It's not really even a sandwich at all. So, the next time, you get bread and cheese and a hot pepper. The next time, you get bread, cheese, turkey, and you skip the hot pepper because it was just too spicy. Maybe you try a tomato instead. Each sandwich gets a little better, until you finally make a great one. And that one becomes the sandwich you love—your own personal favorite sandwich.

In other words, you learn something or resolve something from each relationship and you carry that lesson with you into the next one. Then you figure out what else you need or what else has to be resolved. But always take something with you and, if necessary, leave something behind. It takes a while to get all the parts you need to make your metaphorical sandwich, so don't get frustrated if your relationship history reveals mistakes. I never said it was going to be easy. There are a lot of mediocre or downright unappetizing sandwiches in the world, but that doesn't mean you should give up ever making another one: Just keep tweaking the recipe until you love it.

Honesty is more important here than efficiency, or even optimism. There's nothing to be gained by glossing over your mistakes with excuses for why a relationship failed. Rule #2 is about looking past those stories and fixing the actual problems on the next try.

Take each relationship at face value. Go back over it and look at it, like a recipe that just didn't work. What element needs to go, and which can stay? Do you see any patterns? Label each relationship: codependent, rebound, self-abuse, codependent, rebound, fear . . . are you starting to see a pattern?

Next, think about the core issue that ended your relationships. Whether it was infidelity, money, religion, growing in different directions, intervening life events, boredom, or just bad timing, try to pin it down. Are there more patterns emerging?

Please don't take a lesson from the Bethenny School of Break-ups, which would mean that seven seconds after a breakup, you are calling up every single guy you ever dated, or drinking your weight in Skinnygirl Margaritas, or giving 5,000 men your number for the next three months trying to score another husband-to-be. But if that's you, too, then so be it. Face it, and ask yourself why you keep doing this. The sooner you uncover your patterns, the sooner you can begin to change them. Know thyself!

Finally, in your mind, or on paper, go back and say thank you or I'm sorry to each past relationship: *Thank you for changing my life. I'm sorry for breaking your heart. Thank you for helping me see my own strength. I'm sorry I didn't give you what you needed. Thank you for letting me go.*

This is so healing. You don't have to tell the actual person anything (unless you want to). This is for you. This is to make peace in your own heart, and help you be more objective about your loves and losses. Your past relationships were a necessary part of your journey. What if you don't have to regret anything? Wouldn't that be a relief?

Coming from a place of yes means replacing regret with curiosity: What can you discover when you get past the noise and look at what happened and accept it as the truth? You can't necessarily see this when a breakup is fresh, or when you are right in the middle of it, trying to decide what to do. Once the wounds start to be less raw, however, these are the questions you need to ask yourself: Who am I? What do I want? What did I learn? What will I do differently *next time*?

Relationship Noise

As you delve into your relationship history, also be aware of your *relationship noise*, the noise in your head that foils your good relationships and convinces you to stay in bad ones. Relationship noise can trick you into thinking or acting inauthentically. It can make you want things that aren't really right for you. It exploits your vulnerabilities and takes advantage of your insecurities. It can make you think you are made up of your worst qualities; you are the bad guy; you always mess up the relationship. It can also tip you into blaming mode, so you think it's always someone else's fault when things don't work out.

Relationship noise can prompt you to run around advertising to everyone that you want to be single forever because you are afraid of rejection, or it can keep you unsatisfied, after you've already made a commitment because there might be "somebody better," or it can trick you into becoming a serial monogamist, like I was for years, always in a long-term relationship but never actually able to go all the way with a commitment.

My relationship noise led me to seek financial security from men (as you'll soon see), then fight against them when they offered it to me. I was always the runaway bride. In some ways, I have to give myself props for refusing to settle for something that wasn't right, but getting to what was right was a long, slow, sometimes painful process of self-discovery. It took me years to figure out who I really was and what I really wanted.

The painful process was, in fact, the key to finding my truth. I wouldn't have gotten there if I hadn't first experienced relationships that didn't work, careers that didn't work, done some serious soul searching, and recognized what each failed venture taught me. With each new relationship and each new job I made adjustments, until I was finally on course.

Maybe you are good at running, or good at staying when you should run, or maybe you've finally got it right but you are plagued with self-doubt. In any case, this is your assignment, your action-item to help you find your truth and work on figuring out exactly who you really are and what you really want right now, at this stage in your life: Look into your relationship history. Really think about each one, why it happened, and what you learned. Look back from a place of yes and discover your truth.

To get you started, I'm going to open up my closet of skeletons for you to see. I don't normally like to open this closet or even think about what's in there, but I'm doing it because I've received so much support, I want to return the favor, supporting you by sharing my mistakes with you, and what I learned from them, so you can possibly avoid making some of the same mistakes yourself.

If you've already made some of these mistakes (as I know, from the letters I get, some of you have), I want to help you see that you are not alone, and that sometimes you have to close one door before you can open the next one. Whatever the past, coming from a place of yes means turning it around and making it work for you, turning your mistakes into knowledge. And I'm just going to hope my husband skips this chapter—Jason doesn't want to hear it, but for you, darlings, anything!

As I go through my relationship history, use this process as a model for yours. You might be shocked and enlightened about what you discover about yourself—I was. I've given each story a title based on what I learned.

Listen to Your Gut

The naked truth is always better than the best-dressed lie.

—*Ann Landers, advice columnist*

After my wedding last year, there was a rash of tabloid stories about my "secret first husband." But Peter was never a secret. Peter was my best friend. I was twenty-six when I married him, and he was in my life long before anybody knew who I was.

Peter loved me and understood me. I could tell him anything and he was supportive and there for me. He made me part of his family, and his family loved me—they took me in as if I was one of theirs, and that was very attractive. I could almost convince myself that I had a normal family.

I had the best intentions, being with Peter. I thought I was doing everything right, choosing a relationship the way people are supposed to choose a relationship. However, I was young and I hadn't really found my truth yet. I didn't see the real reasons behind why I chose Peter.

I think I chose him because he was everything my father and stepfather weren't. He was funny and kind, stable and affectionate, and attentive. I knew I needed to find a man who was good to me, so that's what I did. Peter was a *good guy,* and one of the reasons I married him was that I knew he would be a good father. Peter looked great on paper, and everybody supported us. I was at the "marrying age," or so I told myself. He was all the good things husbands are supposed to be. To everyone around us, we looked like we had the perfect relationship. *Except . . .*

Except I wasn't anywhere near being ready to get married. There was so much about myself that I had yet to figure out. Maybe because of that, I didn't really love him the way I needed to love a husband, or the way he deserved to be loved. I *wanted* to love him. I *wanted* to marry a man like him, or so I thought. Peter was the man I *wanted to want,* and I thought he could love me enough for both of us.

Nobody can love you enough for both of you. When I look back on it, I can see clearly that I was with Peter out of fear, not truth. I liked him, but the driving force that made me marry him was my fear. Ridiculous as it sounds to me now, I was afraid, at twenty-six, that I was getting too old to find a husband. I wanted to have it all figured out, my marriage, my career, and I wanted it all tied up in a blue Tiffany box with a big white bow. I was trying to escape the stress of pursuing an acting career (which wasn't going so well—

I'll tell you more about that in the next chapter), and my incessant job-hopping was wearing me down. I was constantly nervous about money and about how I would support myself. Peter seemed so easy.

I felt like if I didn't marry Peter, who loved me so much and was such a good friend, who had such a wonderful welcoming family, that I was never going to get another chance. Peter used to tell me that nobody would ever love me as much as he did, and I believed him. And that terrified me. I wanted stability and upward mobility, and I saw a chance for that with Peter. So I quit acting, took a regular job, and married him.

Blue box, check. White bow, check.

Remembering this, I can't help but repeat the old saying, "Youth is wasted on the young." I had so much evolving to do, and there I was, thinking my life was "fixed." Why was I giving up so early? Why was I selling out? But I refused to see it that way . . . until trouble set in, as it always does when you ignore your gut.

I could feel it under my skin. My gut knew, even before I consciously realized it. I developed insomnia. My skin started to break out. Another big clue was that I wasn't sexually attracted to Peter. If you asked him now, he'd probably say I wasn't someone who was interested in sex at all, and although it's true that I'm no nymphomaniac, I lacked desire for him but didn't want to admit it. He was handsome and charming, so why wouldn't I be attracted to him? What was wrong with me?

I tried to ignore my lack of passion, but the more I ignored the signals my body was sending me, the more I felt trapped and panicked. Desperate to control something in my life, I began to control my food intake with a new strictness, and for the first time in my life, I became drastically thin. When a relationship isn't working but there isn't some major event that ends it, it festers. It's like indigestion. You just know something's not right in your gut, even if you don't know what you ate that was bad. The fear kept rising, and when I realized that getting married wasn't helping the fear but making it worse, the marriage fell apart.

For so long, I kept telling myself that I needed a tangible reason to end the marriage. Otherwise it seemed too extreme, out of nowhere, not justified. Now I know that an emotional reason is enough. Nobody has to cheat or betray or do anything wrong. It doesn't even have to be anybody's fault. I blamed myself for the breakup for years, and maybe I should have known not to get married at such a young age, but I didn't. I thought I was doing the right thing. I just happened to be wrong. And I was young. Not ready.

The marriage ended, but in retrospect, I can see that it happened for a reason. We were both wounded by the experience, but how would we know what we didn't want if we hadn't gone through it? From my relationship with Peter, I learned that I absolutely have to listen to my gut, not my head. My gut knows better than my brain what I should and shouldn't do. I learned that I can't be happy going to bed at night with someone who looks good on paper but isn't the right match for me. I learned (although I would need to learn it a few more times) that when I make a decision based on fear, it isn't going to work.

I also learned that I was right to choose a man completely unlike my father, that a good man can love me, and that I can choose a relationship with the best of intentions, even if it doesn't ultimately work out. I did that part right.

So I took some of the positives and left the negatives behind. And I moved on.

When you look at your past relationships, it's natural to wonder whether your current relationship is on the right track. How do you know? How do you avoid falling into the same old traps and the same bad habits? How do you get a little perspective when you are right in the middle of it, and confused? I can't tell you what your priorities should be, but I can tell you to listen to your gut—it's probably trying to tell you something.

Does your gut feel calm and happy, or tight and anxious? Are you sleeping, or are you lying awake at night, torturing yourself? Are you constantly making excuses for the other person? Are you forcing it? Are you blaming yourself for what's not working?

Breaking up, not to mention divorce, seems like the most excruciating thing, when you are in a relationship and contemplating it. However, when you get past other people's expectations and search for your own truth, you may be able to realize that it's necessary, before you get in too deep. Or not—maybe it's not so hopeless, and finding your truth will help you see that you have the gifts to solve your problems.

Finding your truth in a relationship can help you to avoid wasting months or years in a place that isn't good for you, and it's never too late to start living with integrity, according to your own internal barometer. You may not be able to explain why a relationship has to end, or why it's worth fighting for. You can't always reason your way to an answer. In fact, sometimes you shouldn't. Your mind can play tricks on you. Sometimes you just have to trust your body's reactions.

If you are on the brink of a big decision (moving in together, marriage, divorce), what is your gut telling you to do? Is your gut saying no even while your mind is trying to talk you into something, whether it's getting into or out of a relationship? Now is the time to listen, not ten years from now when it will be much harder to get in or out, and your gut has been torturing you for a decade.

If you still aren't sure, just open yourself up. Be vulnerable to yourself. Let down your defenses. It's just you, trying to know yourself, so give yourself a break and let yourself feel what's going on right now, inside. There will always be a point, in every relationship, when you have to face the question: *Is this right for me?* You have to ask it. And you have to answer it, without any preconceived notions about what the answer should be. It can be scary to end a wrong relationship, to cut that cord that is so familiar, even if it's strangling you. You might think you'll never find love again, but trust me when I tell you that the greatest things in my life happened after I jumped in and did something that I was terrified to do . . . like trading the familiar for the unknown.

And then there is the other question: *Is this right for the person I'm with?* If you've got that gnawing guilty feeling, maybe you know it's not working for the other person, either. If you are in a relationship, you not only have to be true to yourself, but you also have to take responsibility for your partner. If you really love someone, take care of them and be fair, not selfish. A relationship has to be right on both sides, and if you don't both have a calm feeling inside that tells you that you are going in the right direction, then you have to dig deeper to find the answer to the question *Should I stay or should I go?* (Like the Clash song.) The answer is in you. You already know it.

. . . .

TIMING IS EVERYTHING
(OR ALMOST EVERYTHING)

I believe there are many reasons why my first marriage didn't work, and one of the biggest was timing. I wasn't ready to be married at twenty-six. If I had met Jason, my husband, when I was twenty-six, I doubt either one of us would have been close to ready to have a relationship. I guess I'll never know for sure, but I think that because we met when we did, when we were both a decade or so older and much wiser and wanting the same things and had our lives more in order, it worked. I had established my career. Jason had put in his time as the party boy and was ready to man up. We spent our twenties running the same game, and then we found each other.

Still, when I met Jason, I didn't think I was in that place yet. It took Jason—our chemistry and interaction—to help me see that the timing was right. We grew in that direction together. Jason is my proof that the right relationship is a combination of good timing and good chemistry.

. . . .

Be Passion

We welcome passion, for the mind is briefly let off duty.

—Mignon McLaughlin, journalist

After my relationship with Peter, I realized that I had done some things right. I had found a good man, someone who treated me well, someone who wasn't like my father. But I was missing part of the picture. With Peter, I listened to my brain. With Larry, I listened to my heart.

Larry was Peter's family friend, and an usher at our wedding. I had always had a crush on him and I had dated him briefly for a summer before I was with Peter. When I was with Peter, something about Larry still attracted me, but we were just friends. I even fixed Larry up with my girlfriends.

When I was with Peter, he was my life—I was in it. However, after Peter and I separated, for a brief time Larry was a support system for me. And then I fell for him. Or, if I look at it more realistically, I was so relieved that my relationship was over, I ran straight into another one. Five seconds after I was out of it with Peter, I was in it with Larry. God forbid I would be alone for even one minute.

Of course, because Peter and Larry were friends, our relationship was a scandal. It tore the two families apart, causing a rift that has lasted to this day. But Larry and I had passion and we knew that it was worth the price. We were consumed with each other and I can't say I wasn't also somewhat excited by how the relationship had its forbidden aspects.

Our relationship was intensely romantic and volatile. We truly loved each other, but we also clashed, with sparks. For years, I thought Larry and I could have ended up together, but now I doubt it could ever have worked. I always thought of our relationship like the movie *The Way We Were:* full of fiery passion but doomed. When it exploded and we broke up, we both regretted it.

You probably know this kind of relationship. For years, Larry asked me to get back together, and for years, I thought in the back of my mind that he really was "The One." But my relationship—and my feelings of longing after it ended—also had elements of fear. Just as I feared, with Peter, that I wouldn't find another great, stable guy, with Larry I was afraid I wouldn't ever find that kind of passion again. So I held on.

Heroin addicts say they are always chasing their first high, because the highs they get after that first one are never quite as good. They call it chasing the dragon. For years, Larry and I chased the dragon, but it wasn't meant to be. The passion wasn't sustainable. Too much of a good thing . . . isn't. Relationships should be work, but they shouldn't be impossible, and Larry and I weren't right for each other.

Yet falling in love with Larry had been the next necessary step for me, a progression from mind to heart. I took what I learned from Peter—to choose a good man who genuinely loved me, to make decisions with courage, and to listen to my gut. Then Larry taught me to feel real passion, and I would take that with me, too, but leave behind the torture of a relationship that was too intense and unsustainable. At some point in your life, you have to decide if you want to spend your life tortured, or in a solid relationship that you can work at. If I chose Larry, I would be choosing torture, not from him but from myself.

Maybe Larry and I were too much alike. Jason and I fit together so much better than Larry and I ever did, and the same is true with

Larry and the woman he married. Larry will always be important to me, and because we really did love each other, we are both happy that we've each found better matches and happy marriages. When you really love someone, you want them to be happy, with or without you, and that was Larry and me, in the end. In the moment, I thought he was the love of my life. Little did I know how much I had yet to experience.

If you aren't happy in your relationship and you want to be happy, you need to figure out what's really going on. I can't tell you. I can't diagnose your relationship. This is your work. If you don't do it, you could waste even more time. Dig in and fix it based on your truth, or move on based on your truth. Change might be scary, but living a lie is scarier.

· ·

FEAR NOT

How do you know when you are staying in a relationship out of fear instead of truth? There are a lot of little signs. Can you think of more cons than pros? Are you always making excuses? Are you unhappy, but the thought of ending it gives you a stomachache? Are you tempted to cheat? Are you drowning your sorrows too often?

A relationship can hobble along on fear for years, but when the people in it finally get out of it, they are set free and realize they know exactly what they do want. Often, it doesn't take long to find someone who is more suitable.

Sometimes, however, fear makes people want to run when they should stay. Good relationships take work, but it's work worth doing. Working on a good relationship is different than staying in a relationship for the wrong reasons. Only your gut knows which situation you might be in.

I've always run away out of fear, but I've been with people who stay out of fear, too. You have to get to know your fear. Get intimate with it, so you understand what it's making you do. Only then will you see what you really need to do. Only then will you be able to thwart it.

Of course, it's not just about you. I can understand why people stay together for the children. If you have a young child or an adolescent going through issues, I can see a reason to stay, even if your relationship isn't really what you want. But if you are in a relationship just because you fear being alone or you are afraid to hurt the other person (even if setting them free would be better for them) or you just don't know how to leave, then it's time to consider how much power you want to give to your fear.

• •

Learn Your Lesson

Just because you made a mistake doesn't mean you are a mistake.

—Georgette Mosbacher, cosmetics CEO and author

My name is Bethenny and I'm a serial monogamist.

When Larry and I broke up (this is going to sound familiar), God forbid I should just take some time out and be with myself for a while. No, I wasn't programmed to do that. I didn't know how to be alone. I felt like I couldn't be alone. I was too scared. I wanted to be comfortable and safe and not have to look too closely at myself, which is what serial monogamists always do. After all that passion with Larry, I needed some sanity in my life—some security. But I didn't yet know how to find those things inside myself. I wanted someone to take care of me again. Never mind all the lessons I learned from Peter. *I wanted a boyfriend.* I thought I *needed* a boyfriend. So I went out looking for the next man, and I found Jimmy.

Jimmy was a high school boyfriend. An "old flame"—what feels safer than that? I was still working in event production during this time in my life, and I was producing an event in Chicago. I knew Jimmy lived in Chicago, so I called him, and we reconnected over dinner. It had been twelve years since we'd seen each other. Jimmy was handsome, successful, wealthy, a nice guy, and we had a great time. So great, in fact, that we decided to give it another try.

Being with Jimmy was easy and fun. He is a wonderful person, charming, with such a nice family. Being with him felt so effortless and good. He adored me. He also had money. He reminded me of Peter in some ways, but more successful. I was feeling financially insecure, so knowing Jimmy could support me financially was comforting to me. I started to tell myself that maybe security wasn't so bad after all.

Because my work life was stressful and my career was all over the place, I was tired of trying so hard for so little gain. I just wanted things to be easy, for once. I thought, Is that really so wrong? Wouldn't it be so, so easy to just stop all the striving and let someone else do the work?

And Jimmy was a *catch*. Somehow, I forgot that it hadn't worked before to be with someone who was good on paper but wasn't right for me. I poured all my energy into convincing myself that he *was* right for me.

In this way, Jimmy was a setback, like seeing a fuchsia lipstick in the store and buying it without thinking, even though you already have five just like it at home. And forgetting that you don't even look good in fuchsia.

So there I was, a serial monogamist commitment-phobe, obsessed with making my boyfriend commit to *me*. It was wrong in so many ways, but at the time, all I could see was that I had to make him love me, before I had even really seriously considered whether I loved him. I wanted him to do all the hard work, take on all the risk. I wanted to feel loved and safe. It was totally unfair.

Jimmy *did* love me, and he asked me to marry him. Triumphant, I accepted. All my friends told me I would never find a guy this good again. I was approaching my thirties, so the fear reinforced the notion I had that I'd better get married before it was too late. I felt immense pressure to marry well and I was terrified of seeming pathetic. I thought: Being broke and alone is cute in your twenties, but not in your thirties.

I had created, consciously or unconsciously, a random deadline for myself: I thought it really mattered that I would marry a rich handsome guy by the time I was thirty, so I talked myself into it. And I mean I really talked myself into it. I changed my entire life.

I gave up my business. I left Los Angeles. I moved my whole life to Chicago, just to be with him. I wore the big engagement ring, I bought a lot of stuff—I had all the status symbols (yuck!).

And then—big shocker, here—it started to fall apart. Oh, I tortured myself during this time, yes I did. I knew so many women who would kill for a man like Jimmy.

But if you know me at all, even just from watching my show, imagine me at home alone, a bride-to-be with nothing to do, no job, no purpose, in a city I didn't know or love. An idle mind truly is the devil's playground. I thought I was going to go insane. I would go to the gym and try to stretch it out for as long as I could, just so I wouldn't have to go back home and be alone. I took long lunches, ran errands for hours, bought everything I could.

And I tortured Jimmy. I tortured myself. I was miserable, absolutely miserable, but not because of him. Because of me. I had acted contrary to my truth, and this was the payback. Jimmy would come home at 5:00 every day, happy to see me, and I would be so depressed and miserable that I couldn't bear the thought of going out again. I didn't want to go anywhere. I just wanted to crawl into bed. I was depressed.

If you watched my show, *Bethenny Getting Married?*, and saw my temporary descent into bridezilla hell when I had too much to do, believe me when I tell you that this was nothing compared to the

misery and stress I endured when I had *absolutely nothing to do.* I
would lie in the bathtub or on the bed every night, willing myself
to be happy, praying to be happy, wanting so badly to want this life
while everything inside me rebelled against it. It's ironic because
now, I lie around the house doing nothing at every possible opportunity. Because I'm happy, I love to do that. Back then, I blamed
Jimmy for my loneliness and boredom and, truthfully, for my stupid
mistake in uprooting my life and derailing my career just because I
was afraid of turning into a spinster.

It was a disaster. I felt paralyzed and trapped. I couldn't just
break up with him and go on my merry way. I had given up *everything.* I was in *Chicago,* for God's sake. (Nothing against that lovely
city, but it just didn't feel like home.) What the hell was I doing?
How did I make such a drastic mistake? What was wrong with me
for not wanting this?

In an effort to try to fix things, I convinced Jimmy that we should
move to New York, just for a while. I thought maybe if I was in a familiar place, things would be better. I thought I hated Chicago, but
I really hated where I was in my life and what I was doing. I was
going against everything that really mattered to me, just to escape
my problems. What I didn't see was that I created more problems.
Really, moving back to New York was just running away.

In retrospect, I think this is the relationship I beat myself up
about the most. I can be pretty hard on myself sometimes, and I
hated that I made this mistake. I felt as if I should have known better, and that I hurt someone because I wasn't self-aware enough.
Jimmy never did anything wrong. The old excuse, "It's not you, it's
me," couldn't have been more true in this situation.

Moving to New York was the beginning of the end for us. When
I arrived, I knew I wouldn't be going back to Chicago, and I knew
Jimmy could never stay in New York. I had my escape. Runaway
bride again.

The fallout from that relationship was brutal. It was a messy
breakup, as breakups often are. I hurt him, but he moved on and

found someone who was a much better match for him, and I'm glad. Once again, I recognized that you have to take responsibility for the other person's feelings, even if it means leaving them. If you are not really into the relationship and you are just staying out of fear or settling because it's easier, you can't just think about what that does to *you*. What does it do to the other person who loves you and thinks you are really invested in the relationship? How will they feel in ten years when you pack up and leave and they are blind-sided? It's selfish to treat someone else that way, and it will end up hurting you, too, in the end. It hurt us both.

I remember a girlfriend of mine trying to convince me to go back to him. In weaker moments, I was tempted. I even tried, and thank God he didn't take me back. It wouldn't have been right for either of us.

Here's the really surprising thing I learned from my relationship with Jimmy, and something I hope you can learn from any relationship where you think you really screwed up: There was nothing wrong with me. I was not fatally flawed. Jimmy and I weren't right for each other, because of who we were, because of the timing, and a million other reasons. Each of us is perfectly fine. We just weren't meant to be together. We didn't want the same things. It was that simple.

Incidentally—and this is just one of those "holy shit" stories— once, when Jimmy and I were still together, we were having dinner in a restaurant, and a girl walked in. I happened to notice her. She looked like a very nice, pretty, normal girl, and I said, jokingly at the time, "Jimmy, if it doesn't work out with us, I could see you being with a girl like that." Amazingly, after our relationship was over, he coincidentally ended up being set up on a date with her, and they got married and have children now. Even then, somehow, at some level, I not only knew Jimmy and I weren't right for each other, but I had an idea of the type who *was* right for him. You know more than you think. We all have instincts about these things.

Of course, it didn't feel simple at the time. It never does. It was devastating for both of us, and for our friends. I'm sure they all had their opinions about what happened, but unless you were there, you can never really know what happens between two people. The judgment of others shouldn't distract you from what the relationship meant and what it taught you, and most of all, whether or not it's right for you now.

No matter how it looks on the outside, a relationship that doesn't work falls apart for a reason, and it's a reason that can help you move forward. So stop blaming yourself. It's a waste of time. It's coming from a place of no.

Instead, focus your energy on figuring out what went wrong. Let it teach you. Let it make you better. Open your eyes and find the pattern. Find the truth in it.

As I examined my relationship with Jimmy later, in retrospect, I came to some important conclusions. I believe Jimmy loved me, but I also think he loved the *idea* of me. Are you someone's idea? Or do they see the real you? Does someone like you because of how you look or what you do, or are those things secondary to who you are? Or are you doing this to someone? Do you love the idea of someone, not who he or she really is? Do you like to say you are with someone because of what they do, or because of how they look? Can you see past those external trappings to the person underneath? Because that's where the truth is.

One of the reasons why I know that Jason really loves me is that he doesn't care how I look. Well . . . of course, he likes it when I look good, but when I don't look good, when I've got bags under my eyes and I just woke up in the morning, he loves me just as much as he does when I'm wearing a short skirt and high heels. I didn't even notice Jason's eighties jeans until fans noticed them. That's when I took him jean shopping, but I don't care what he wears, because I love *him*, the Jason underneath the jeans. (Ha ha, I know what you're thinking, but you know what I mean!)

I also realized that sometimes, you can have the very best intentions entering a relationship, but that doesn't mean it will work.

Before you really take the plunge, you have to look ahead, and look at the big picture. I think that the high divorce rate is a result of how seldom people subject their potential marriage to the hard questions before they jump in. You really have to assess what you're doing and how it will affect everyone, now and in the future. Of course you can't ever know what will happen, but you can listen to your gut, and you can consider if the relationship conforms to your personal truth and values. You have to take responsibility and look beyond the immediate feeling of being in love. Take a good hard look at yourself. Are you acting on purpose, or out of bad habits and destructive patterns?

Depending on where you are in your life, you can do this right—or you can do it right the next time. Don't let the pressure to see the big picture scare you away from commitment, but please, please do let it scare you away from settling for anything less than what's in line with your truth.

I can't speak for Jimmy, but in addition to what I discovered about myself, some good did come out of that time in my life. The best thing of all was Cookie, my dog. I found her in Chicago, she was my first baby, and she has been my best friend ever since.

Another important thing that happened to me when I moved back to New York was enrolling in culinary school. At the time, I did it so I would have something to do, not knowing where it would lead. Ultimately, it led me away from Jimmy and toward a new career. I had no idea how much I would love it and how important it would become. It was something I was good at, and it was the beginning of a new life.

• •

ABOUT SEX . . .

Let's talk about sex. Your level of desire is an important clue, like it or not, to the validity of a relationship. Lack of desire may not be a deal breaker, but you have to consider what it means.

I'm not a doctor and there are plenty of reasons for intimacy issues, but keep your eyes open when you're feeling the urge to keep your pants on.

However, there's a difference between being turned off and just not being in the mood. You can do something about your mood. I'm not someone who wants it seven days a week, or even four days a week. I'm good for maybe once or twice a week. Sure, I have my horny-as-a-rabbit days, but on other days, the shop is closed.

However, I do believe that in a good relationship, sometimes you have to compromise. My husband has a higher drive than I do, but I drag him to book signings or department stores or I make him pick out furniture with me and he does it because he loves me. That's what marriage is. When he wants a little love and I'm not necessarily in the mood, I can give that to him anyway. I like to wear granny panties, but once in a while, I'll make the extra effort and wear, if not lingerie and cowboy boots, at least the lingerie. And maybe high heels.

Throw your guy a bone once in a while, and then maybe he won't mind so much following you around the mall. Men want to get laid. The penis knows what it wants and some men could practically shag your next-door neighbor and not consider it a big deal. If you go for too long without giving your husband sex, if you start to get bitter and angry and turn him away, at some point he's going to give up and he may even look for it somewhere else. I'm not saying it's right and I would never condone cheating. I'm just calling it like I've seen it.

It's also not impossible that sometimes you're the one who wants it and he won't be in the mood. What I'm saying is that sex matters in a relationship. It maintains the relationship. It's like keeping your kitchen clean. If you don't do it regularly, you can end up with vermin.

So take off those flannel pajamas and that ratty old robe and get a little creative. It doesn't mean you have to be his blow-up doll every night, it just means you care about him and you want to make him happy. When you both do things for each other because you want the person you love to be happy, it's coming from a place of yes. You say yes, he says yes, and you both get more of what you want and need, whether it's a blow job or two hours at The Container Store.

. . . .

Move Forward, Not Backward

Things that don't get better, get worse.

—Ellen Sue Stern, relationship coach and author

It's almost comical, but after repeating my mistakes with Peter by almost marrying Jimmy, I went back to Larry. Maybe I need to learn every lesson in life twice.

I still wasn't over Larry—he wasn't out of my system. And honestly, my serial monogamy wasn't out of my system, either. I still felt I *had* to be in a relationship, and Larry had been after me to get back together for years. When I didn't have someone, there he was. And there I was, alone, no fiancé, no boyfriend, no financial support. Just me and my fear.

So I decided that maybe Larry really was the one for me. We had the passion. I really did love him. Most of all, he was comfortable and familiar, so I told myself that maybe it would be right this time. Maybe it would finally work. I would give it another chance. Maybe I was ready now, maybe the timing would finally be right. And I felt like I had to be sure he wasn't "The One."

Larry was in. He took me to the Caribbean for sixteen magical days. We were in love again and it was romantic and perfect. I didn't think about the fact that we were totally removed from the real world and that's why things worked so well. All I thought was that after all these years and arguments and water under the bridge, we still had passion, and that alone would be enough to make it work. I felt happier with him than with anyone else I'd been with— at the same time, I was forgetting that I was more miserable with him than with anyone else, too. A reality check was imminent.

I'll never forget that night in our hotel room when I finally told him, after years of turning down his proposals, that yes, I would marry him. And I'll never forget the look on his face.

He was paralyzed. Stunned. He didn't know what to do or say.

Suddenly, I had this sinking feeling. I realized that he had been chasing me for so long because he never really believed I would say yes. That's what made me the irresistible challenge. He was as commitment-phobic as I was—what a kick in the balls that was.

And that was the beginning of the end. (Again.) The magical time was over and reality slapped us both in the face. We fought for two days, my eyes were swollen from crying, and when we got back to our respective cities, I cut him off and told him never to speak to me again unless he had something new to say. But I still wanted him. I was so hurt that he didn't want me, that I wasn't even able to see past the marriage proposal part to what might lie ahead. Neither could he, I suppose. We were both shell-shocked.

Sixty days later, back in New York, my doorman buzzed and said I had a delivery. When I got to the elevator, there were flowers with a note: "I'm coming to New York. I have something to ask you." I couldn't believe it—the big moment was here and all my dreams were about to come true. Another buzz, and suddenly, he was at my door.

It's hard to remember all the details of that night, but he proposed to me and I accepted. Larry and I went to a party together, and we began our engaged life. Or shall I say, we began another mistake?

Those next few weeks, Larry was ecstatic, manic, passionate.

He'd decided to wrap up his own life in his own Tiffany box. He had it all figured out. He already had a credit card with my name on it. His mother was already voicing her opinions about our wedding. Everything was arranged. I would move immediately to Los Angeles, into his house. The process was under way, and I got the sudden, horrified feeling that I wouldn't be able to stop it. That I was doing it again. My gut has the most inconvenient habit of throwing a wrench into the most perfect-seeming plans.

Now, I was the one who was stunned. *Wait a minute.* It was all happening, everything I had dreamed of and desired for years, or so I thought. Marriage, to the one I loved, the passionate one, The One. Wasn't he? The one who would finally take care of me and take away all my problems? Wasn't my long, hard search over? Hadn't I finally, in my thirties, found the man of my dreams? Wasn't I defying the odds and living the fairy-tale ending, the romantic story I could tell all my friends, and children, and grandchildren?

Thrashing around for the panic button, in characteristic fashion, I began creating excuses to get out, dismantling the relationship piece by piece, tearing apart the fairy tale.

I've said it before and I'll say it again: It's never about what it's about. It wasn't that I loved Larry or hated Larry, loved New York or hated Los Angeles. It wasn't about sex or money or anything obvious—it wasn't even about marriage.

It was about *me.* By this point, I had so much emotional baggage to drag with me to Los Angeles, I never would have made it onto the plane. The ring was very beautiful, but of course it wasn't the ring I would have picked. Like a spoiled brat, I complained and obsessed until he took it back and got me exactly the ring I wanted. I took every possible opportunity to make it clear how unhappy I was, and it didn't take Larry long to realize there was no way to fix it.

He asked me why I always had to struggle, why I couldn't just let him take care of me. But I still had something to prove. I began to realize that I was terrified of becoming too complacent, too comfortable. What if I would never be motivated to make something of my life? I would lose myself again.

You can guess what happened next. I left him, much to our mutual relief. When you are chasing the dragon, at some point, you have to realize that you aren't ever going to catch it. You have to turn your back. It's the only way to see what you really want, and what I really wanted, what I really needed, was to have a relationship with myself.

· ·

EGO NOISE

When someone doesn't want you, it's easy to freak out. It brings up all kinds of noise: self-esteem issues, ego issues. You forget what you really want, or you don't even know what you want because you are so upset that someone doesn't want you. I see people making this mistake all the time, and I recognize it because I've made it. Or, you break up with someone because the relationship isn't working, and then they get engaged or married and suddenly you are consumed with jealousy and you want them back.

In the movie *My Best Friend's Wedding,* Julianne (played by Julia Roberts) always knew she could never marry her best friend, but when he gets engaged to Kimberly (Cameron Diaz's character), she panics. Because he found someone and she hadn't, she suddenly thought she wanted him after all.

If you've ever been rejected or regretted the end of a relationship (and who hasn't?), the only way to keep your perspective is to step back from it, take a deep breath, and reconnect with your truth. I once saw a quote by Beyoncé Knowles: "When you really don't like a guy, they're all over you, and as soon as you act like you like them, they're no longer interested." Hey, if it can happen to Beyoncé, it can happen to anyone. Other people aren't always going to act the way you want them to act.

So if someone breaks up with you and you are blindsided, you have every right to stay home, wallow, cry, and drink Skinnygirl Margaritas. For a day or two. I give you my blessing. After that, even if you feel heartbroken, try to come from a place of yes, realize that the relationship ended for a reason, and start planning the next stage of your life—one that can be even better than the last one. Be good to yourself. You're going to be okay.

And if you're the one who breaks it off, just don't involve your ego. Be kind. Keep it clean. Otherwise you'll miss the cues from your voice telling you what's real and what's right. Don't get distracted from what's important. Your truth will guide you, even when your noise tries to send you down the wrong path.

. . . .

Learn to Court Yourself

I want to be alone!

—Greta Garbo, actress

After Larry, there were a few short-term relationships, but after one particularly destructive one, I didn't date anybody for three years. Finally! It was a much-needed hiatus. I needed time to think and put things into perspective. I needed to get reacquainted with Bethenny Frankel.

I began to focus on me. I nurtured my career, began to network and clarify my business strategy, and poured all my energy into my business. It started to pay off.

Slowly, I was getting closer to the person I had always imagined I could be. And I started to change—or, not change exactly, but know myself better. The more I explored my own intentions, desires, and truth, the more I began to see where I had been fooling myself and misleading myself about what I really wanted.

It was a revelation when I finally realized that I didn't want money from a man. That wasn't me. I am not my mother. I don't have to be financially dependent on anyone. When I was totally, utterly honest with myself, I realized that I wanted to be dependent on myself. I didn't want a fairy tale, I wanted reality. I wanted a life that was true to me, not some idea I had about what a woman my age was supposed to be. And I began to see that I could never be happy with even the most wonderful man on the planet, if I had to rely on him for financial support.

It might be different for you, and I know a lot of people who do need support from their husbands and are fine with it. I needed something else from a husband, and I started to see that as long as money was in the way, I would never be able to find it. If I could make my own money, if I didn't have to depend on anybody else for a single cent, then maybe I would have a chance of getting past my money noise and moving on to something more important. As long as I was focused on money, I was never going to be able to find out what that something else was.

So I would make my own money, and then I would just see what happened next.

· ·

MUST BE THE MONEY

When I became engaged to Jason, I decided to do some informal research. I asked all my friends about marriage and where things go wrong and what you can do about it. I asked about sex and children and schedules and money, and overwhelmingly, it seems that problems always arise around money.

I believe almost everyone has some form of money noise. When you marry someone, of course your money noise is likely to clash with theirs, unless you both just happen to see money

in exactly the same way. Whether you are fanatical about having your money in a separate account or you don't want to know
anything about money, your noise can cause a problem. It's good
to see it up front and be ready for it if you want to avoid the kind
of blow-out that destroys a lot of marriages.

I have a friend who used to work and kept a separate account, and said this was very important to her. She had a lot of
noise about this account. But when she quit her job and stayed
home with their child and her husband made all the money,
suddenly her money noise dissolved.

For other people, it is the opposite: having their own money
calms their noise, and relying on someone else's money revs it
up. There are no rules about what will generate money noise,
and what will help make it better. It's as unique as you are.

I think the key, though, is communication. People always
seem to want to hide their money noise, like a dirty little secret.
The husband makes money and doesn't want the wife to spend
it, so he doesn't give her access to it or doesn't tell her how
much he's got. Or the wife spends it in secret and hides her
purchases. Or the wife makes more than the husband and he's
overly sensitive about it so they never mention it. Or neither
one wants to share. Or one person can't deal with money at all,
spends blindly, and refuses to acknowledge any problem, while
the other struggles to save it, and they never admit that it's tearing them apart.

I say, stop it. Talk to each other. Without open communication, you've got nothing. What's the money situation? If one
of you spends too much without regard to your joint financial
well-being, that has to come out in the open. If one of you is so
cheap that you can't even let the other one enjoy a few simple
pleasures, then that's a problem, too. Where's the balance?
Where's the compromise?

Money could have been an issue for Jason and me. He's got
a solid job with a good salary, but right now, my career is really

going strong. I realized early on that this could be a problem. On one of our first dates, we went to a restaurant, and I ended up paying the driver who took us there. That really upset me, not because I couldn't afford to pay the driver, but because I didn't want to feel like the man.

All my life, I had been supported by men, and my recent financial independence was still new to me. It's ironic, because I know I am not someone who can be financially dependent, but at the same time, I hadn't yet figured out how to handle my financial independence. It was uncomfortable, but I knew we were going to have to talk it out, no matter how it might reflect on either of us.

So I was completely blunt with Jason, and it was one of the the most difficult conversations I have ever had to have. I admitted to him that it might be wrong, but that it really bothered me to have to pay for the little things because, money or no money, I still need to feel like the woman. We feel the way we feel even when it isn't entirely logical. Know thyself!

Luckily for me, Jason is confident enough not to be threatened, and he understood exactly what I meant. He understands me. I felt petty bringing it up, but I had to come clean or it would have destroyed us, stupid as that would have been. It has been one of the ways we've both had to learn to compromise, and to accept the other person, warts and inconsistencies and all.

So we've been working it out, one little issue at a time. For example, when I had Bryn, I wanted a baby nurse to help me, so I could keep working. This isn't something Jason would ever do on his own. His mother never had a baby nurse. He thought it was a frivolous and unnecessary expense, and it took me a long time to get him to see that we really needed it and could afford it. It was worth it to me to be able to keep working.

Jason is proud and there was certainly ego involved, but I often work at home and although I'm there with Bryn, sometimes I need to get on the phone with a book editor or a magazine or a producer. I need to be able to write my books and commit to appearances and film my show. I consider myself a mother first, and I love to stay home with Bryn, but the reality is that at this time in my life, I can't do that every minute of every day. I would always rather take my family with me when I have to work, but it's not always possible, and I need to be able to work. It makes me a better mother, not a worse one.

But because of our dynamic, it became a money issue, as so many things do—it's never about what it's about.

When you are in a relationship, you don't necessarily have to agree about every single aspect of your financial lives, but you do have to say how you feel and admit to each other who you really are. Nobody can fault you for being honest. Even if you feel disgusting or petty or shallow for how you feel, you have to say it. Come clean. Maybe talking about it will change your mind, but never pretend something doesn't bother you when it really does. It's crucial for the health of a relationship. Admit who you are, and you've taken one more step toward finding your truth.

. . . .

Be a Team Player

Michael, if you can't pass, you can't play.

—Coach Dean Smith to Michael Jordan
in his freshman year at UNC

As I began to get a handle on myself and come more into my own life, my choices began to change. Finally, I had a sense of who I was. I was finding my truth. After three years, I felt like maybe I was ready to try a relationship again. Maybe I'd finally, actually learned enough to make a relationship work.

Kevin was a handsome, free-spirited, down-to-earth rock-and-roll photographer. I had met him years earlier at the Sundance film festival, when I was dating someone else and he was married. When I ran into him again, he was free and so was I. We found each other at a time when we both needed someone like each other in our lives.

Kevin was generous and loving, sweet, caring, and fun. We were young and busy with our work, and it was a great time. Being with Kevin really felt like being part of a team. We shared our time and our lives; we bounced ideas off each other, and were really partners. It was rewarding, a kind of relationship I'd never had before.

Kevin had to travel all over the world on assignments and sometimes I went with him—we surfed in Hawaii, traveled to Venice, and shared one of the greatest entertainment experiences of my life, a Billy Joel concert at the Roman Coliseum. Absolutely amazing.

Kevin shared my passion and drive for work, and he knew a world I hadn't yet learned about. Kevin was a photographer, but he was really in the celebrity business. Although I had been on *The Apprentice: Martha Stewart* by this time (I'll tell you about that soon), and I understood at least a little bit about running a business, I had never seen this side of "the game."

Before Kevin, I thought a party was just a party, an event was just an event. I never really noticed that there was this whole organized process with press and a red carpet. I had done event planning, but I was always inside dealing with lighting and sound and staging and whether there were enough chafing dishes on the buffet. I had never dealt with invitations and press lists. I didn't know what a step and repeat was. (In case you don't know either, it's a backdrop along the red carpet, where celebrities line up and move along the line to be photographed and to answer questions, making it easier for the press to have access to them.)

Kevin knew how it all worked, and I watched him participate. He was very connected, part of the press, taking pictures of movie stars and rock stars, and he knew how to play the game. I was trying to market myself as a personal chef to celebrities at the time, and Kevin was helping me get this business off the ground, trying to get me in front of the camera. He would have his staff of photographers take pictures of me, although I could tell it irritated some of them. I wasn't anybody. To them I was a waste of film, but Kevin kept trying to get my face out there.

It was all so new to me that I was embarrassed and stiff in front of the camera. I thought I had no right being there, walking behind Anne Hathaway on the red carpet. Nobody had any questions for me. Nobody was selling my pictures to the tabloids, but it was a great experience for me.

I helped Kevin, too. While he knew about celebrities, I knew about marketing, and I helped him market himself more effectively. I think I also helped him emotionally, as he was newly divorced. However, that was also part of the reason why our relationship ultimately didn't work. Kevin made plans with me for major holidays, then often canceled at the last minute to be with his kids. He was free-spirited but also disorganized, and although I admired his desire to be a good father, he was an unreliable boyfriend.

Again, the timing wasn't right. Something felt wrong for me about the fact that Kevin already had children. Originally, I had convinced myself that a built-in family was all I would ever get, all I could handle but something didn't sit right. This was a recognition of my truth—I didn't know it at the time, but I was waiting for someone who hadn't had children yet, so we could both share that new experience.

I began to see that Kevin's life was not the life I wanted. Although the celebrity world was interesting and the travel was fun, it was too much on-the-go for me. I really am more of a homebody. I'd rather stay home in my pajamas and cook dinner and snuggle than go to the Academy Awards. I like a good night out as much as the next girl, and I'll attend events for the benefit of my career, but I didn't want to do them all the time, especially when it was just for "fun."

I began to recognize that I couldn't spend my life running around after Kevin. In my life now, Jason and I work as a team, and he is accomodating when I have to travel and do everything I do, and that works better for us. You have to find the right partner for who you are. You have to fit together, and while Kevin and I had fun for awhile, we weren't meant for each other.

But Kevin helped my career, and I think I helped Kevin get over his divorce and his fear that he couldn't love someone again. We both helped each other get to the next place we each needed to go on our own emotionally and careerwise. The beginning was exciting, and I still think of him fondly, but in the end, it fizzled.

But I was back in it. I had my head on straight, and my time alone had finally helped me to integrate the lessons I had learned from all my past relationships. My career was on track and I was driven by the passion I had finally discovered in myself when I quit looking for a man to replace it. Even after Kevin and I parted, life was good.

. . . .

EDITING

I am a compulsive editor. I edit everything in my life, and by that I mean that I get rid of anything that is not immediately necessary and crucial for my existence. Old black tank top? Toss it. Shoes I haven't worn in two months? They're gone. A chair I haven't sat in for a while? Get it out. That extra spatula? Toss it. Extra words in a sentence that don't say exactly what I mean? Cut, cut, cut.

I edit my kitchen tools, my wardrobe, my jewelry, my furniture, my writing, my counters, my drawers, the contents of my refrigerator. If I no longer need it or want it or love it, I get rid of it. To me, moving on from something that doesn't work is not just liberating, it's essential for my sanity. But I get extreme about it—you wouldn't believe the things I've tossed. I have *nothing* from my past. I compulsively purge my possesions. It's borderline straitjacket, it's loony-bin, I know, you don't have to tell me. But it's the way I am. Sometimes I ask Jason if, when they finally put me away, he will visit me in the insane asylum and bring me muffins. Maybe because I moved so much as a child and always lost things along the way, editing has become a way for me to control my environment.

Here's one way I like to edit: When I go on vacation, if I wear something and I don't like how I feel in it or Jason makes a comment about how it's not his favorite thing, I'll just leave it in the hotel room. Maybe the next guest or someone on the hotel staff will find it and it will work for them. I consider it a form of recycling. If I decide it isn't right for me, I am not putting it back in my suitcase.

I definitely take it too far, but I maintain that editing is a great practice—in moderation—and most people could do more of it. Being an editor of your life is a good way to keep things simple and clear.

Of course, relationships aren't like clothes or spatulas or earrings or extra words in a paragraph. You can't just cast people aside. However, if a relationship—romantic or otherwise—has become useless or lifeless or even worse, detrimental or painful or abusive, think about how you might edit it. Can you simplify it, so you can see it more clearly? Maybe the relationship has to go. It might be better for both of you.

In a way, being your own editor is like being your own advocate. It will help you find your truth, when there is just too much stuff in the way to see it clearly. See how you can apply it in your life—start with your closet, and end with your relationships.

You Can Still Pitch for the Yankees

Diamonds are only chunks of coal that stuck to their jobs.

—Minnie Richard Smith, poet

I make jokes about the name Jason. I think I've dated every Jason on the Eastern Seaboard. Although there have been a few minor Jasons I've dated here and there, the first more serious Jason (it amuses me to call him Jason number one) was a friend of an ex of mine, and if you watched the first season of *Real Housewives,* you may remember him—the introverted, quiet investment banker who obviously didn't want to be on a reality TV show. People didn't necessarily respond well to Jason, as he was portrayed on television, but that was unfair. The truth is that he wasn't comfortable on air, or with my lifestyle. It can be frustrating when you love a lot of things about a person, but your lifestyles clash. But we tried to make it work.

Jason had a lot of qualities I loved. Like me, he often preferred to stay in more than go out. He was kind and loving, but there were also some major aspects of his life that I didn't love. His ex-wife was still in his life, and he had three adorable children who were caught in the middle of their divorce. I'd gone through some of these issues with Kevin, and I knew, even as I tried to deny it, that I wasn't a good fit with someone who already had children. I thought Jason's kids were great, but I realized, the more time I spent with them, that no matter how good a stepmother I might try to be, I would never be their mother. I wanted my own child, and Jason seemed to be done in that department. He might have done it for me, but I don't think it would have been best for him. I felt a responsibility, not just for my own happiness but for his. It just wasn't quite right for either one of us.

But the final nail in the coffin became evident when we had the conversation people always have when they decide to break up and think they should talk about it: We were discussing our futures. He wanted me to accept his kids and make a quiet life with him. I wanted my own kids, and more—more than he wanted, more than he could give me.

I said I really couldn't imagine my life continuing the way it was going. When I told him I still had dreams I needed to chase, he said something I'll never forget. He said, "Every nine-year-old boy wants to pitch for the Yankees."

He meant that we all have big dreams but they aren't all going to come true. At some point, you have to accept that and go with what you've got. You have to compromise or give in or settle because it is realistic. He added, "I'm not pitching for the Yankees, am I?"

I immediately replied, "But I still want to pitch for the Yankees." It was a defining moment. In my own mind, I wondered if I was being unrealistic—if it was even possible to have more. Was I being too much of a dreamer? Shooting for the stars? But some part of me was insistent—some part of me couldn't give up or give in.

Jason thought it was unrealistic of me, but I knew I had more to do than settle down. I'd learned that lesson already, too many times over. I was coming from a place of yes. I believe anything is possible and I still do—if you want to be really successful, you have to be one of those people who sees yourself as more than a number or a drone or a cog in a machine. You have to see that you are special and believe that you can do it—and you have to surround yourself with people who believe you can do it, too. It doesn't mean you won't have doubts, but you have to keep seeking your truth, and my truth was rooted in my belief that I was destined for something more. I could feel it in my gut. I was on the verge of something bigger, and I needed a partner who could go there with me.

It's not that Jason number one didn't believe in me. He did. He was always supportive of my career, but that conversation was a watershed moment. He was content in his life and his path. I was still fighting. It doesn't mean that what he was offering me was bad, it just wasn't for me. I was not going to give up my dreams. Jason has his own noise, and I'm sure he has his own memory of that conversation, but to me, he was asking me to settle, and I had to say *no*. And so it ended.

Some people do end up pitching for the team, dancing ballet, running their own companies, even finding their books on the *New York Times* bestseller list (which is my equivalent of the World Series). I was still going for it, and I had to believe in it with everything I had.

Ironically, by implying I should be more realistic, Jason taught me to try even harder, to keep coming from a place of yes. So I did, and that's when it finally happened for me. After that, my career skyrocketed—and I met the final Jason, the only Jason, the Jason who would become my husband and the father of my child.

Wait for It

Waiting, done at really high speeds, will frequently look like something else.

—Carrie Fisher, actress and author

I love this Carrie Fisher quote because I feel like I've been moving at high speed for most of my life, and yet, I also spent years of my life waiting, in a way that never looked like waiting—waiting for the right person at the right time, waiting for the right career, waiting to find myself, and waiting for the man who really could be my husband.

Jason has been a miracle in my life. He's the one who defied the odds. He has changed me forever. At the age of thirty-nine, I found my perfect man, I had a baby, and my career went wild. All my dreams came true at once. Jason proved to me that waiting was worth every second, and that it's never too late. Sometimes what seems like too late is right on time because you are only just ready. Please remember that. When you come from a place of yes, anything can happen.

I don't think I could have met Jason any earlier than I did. Of course, I can speculate about how it might have gone, but I probably wouldn't have been ready. I had to get to that place where I didn't think I needed anybody anymore.

I see a lot of independent, strong women these days who aren't concerned about meeting men. They are too busy with their careers. That's the place I had to find, and ironically, that's the only place I could come from and find the right man for me. The least interested party always wins—and desperation kills. For me, not needing a man was what finally allowed me to find one I could love. Every single step I took toward myself and my truth prepared me for the moment I first saw him.

Our meeting wasn't fairy-tale. It was ultimately modern, just like we are. It was *us*. I wouldn't trade it for ten Prince Charmings on ten white horses.

As people often say when they tell the story of meeting the right one, I wasn't looking for a man. That night, I was running around with a group of friends from out of town, going from one event to another. One of our stops was at a nightclub, and when we tried to go inside, they said I could go in, but my friends couldn't—I guess they looked like they weren't from New York. I was furious. I knew the owner of this club, so I decided to call him and complain. He told us to come back, and that we could all go in.

When we got back to the club, I went up to the doorman and started yelling, "Just because my friends aren't New Yorkers dressing fancy and wearing seven-inch heels, you aren't going to let them in?" But just think if I hadn't called—if we had given up and gone somewhere else instead, I might have never met my husband that night.

This confrontation had fueled the attitude I already had—I walked into that nightclub as an independent woman who frankly didn't give a damn, and it showed.

And there he was, my beautiful-inside-and-out future husband, working his magic. I was posing for a photo, smiling when the cameras were up and going back to my usual smug face when they were down. He took one look at me and said, "Are you ready to get that stick out of your ass now?"

It may not sound romantic, but there was no more perfect pickup line for someone like me. If he had come up to me with a, "Hey, nice to meet you!" I wouldn't have given him a second glance, but that line drew me in and got my attention. It intrigued me. I almost felt like he understood me even before he knew me at all. Who *was* this guy?

He was actually working some other girl that night, and he did go on a date with her after we first met. I went on a few dates with other guys after that night, too. But somehow, in retrospect, it was always all about the two of us, more than either of us realized when we danced that night and kissed and bantered and didn't know but somehow also *knew*. Chemistry is chemistry. Jason saw right through me from the beginning. He saw *me*.

Jason said I was a tough nut to crack. He's competitive and he loves a challenge. It took me six months to come around and Jason wasn't pining for me, but he was definitely interested. He would get it to happen. That's why we're together—because he approached me from a place of yes. He'll always be chasing me a little, but that's part of what he loves about me. I love that he won't ever give up. It took us a while, but at last we admitted it: We were in love. I said yes to myself, and that opened the door for me to say yes to him. Before I knew it, I was pregnant. And now we have our little family: Jason and me, baby Bryn, and of course, our dog, Cookie, aka Dabooboo.

I finally found the right man for me. Jason doesn't try to be anything other than himself, and I love who he is. He goes to church and prays for people. He loves children. He cares more about me than he cares about money or his job. When my father died, he was with me. When I had Bryn, he was with me every second in the hospital, from the time I checked in to the time I checked out, six days later. He's completely hands-on. He's up with me in the middle of the night. He's my partner in every way. I've never met anyone more committed to family. And the timing—it was finally, wonderfully right.

Jason once told me to let him love me. "Let me love you." I'll never forget that. It's been the hardest thing I've ever done, but I did it because of what I'd been through, and what Jason has been through, and what we've now been through together. He won me over, just by being who he is. Jason knows his truth, so we're the perfect match—the final piece in the relationship puzzle I've been assembling all these years.

Jason taught me so much about myself. He taught me that I can be softer than I thought I could be. He taught me, finally, after decades of shutting people out, that there are a few I can let in. He taught me how to let go, that I don't have to control every single thing in my life. He taught me how to trust and maybe most important, he taught me how to stop running away.

So I guess the lesson in this chapter is about finding your truth, but also about finding—or reconnecting with—the person who can help you get there. Your relationship voice will tell you when someone loves you and when you really love someone.

When my own inner voice finally spoke up and helped me find the love I'd been seeking, it was such a revelation—about love and about *me*. Jason is the person who will be there when I'm sick, who will never hurt me, who will sit beside me on the park bench when I am ninety years old. And I'm finally the person who can be there on the park bench beside him.

Jason doesn't have to try to be loving and emotionally supportive. He just *is*. It's part of him, and I'm learning how to be just as supportive and open to him. He loves me no matter what I do, for who

I am, not for what I will or won't do for him. I used to try to create problems so I could run from my relationship. Now I try to make solutions. I don't need Jason's money, but I do need his love. I can finally see that. Emotional support was what I needed all along, what I didn't get as a child and what I had always been seeking. Jason taught me what emotional support really means.

I know he's learned things, too. He's softened, in his own way. When we first started dating, he couldn't stand dogs. He didn't want to be near Cookie, and when we were lying in bed, I had to lie between them because he didn't want her fur to touch him.

Now Cookie is practically *his* dog. When he gets home, he says hello to her first, and she loves him dearly. Recently, Cookie had some minor surgery and had to wear one of those cones around her neck so that she wouldn't scratch at her stitches. Jason went out at 8:00 in the morning to get her a softer cone, so she would be more comfortable. At one point I caught him upside-down on the bed, with his arms around her, scratching her neck under the cone to help make her more comfortable. Of course, Cookie has a way with people—even when she practically mauls people on my show, we all still love her, and she has her own fans. She even has her own Twitter account.

In fact, Cookie and I have a lot in common, and we've both decided that Jason can sleep in our bed. He loves us, and we aren't going to bite him.

So that's my journey, and my relationship advice. Take it or leave it—but please take it. I've suffered, I've pounded the pavement, I've dated rich men with big planes and small penises, and I've dated poverty-stricken losers with no planes and big penises (I'm still not sure which I liked better). I've done it all in order to be able to give you this advice! Consider all my torture and my bad choices, and learn from it. I have very smart friends who come to me for relationship advice, because I've been around the block.

You are on your own journey, and more than anything else, that journey must be about finding your truth. Not finding a husband, a boyfriend, a partner—but finding *yourself*. Shine the flashlight into those dark places you haven't wanted to face before. Face up to your qualities—all of them. Look at your patterns. Analyze them. Only by looking back over your past relationships and deconstructing the noise that's led you in the wrong direction will you discover your strengths, your desires, the things you really need from a partner, and the things you really can do for yourself.

You'll find truth, and then you'll be able to take your life to the next level.

Rule 3
. . . .

Act on It
My Dream Evolves

Destiny is not a matter of chance. It is a matter of choice. It is not to be waited for, it is a thing to be achieved.

—William Jennings Bryan, politician

The first two rules, *break the chain* and *find your truth*, are about introspection. You go inside and figure out what you are doing, and why, leading to a clearer vision of who you are and what you want.

Now it's time to do something about it.

Rules #1 and #2 can change everything, but they don't actually do anything. When you understand them, however, you are set free to move forward, transforming from insecure to self-assured, from paralyzed to proactive, or even from know-it-all to take-it-back-to-the-drawing-board. Accepting and working with the first two rules enables you to act because you learn who you are and what you want. You are now perfectly positioned to practice rule #3: *act on it*.

Act on it means taking positive control of your life, and actually doing something about your goals. It means taking real, tangible steps forward. You stop thinking and start doing, even if you aren't sure where it will lead. It's time to start shaking things up and making changes in your life, big or small. Rule #3 helps you put things in motion, so your life can start unfolding the way you want it to.

You can act on your vision and goals at any time in your life, though there is no more important time to *act on it* than during transitions. Whether you are graduating from school and heading out into the world, quitting or starting a new job, leaving or entering into a relationship, or moving to a new city, you are automatically in an active mode. But your transition doesn't have to be that dramatic. Maybe you just feel ready for a change. Maybe it's just a change of mind. Maybe you're just tired of the way things have been going.

Act on it, now, not later. Don't wait around until you're absolutely sure that you're doing the right thing. You'll never be absolutely sure. Go with your gut and act in line with your nature, and you'll be on the right course. You may need to make adjustments later, but that's better than not doing anything at all.

Making things happen for yourself is how you gain the experience that will help you continue to practice rule #2, *find your truth.* The more you do, the more you act, the more you learn about your truth, refining it and perfecting it. Rules #2 and #3 become like a propeller, each rule cycling around to the next until you lift off the ground. Find your truth, act on it. Find more truth, act on it. Find still more truth, act on it, and so on. Self-analysis is great, to a point, but it has to lead to action or it will never come to anything.

That's not to say you'll always know exactly what to do. You won't. Don't paralyze yourself worrying that you might not do the right thing that will lead you to the fulfillment of all of your dreams for the rest of your life—that's just too much pressure. You'll scare yourself into doing nothing. Instead, make acting on it a habit, your default mode. Just get out there and start working and learning and doing. Start your life.

It doesn't matter if you don't have the perfect job, or even the job you deserve. It doesn't matter if you aren't living in the best place yet, or wearing the clothes you wish you could afford, or spending every minute doing what you want to do. It doesn't even matter if you really don't have a plan. Welcome to the world—what matters is that you are doing something, working for something, proving yourself, gaining experience. If you don't get out there and let people know who you are and what you want and what you can do, you may never find the job or house or relationship or whatever else you want.

This rule reminds me of that old joke where a man gets down on his knees and prays: "Dear God, why didn't you ever let me win the lottery?" And God answers: "Why didn't you ever buy a ticket?" The world is filled with people who have great ideas, but never put them into practice. Be the one who *acts* on your great idea, and you'll never have to live with "what if?" Stop making excuses. Stop saying you want things to be different, then doing everything the same. If you want things to be different, change them. Now is your time to act on it.

What's the next chapter of your life going to be about? Don't just plan it. Start making it happen, even before you've figured it all out, whether it's signing up for a cooking class or becoming more active at your church or joining a gym so you can get control over your health, or actually saying yes to that guy who asked you out. So what if he might not be Mr. Right. Get yourself out there. Shake it up. Make it happen. Make *something* happen.

Or maybe you want your life to be simpler, more organized, easier, healthier. Don't just say to yourself, I want to simplify. *Act on it.* Start ditching the junk you don't love—clean out your closets, drawers, kitchen cabinets. Clean off your desk, your beside table, that counter where you pile all your mail and junk. Get rid of your baggage, in a very literal way. This simple act will make you feel so much calmer and cleaner. Don't just say, "I'm going to get healthy!" Go for a walk. Have a big salad. Take a deep breath and calm down before you eat, so you can be sensible. Do it *now.* You don't have to have a master plan. You just have to muster the will to act.

It all comes down to saying *yes*. Acting on it—making real things happen in real life—comes from a place of yes.

Focus Noise

One reason so few of us achieve what we truly want is that we never direct our focus; we never concentrate our power. Most people dabble their way through life, never deciding to master anything in particular.

—Anthony Robbins, motivational speaker and author

As always, there is noise that can get in the way of this process of self-discovery and taking action. I call it *focus noise*. Focus noise is that noise in your head that tries to distract you from your goals. If you want to excel in your career, focus noise can convince you that you're young, you want to have fun, and you shouldn't have to take work all that seriously. You *should* enjoy your life, of course. Don't waste your youthful years being too serious, but don't let your focus noise distract you from the things you really want, either. Play makes life sweet, but work makes life rich, and I don't just mean financially. Find something you are passionate about. Create something. Build something. Fix something. Make the world better—begin with your own life.

Focus noise can keep you watching TV instead of taking a walk, reading junk email when you could be spending time with actual friends in real life, looking up random things on the Internet when you could be working on your novel, or lying on the couch eating cookies when you could be going to yoga class or catching up on a project you've really wanted to finish. There is always a line between too much focus and not enough, and this is the time to learn how to walk it.

Another way to lose focus is through excessive worry. My assistant, Julie, gets anxious sometimes that she hasn't figured out everything in her life. She's twenty-six. To her, this anxiety seems founded and real, even though it seems to me that she's so young, she shouldn't have to worry about anything yet. But I remember feeling that way, too, and I know a lot of women who felt like that in their twenties . . . or thirties . . . or forties . . . or any time. Anxiety and fear about what you are doing or "what it all means" can distract you at any time in your life, keeping you from actually seeking meaning through action.

Focus noise can convince you that you have to have all the details worked out in advance, but you don't. *Acting on it* only requires a sense of yourself and your general direction. You can't know how it's all going to play out later, so don't let that hold you back.

Focus noise can also turn into *future noise,* when you get so preoccupied with what might happen later that you forget to live right now. You have to live now. That's what this rule is all about.

This is the time to get in the game. Dip your toe in the pool, and eventually, you'll be all the way in. You are learning, and everything you do will teach you more about yourself. It doesn't matter that you don't have your ultimate job right now. There are no shortcuts and there is a path to greatness that you have to follow, no matter what anyone says. Sometimes you'll have to work hard. There is no easy way out. You'll have to do things you don't always like, that aren't always fun. You have to put in your time and not let yourself get distracted. Just chart a general direction, and *go.*

Learn Everything

I am learning all the time. The tombstone will be my diploma.

—Eartha Kitt, actress and singer

Acting on it is also about learning, in real life, in real time. It's about accumulating experiences that you can use later, when you might need them. Even when that crappy job doesn't seem relevant or your life isn't going so well, the point is that it might become relevant, or some aspect of your life now may become relevant later, just when you need it. No matter what you are doing, always learn—it's all life experience.

There is no better classroom for life than work, so in this chapter, I'll share some of my stories about my colorful employment history—because more than anything, the jobs I've had have taught me how to put rule #3 into practice.

I've had a lot of jobs. Some have been great and some have been horrible. I've done it all, from stuffing envelopes in a cubicle to waitressing to event planning to being on television. I will never have to look back on my life and say I didn't have a good time, but I've also worked really hard to get where I am. I've learned a lot and taught myself how to ignore my focus noise (most of the time—nobody's perfect). Some of those skills seemed pointless at the time, but they turned out to be surprisingly relevant later.

For example, when I first moved to Los Angeles, I went to bartender school. I didn't become a career bartender, so was that a wasted experience? No. Now, years later, I'm in the liquor business with my Skinnygirl cocktails. Who knew?

I didn't know when I went to culinary school that I would later start a natural foods business. I didn't know when I took acting lessons that I would later have my own television show. I certainly didn't know, when I was a teenager spending my weekends at the roller rink, that I would someday be on *Skating with the Stars*.

Whether you're working in an office, bussing tables, transcribing medical records, or doing the accounting for somebody else's small business, you just never know when you'll learn something that you'll need. Your experience is your toolbox, and you're filling it up right now by *acting on it*. Someday, you might suddenly have to have that one special wrench you never thought you'd need.

When teenagers whine about school because they'll *never need to know* what they are learning *in real life* (I whined about it, too), I know now that we were wrong. What if you blew it off, whatever it is, algebra or grammar or U.S. history, and then miss your big chance? What if you end up on the TV show *Are You Smarter Than a Fifth Grader?* as I did recently, and you don't remember a damn thing, and then you look silly on national television?

I've had my share of "I don't need to know that" moments, but in general, I'm so glad I've always been into a lot of things because now I know a lot about a lot of things, and it's paid off a hundred times over. Learn everything you can, every day of your life. Prove the naysayers wrong when they say that youth is wasted on the young, or that you can't teach an old dog new tricks. Act on it—"it" being your life. At any age, at any stage. Because your life depends on it.

Work hard, learn, do your best—and have fun. Take action, to thwart your focus noise and get you on track for something bigger and better, if that's what you really want. The people who make it big when they are young are unusually focused on accomplishing something, whether it's winning an Olympic medal or starting a company or inventing Facebook, but plenty of people finally hit their stride later in life, too—just look at me.

I don't always follow my own advice, but in retrospect, I can see times I should have followed it more. I didn't always know what I wanted to do, but I've always had a lot of interests. So, to show you how rule #3 can play out, I'll tell you about a particular time in my life—the victories I achieved and the screw-ups I committed when I first started trying to get career #1 off the ground.

Trying to Live My Dream

Inaction breeds doubt and fear. Action breeds confidence and courage. If you want to conquer fear, do not sit home and think about it. Go out and get busy.

—Dale Carnegie, author

Careers are like kites. They can be hard to get off the ground. You run and run and run and the kite still bumps along in the dirt behind you. When the kite finally lifts up into the air, sometimes coaxed by a random gust of wind or a little dumb luck, then you've done it. You've taken it to the next level, and get ready to hold on, because it's a whole new life.

But if you never try to fly the kite—if you never *act on it*—then you'll never know the thrill of achievement you could have experienced when all your hard work pays off and you end up in an amazing place you'd never even dreamed about.

For years, I tried to get my career into the air, so to speak. Sometimes it was maddening and I despaired that I would never get it right. But I kept trying until it was finally airborne. I acted on it, even when I wasn't always acting in the most efficient or direct way. The point is that I was running with that kite, and come hell or high water, I was going to get the thing airborne.

Success is hard, at any level, whether it's making partner in a law firm or getting elected to political office or raising happy, healthy, well-adjusted children. But oh, it's so worth it in the end.

So now I'm going to tell you the story of another relationship—this story isn't about a man. It's about a dream. It's about what I used to want to be when I grew up, and how I acted on it, and how it taught me some surprising lessons, and eventually, in a round-about way, got me here. It's the story of Bethenny Frankel: Actress.

Ever since I was a little girl, I wanted to be a performer. It may not have been the most original dream, but it was mine. I believed it could happen. I still believe that when you envision something for yourself, and you can really see it, and feel how it would be, then that means it's attainable.

Even when I was very young, I knew performing was something I could do. You could psychoanalyze it and say I just wanted more attention than I was getting at home, and maybe that's true, but who's to say that invalidates the dream? Plenty of famous actors sought out the profession because they didn't get enough attention as kids. I thought I was born to do it. Acting would be the ultimate career for me. I thought it was my destiny. I was hungry to *act on it,* long before I had the resources to do anything about it.

I remember looking up "Acting" in the phone book and finding lists of acting schools, and poring over the lists, trying to figure out if any of them were any good. I wondered if a really good acting school would even be listed in the phone book, and I also felt completely helpless because I was too young to drive or pay for acting school or know how you were "supposed" to become an actor. I didn't have enough information, and my mother was completely un-interested in helping me become the next big child star. She ignored my requests for help. There is nothing more frustrating than having ambition as a child and having no possible way to do anything about it. Please remember this as a parent—I plan to remember it with Bryn! If your child expresses interest in something, you can act on it by helping them explore their developing passions.

Later, I went away to private boarding school in Florida for high school, and although I still planned on becoming an actress, school and socializing and adjusting to living away from home took center stage in my life. Still, I was in a few plays—I had a small part in *A Christmas Carol,* and a few other plays. In ninth grade I got cast as the understudy for Maria in *West Side Story,* and although it was rare for a ninth grader to get cast for a role that big, I was angry that I didn't get the lead, and I turned down the understudy part. Now I see that as a mistake. I was a poor sport about it, and I was impatient to be in the spotlight. I didn't realize at the time how you have to earn parts like that, and the value of working for it. (I've definitely learned this by now!)

When I went off to college at NYU, I took theater classes, but I didn't major in theater because I suppose part of me was holding back—and I probably wouldn't have gotten into their incredibly competitive theater department, anyway. I really didn't understand what it takes to be a real actress. I had this passionate dream, but I didn't know how to make it come true—I didn't know how to kill for it. I wasn't focused.

Yet my dream persisted. I wasn't acting on it yet, but I was waiting . . . waiting for something to happen. Anything. Waiting for my adult life to begin.

And something did happen—my first foray into the entertainment industry came when I was nineteen. I was traveling to L.A., and I just happened to be late for my flight. I almost missed it, and they had already filled my seat, so they put me in the last available seat in first class. As luck would have it, I sat next to a producer for the TV show *Saved by the Bell*.

We chatted throughout the flight. I asked him questions about what he did for a living, and he told me he was impressed that a young woman could converse intelligently and be interested in what he had to say. (Now when I'm on airplanes, I always see young people hunched into corners, listening to their iPods and doing everything possible not to speak to the people next to them—but you never know who might be sitting next to you or what you might learn from them. Don't tune out the world—you might miss *your* next big break!)

My new friend the producer told me that he would never normally do this, but he thought I had potential, and he just might have a position available as a production assistant for an upcoming series of *Saved by the Bell* episodes. If I followed up with him, he said, he would see what he could do.

I was ecstatic—*this* was what I had been waiting for. I handled myself professionally and expressed my gratitude. As soon as I got home, I called the number he gave me and very calmly and maturely made arrangements for an interview. I was jumping up and down on the inside at the thought of my big breakthrough in Hollywood, but I knew I had to handle it the right way. Still, I thought I was finally on my way. Oh, how little I realized what a long road lay ahead of me, but what might have happened if I *hadn't* acted on it? So often, people just don't bother to follow up on opportunities because they think they won't be chosen, it won't really come to anything, it would be too hard, or too much of a risk. No! Act on it. Why shouldn't you be the one?

I got the job. It was a temporary one, for the summer beach episodes, and my job was to run errands for the producers, get coffee, answer phones, keep track of schedules, and basically do whatever anyone needed. I was still in college, but this job was so much more interesting to me than my classes. I was fascinated by the whole process of filming a television show, and I couldn't take my eyes off the kids on the show. I worked hard and I was all business, but truth be told, I was envious of those young actors who, in my mind, had everything. They were all so beautiful and got so much attention, and they were all involved with each other in complicated off-screen hook-ups. It all seemed so glamorous to me at the time, so Hollywood. I would have loved to be in their shoes.

Every day at work was a new experience, and I loved every minute. I was particularly fascinated by the behind-the-scenes politics. For example, all the girls wanted to wear sexy outfits on the show, but some were allowed to wear bikinis and gorgeous dresses, and others weren't, according to their characters—that resulted in some off-camera fireworks.

There was always sniping and emotional drama on the set, just like a junior version of what I would experience years later on

Housewives. As I worked behind the scenes, I dreamed of being one of the people in front of the camera. I remember, during one of the breaks in filming, I was talking to a young guy who was a guest star. I don't remember his name, but I still see him in a lot of commercials. He said to me, "Oh my God, I love this so much! I would do this for free!" I replied, "Don't ever tell *them* that!" But secretly I agreed.

I met a lot of people who were on that show before they were famous, like Denise Richards, Tori Spelling, and Leah Remini. During that time, I became chummy with Mario Lopez, who played Slater. (I'm on *Extra* fairly regularly now, and am business acquaintances with Mario—it's funny how each of our careers played out and it's amazing to know each other again in our current roles.)

Working on *Saved by the Bell* galvanized my desire to be an actress. This was the world to me; I soaked up everything I could and made all the connections I could and tried to get my foot in that brightly lit, diamond-encrusted door. Maybe it was for all the wrong reasons—fame, attention, wealth, everything I perceived those other people had that I didn't have—but I was nineteen. I had a lot to learn.

Now, when I think back on that time, I have to smile. I was so young and inexperienced! When they were casting a spin-off show called *California Dreams,* I talked my way into getting the producer to let me audition, but when I got in front of that camera, I totally choked. The pressure was too great and I was too daunted. It's hard for me to imagine being so intimidated by a camera now. I tried to read the lines the way I thought they wanted to hear them, but it didn't really occur to me to try to really listen to the other person's lines or access the character or be myself. But at least I tried—I was *acting on it*, but I didn't have enough experience to get the part. Yet, just doing the audition was a good experience.

When my stint as a production assistant ended, I wanted to keep going, and I tried to take advantage of every opportunity and every connection I made on that show. They didn't all pan out. During that time, I met another NBC producer who offered me the chance to work on *Saturday Night Live*. This remains a dream of mine, to appear on this dynamic, iconic show. At the tender age of nineteen, I thought this would be a huge step forward in my so-called career. However, I learned that *SNL* had a policy that interns could work there only for college credit, and NYU didn't participate in the program, so I wasn't able to do the job. I was so disappointed—it didn't even occur to me to fight the system. If today's Bethenny had been in that situation, you better believe I would have been in the dean's office wheedling my way into it and trying to get them to make an exception to their policy. I would not have taken no as an answer, or certainly not as readily as I did back then. But at the time, I didn't even know there *was* a dean's office.

So there I was, sometimes encouraged, sometimes foiled, but all the more inspired to get out of college and move on with my new life—the life of an actress. As soon as I graduated from NYU, I moved straight to Los Angeles. I didn't even go to my graduation ceremony. I was going to be a star.

. . . .

NOTHING MAJOR

Interviewers and fans frequently ask me what my college major was, but the answer isn't anything revealing. A lot of students obsess about what their major will be, but how many of them really have a clear plan when they are eighteen? When I was in college, I was floating. I didn't know what to major in, so I chose communications and psychology, simply because those were the classes that worked in my schedule. There was no rhyme or reason to it; I had no dedicated focus at the time.

College can be an amazing experience and it's almost always going to benefit you later, in ways you can't even imagine when you are doing it. However, like anything else, college itself isn't for everyone. Truthfully, if I had skipped college, I would have had the opportunity to do more professional work, earlier. However, I know that even though I didn't progress from a dedicated major to a specific career in the traditional way, college taught me so much about the world and dealing with people and how to reach goals and finish things.

Depending on who you are and what you want to do, your major matters less than what you choose to do now. So what if your college major has nothing to do with your current passion, whatever it is? It's never too late to act on your interests. If I had had a clearer vision when I was younger, I might have gone to school for broadcast journalism, or studied nutrition, or even theater. Then again, if I had been more focused in college, I might never have ended up with the life I have now, in which it has been so beneficial for me to know a lot of about a wide range of things. So, in some ways, I'm glad I didn't know what I was doing. At the time, I just wanted to get in and get out.

If you feel as if you chose the "wrong" major or you never finished or went to college, that's all part of your path—but choose a path, whether you get a job straight out of high school or you spend years earning your PhD in a specialized field, whether you take a year or two off to work or see the world first, or join the Peace Corps, or whether you never went to college at all. Be proud of your life and your path. In the real world, you can change your "major" whenever you choose.

· ·

Life in L.A.

I love Los Angeles. I love Hollywood. They're beauti-
ful. Everybody's plastic, but I love plastic. I want to be
plastic.

—*Andy Warhol, artist*

Returning to Los Angeles was an exciting time for me, one filled with promise. I felt like it was a whole new start, a whole new life. L.A. was going to be the exact opposite of my life in New York—full of success and glamour and personal fulfillment. I was finally out on my own, making my life happen, with no rules and nobody to dictate my possibilities but me.

Like a million other hopeful actors, I found an apartment and spent a lot of money on head shots. I sent them out to dozens of agencies, and I didn't get a single response. It was such a waste of time and money. I tried to meet as many people as I could and I met and even dated some agents and producers, but I was embarrassed to admit I was an actress and frankly, I poured most of my efforts into networking for the sake of getting dates, rather than for the sake of getting jobs. I had never done anything like this before, and I really didn't know how to do it. It made me uncomfortable—I didn't like being at the mercy of a casting director, and besides, I felt like every girl in L.A. was trying to be an actress. It was such a cliché, so I underplayed it—I lost focus and didn't commit wholeheartedly to acting, so it wasn't surprising that I was getting nowhere fast.

If I had it to do again, I would have done so many things differently. I would have saved that money I spent on head shots and concentrated on acting school and real networking. I would have approached it with confidence instead of embarrassment. I did take acting classes, but I would have taken more, and taken them more seriously. I would have worn it, owned it, committed to it. Not that I shouldn't have been out there having fun, but if you really want to accomplish something, you have to find a balance. If I had been more focused, people's reactions to my aspirations probably would have been much different than the total non-acknowledgment I received. But I was young and inexperienced and I didn't know how to do that yet.

This was also a time of struggling with body image noise. Living in Los Angeles, there is so much pressure to be thin and beautiful. As you know, I already had body image noise from growing up. I was already obsessed with dieting, and I was actually afraid of food. I'll never forget when Aaron Spelling's casting director told me I needed to lose weight because I wasn't skinny enough. It really upset me. I felt it was a call to action, and I began to obsess even more about food. In some ways, it was just one more way to distract myself from what I was really trying to do. If I could focus on avoiding fat, I would be distracted from the other parts of my life that weren't panning out.

Does anybody remember Susan Powter, the '80s diet guru, who used to be on television screaming, "Stop the Insanity!" and telling everybody that they could eat six baked potatoes and still lose weight, as long as they didn't use butter? She was in the media a lot back then, and I think of her as the founder of the fat-free phase of dieting in America. She made us all terrified to eat a single drop of fat.

This craze fed right into my obsession with dieting. I became pathologically obsessed with avoiding fat. Pursuing my acting career should have been my mission. Instead, my mission was to eat no fat. I thought that somehow, if I could just do that, everything else in my life would fall into place. Talk about *focus noise*. This is what I did:

Every morning, I woke up and went to the Big Chill, a frozen yogurt store, and bought a giant fat-free frozen yogurt or a big fat-free muffin. Although both items probably contained obscene amounts of sugar, I thought they must be healthy because they were fat-free. Ironically, both options were far more "fattening" than the toasted whole wheat bagel I often eat for breakfast, now that I don't ever diet anymore. I know now that if it tastes too good to be true, it likely isn't true. Those fat-free monstrosities were anything but good for me.

For lunch, I bought cheap quarts of plain brown rice from a nearby Chinese restaurant and divided them up into portions. For dinner, I'd have more frozen yogurt, or more brown rice, or fat-free "diet" candy.

I was getting hardly any protein, but I didn't really think or care about that. I also didn't have any money, and brown rice was cheap. If I ate anything else, it was steamed Chinese food—steamed, steamed, steamed, it couldn't be prepared any other way. There was no logic to it. When I wasn't doing this, I was going on every diet known to womankind, one at a time. I ripped out every page in every magazine that had a meal plan that promised I would lose weight. I tried every quick fix. I refused to drink alcohol, but then I'd binge on fruity frozen drinks.

One day, I would feel thin and virtuous. The next day, I would feel so fat. The scale was all over the place, and the number I saw on it every morning would influence how I felt about myself for the rest of the day. It was crazy and abnormal, but at the time, it seemed normal to me.

For one thing, everybody I knew ate that way in L.A. But by the end of the day, I was completely exhausted. I remember falling asleep in a movie theater one night. Now that I know more about nutrition, I realize that my blood sugar was crashing, but I kept pushing through the fatigue and doing it all over again. The next morning, I would wake up ravenous and all I could think about was running right out to get another fat-free muffin or fat-free frozen yogurt.

I also had an exercise addiction, which was another part of my body image noise. I went to the gym every day, obsessively, but if I missed one workout, I gave up and wouldn't go again for weeks. It was all so extreme, up or down. There was no stability, no regularity, no moderation. It wasn't rational. Because I couldn't control what was going on with my career, I thought I could at least control this one aspect of my life, but I wasn't really in control of it at all.

It's not that I didn't have confidence during this time. As I said, a lot of women lived like this in L.A., so I had plenty of context for what I was doing (unfortunately). I wasn't walking around with my head down or feeling dysfunctional. Actually, I thought I looked pretty good and I was proud of myself, in a warped way, for being extreme enough to do what I thought it took to stay thin and attractive. But the truth is, I felt like crap.

I think many women get slammed by body image noise at some point in their lives, just because of the cultural expectations and role models out there. We're under all this pressure to conform to someone else's standards, but just take a moment and ask yourself, for *what*, and for *whom*? It's never about what it's about—feeling chubby shouldn't ruin your day. What else is really going on?

Rule #3 can definitely apply to your health. I cover this extensively in my book *Naturally Thin*, and that book has changed many people's view of food and dieting. I get letters every day from people who say it changed their lives. Women tend to beat themselves up constantly about food, dieting, and body image. More and more men do this to themselves, too. I cannot stress to you enough how important it is to focus on all the great things you can eat, instead of everything you've decided is forbidden. Nothing should be forbidden. Especially during stressful times, you have to act on your conviction to be healthy and take care of yourself. Focus on your life. Food is just food. What are you using it for? How is it fueling your focus noise?

I wish I would have known then what I know now. Eating would have been so much easier and healthier. I would have focused on portion control rather than making fat the devil. I would have spent less time pounding it out in aerobics or spin class and more time doing yoga or something else soothing. I would have treated myself better.

Fortunately, I was able to work out these dietary issues later

myself, by being analytical and learning more about nutrition, but
it took a few years. You really can take control over your eating and
your emotional attitude towards food. I have to say that if you have
serious issues with food, dieting, binge eating, or starving yourself,
and you don't think you can get a handle on them yourself, please
talk to a professional counselor.

. . . .

EATING IN COLLEGE 101

I get a lot of mail from girls transitioning from high school to
college, who want to stay focused on their health and eat for
energy. When you're in college, or really, at any time in your life
when you are thrown into a new environment or stressful situation, it can be really difficult to eat well. Eating late at night,
drinking too much, snacking all the time, bingeing as a response
to stress can all add to a loss of focus and productivity, weight
gain and even health problems.

On my website, I recently published some "back to school"
eating tips, and I think it's relevant to include those here
whether for you or your college-age daughter. Anyone can benefit from these. The underlying message is: Don't be afraid of
food! Instead, eat what you love in moderation. It's all about
reeling it in. Turn the "freshman fifteen" (or the "midlife fifteen"?) into a myth with these three principles:

1. Stock that tiny little refrigerator and small kitchen of
yours with fun yet healthy snacks. Some good ideas include:

- Handful of raw nuts and dried fruit
- Hummus or nut butter on whole-grain bread
- Frozen edamame (most supermarkets sell it now)
- Whole-grain pretzels with a small piece of cheese

- Sliced turkey with a bit of mustard (excellent high-protein snack)
- Natural meal bars (I'm not a fan of these in general, but there are a few great ones—choose the ones with ingredients that you can pronounce)
- Canned or boxed all-natural soups (good comfort food and easily prepared in a microwave)
- Salty snacks like Popchips, soy chips, baked chips, and salsa
- Fresh fruit
- Greek yogurt, instant Irish oatmeal, and Kashi Good Friends cereal (add fruit and a bit of sweetener for a great snack or breakfast)
- Half of a sandwich
- A small portion of anything you are craving

2. Don't diet. Don't deprive yourself. If you want pizza, have it, but just have one slice, and add veggies if possible. Even better, first eat a salad with vinaigrette (skip the cheese—you chose the pizza), or a bowl of vegetable soup. Fill up on good stuff first. The key is to pick your battles. Hamburger? Great. Eat half the bun and forgo the cheese if possible. Turkey burgers are fine, but don't be fooled into thinking they're "diet food." Burger rules still apply. Veggie burgers are a good choice; Boca Burger makes good ones. With low-fat cheese on a whole-grain English muffin, it's a great choice.

3. Cut back on portions. As I said in *Naturally Thin*, cancel your membership to the clean plate club, and remember that you can have it all—just not all at once. Because there aren't always the healthiest options at colleges, don't deprive yourself . . . but don't overindulge, either. Understand that nothing in small portions is fattening, so you can have more of

a good investment choice or less of a bad one. From now on, through the rest of your life, you will be faced with choices. Make the right ones for you.

. . . .

Making Progress . . . and Mistakes

A man's errors are his portals of discovery.

—James Joyce, novelist

Because woman can't live on diet candy alone, I was still trying to build my career, and I was definitely enjoying life in L.A. I had a lot of fun, and slowly but surely, I was starting to get more experience. I started to get small parts here and there. I did a stint on the soap opera *Santa Barbara*, which is how I got my SAG (Screen Actors Guild) card. I had roles in a couple of truly crappy movies. I don't think I even got paid for them.

In one I had a topless scene, and whether or not I should do that was something I pondered for about one minute before agreeing. It crossed my mind that maybe it was a decision I would regret later, but I was mostly just excited to get to be in a movie. (A common Hollywood pitfall, I'm sure.) Besides, I told myself, it's not like I'm going to be running for president. (What if I did want to go into politics? I guess that's shot now!) So I did it. I thought it would be a good experience.

Sometimes, if you aren't looking at the big picture, or thinking about what that big picture might look like five, ten, or fifteen years down the road, you might make a wrong move. Acting on it doesn't always mean you'll make the best possible decision with wisdom and forethought. Every little thing you do could have repercussions later. I knew that movie wouldn't be a huge success that many would see, but I still think it was a stupid decision. Performing in that movie didn't destroy anything for me. It just turned out to be a slight embarrassment. It's come out now, of course—little did I know where I would be a decade later, or that I would have a high-profile career. Truth be told, I never really cared. I live by the motto: Don't complain, don't explain. But maybe for someone else, it could have turned out worse.

Listen to your gut in the moment. Some decisions are, frankly, a crapshoot. They might have a high upside and a high downside, and you have to choose. Think it through. You won't always know what to do. I'm a gambler, so I tend to take more risks. Maybe that's not you. Act, though—act, one way or another. Don't let decisions fester. Learn your own risk tolerance so you can feel good about your decisions. And if you screw up anyway? Suck it up, admit it, learn from it, and move on with your life.

In any case, that movie was one of my stupid mistakes, although I won't say I wasn't ever nude on television again. (I'm thinking back to the infamous PETA photo shoot on the third season of *House-wives*, or the skinny-dipping scene on my honeymoon in *Bethenny Getting Married?* Then again, those had the R-rated bits blurred out, and I'm very proud of those moments. I did those on my own terms.)

In the meantime, as I struggled to make it, I also had to pay my bills, so I took other jobs, too. In many ways, those other jobs became more interesting and rewarding to me than acting.

. . . .

FROM MY IN-BOX

⤙o⤚

This note came to me from Arianna Huffington,
author and cofounder of the Huffington Post:

"My mother was the ultimate place of yes person. She taught
me that there is always a way around a problem—you've just got

to find it. Keep trying doors, one will eventually open. She also taught me to accept failure as part and parcel of life. It's not the opposite of success; it's an integral part of success.

"I had this lesson brought home to me in a very powerful way in my midtwenties when I was writing my second book. My first book, The Female Woman, *had been a surprise success. Instead of accepting any of the book contracts I had been offered to write on women again, I decided to tackle a subject I'd been preoccupied with through college (and indeed remain preoccupied with today): the role of leaders in shaping our world. I locked myself in my London apartment and worked around the clock on this book. I would write until I couldn't stay awake—sometimes into the early hours of the morning.*

"The book was finally finished, and I don't remember ever before or since having been as happy with the work I'd done. So imagine my surprise when publisher after publisher rejected it. Indeed, thirty-six publishers turned it down before it was finally published. It was the kind of rejection that brought up all kinds of self-doubt, including fears that I was not only on the wrong career path but was going to go broke in the process. 'What if the success of my first book was a fluke, and I was not really meant to be a writer?' I would ask myself in the middle of many a sleepless night. And this was after all not just a theoretical question; it was also a crassly financial one: 'How am I going to pay my bills?' I had used the royalties from my first book to subsidize writing the second, and now that money was running out. I seemed to have no choice but to get some kind of 'real' job.

"But my desire to write turned out to be stronger than my fear of poverty. Had I been afraid, I might have tossed the manuscript in the wastebasket somewhere around rejection letter fifteen and taken a job that had nothing to do with my passion. Instead, I walked into Barclay's Bank in St. James Square in London and met with a banker named Ian Bell. With nothing more to offer

than a lot of Greek chutzpah, I asked him for a loan. And with a lot of unfounded trust, he gave it to me.

"Although never a commercial success, the book did finally get published and garnered lots of good reviews. More important, the book was like a seed planted in my twenties that finally sprouted in my forties when I became seriously engaged in political life.

"I had abundant passion and abundant hope (not to mention abundant nerve!), all of which pushed me past my financial fears. I would never have gotten there without coming from a 'place of yes'!"

—Arianna Huffington

. . . .

Clues to My Next Move

If you go to heaven without being naturally talented for it, you will not enjoy it there.

—George Bernard Shaw, playwright

In Los Angeles, it seems that almost every job has something to do with the entertainment industry. While I lived in L.A., I worked at many different jobs. One of the most memorable was as a hostess at La Scala, an Italian power-lunch spot in Beverly Hills (famous for inventing the chopped salad). I applied for the hostess job. I had no idea how many powerful people I would meet there—I just needed to make some money, but this was a lucky break. I got the job, and I loved it because I was able to be in control and make things happen for people, getting people just the right table and finagling to get them seated on time.

I made a lot of connections at La Scala, connections that later led, to jobs as personal assistants for both Linda Bruckheimer

(movie producer Jerry Bruckheimer's wife) and Kathy Hilton (mom
of Paris and Nicky). People now tell me that they remember me
from those days as being funny and fair and friendly, and treating
everyone equally. I gave that job everything I had, and it was fun—I
got to meet a lot of the people pulling the strings in Hollywood.

I also worked at Island Pictures, part of Island Records, and one
day, I offered to organize a party my boss was having, just because it
sounded like fun and I thought I would be good at it. It was a huge
success, my first informal foray into event planning since my high
school days of throwing big parties (complete with catering and security—back then I never dreamed it would become a career).

Other jobs included stints at Merv Griffin Productions and
Broadway Video, Lorne Michaels's company (he is the producer who
created *Saturday Night Live*), where I volunteered to work on the
premiere for *Tommy Boy,* and grabbed the bull by the horns with that
one. It turned out to be a fantastic event. I was in my element and
loving it.

But after a few years in L.A., nothing had really changed. I was
still doing the same things every day. I give tons of credit to the
actors who pound the pavement for years until they get their big
break, but for me, it just wasn't right. Life as an actress wasn't what
I had envisioned, and truthfully, I enjoyed some of those other jobs
more than I enjoyed acting.

I have all the respect in the world for the profession of acting,
but at this time in my life, it just wasn't clicking, and I became increasingly dissatisfied. When you are an actor, you go to auditions,
and you get cast or not. You do the show or the movie or the commercial, and then it's over and you start all over again. I felt I wasn't
getting any traction or building anything.

I also didn't like what I perceived to be a lack of control over my
work. When you're an actor, a scriptwriter tells you what to say. A
director tells you how to say it. A producer tells everybody how to
do everything (unless you're Tom Cruise). You can feel as if you are
at the bottom of the pile, and—believe it or not—that's not a place

I like to be. Even the most successful actors in the world often end up directing or producing, and I suspect it's because they want to gain a little more control.

I began to think that maybe I was trying to be an actress for the wrong reasons. I was always looking for a shortcut, a quick easy road to fame and fortune, and I was beginning to see that there are no shortcuts to a successful acting career. Most of those people who appear to be overnight successes in acting have actually been out there working their asses off for years. I was getting better at acting, and by this point I'd had a lot of training, but I still wasn't sure how good I really was. I wasn't sure, after all this time, that this was the right career for me.

Instead of making a character real by accessing my own feelings and experiences, I created stereotypes of whatever character I played. I couldn't figure out how to go deeper—or maybe I didn't really want to connect to the characters I played. This is the great challenge of acting, of course—you find yourself in every character, and that's the key to becoming that character. I just couldn't get there. I couldn't relax into the part and make it my own. My noise was too loud, my desperation too great, my financial situation too precarious, and my heart too disillusioned.

Or, to put it more simply, I think I really only knew how to be Bethenny Frankel.

I remember going on an audition with a girlfriend of mine. I was nervous and desperate, so I talked her into going with me, even though she didn't really want to go. And they were more interested in her for the part. It's like when you are desperate to meet a guy, so you go out with your girlfriend, who doesn't want to meet a guy, and all the hot guys go for her and ignore you. People can tell when you're in it for the wrong reasons. That's how it felt.

I was beginning to think that maybe I didn't really want to be an actress after all. I didn't want to be a mediocre actress, when I could be really great at something else. I felt like I was in a boat trying to get to an island, and I could always see it out there in the distance, but I couldn't figure out how to get there. Maybe I was in the wrong boat, or looking at the wrong island. I wasn't coming from a place of yes, and there was a reason for that. I had no path, no ideas. It all seemed so random, and I think I was scared that I would never be very successful—that I would get old and have nothing to show for it.

During this time, I had many moments lying in bed and think-ing, *This is crazy. Why would it happen to me? Why do I think I'll be the one-in-a-million who makes it? Why me? What if it doesn't hap-pen? What if I just keep getting older and it never happens?* I'm sure you have played those anxiety games with yourself. It's career noise you're hearing, but it sounds very convincing in the middle of the night, especially when it's mingled with misgivings from your gut that maybe you aren't on quite the right path.

I had a very hard time admitting that maybe I was wrong about my great passion. It was hard to give up this dream I'd held for so long. I really did want to entertain people. I knew that in some way, this was my gift. Acting was almost, but not quite, right for me. It was a time of great crisis in my life.

I think a lot of people get to this stage in a career (or in a rela-tionship or in life in general). You go for something you think you want, and then you discover it isn't exactly what you really want after all. You've been acting on it all along, but then you realize that "it" isn't what you really want. That's when it's time to change course.

Remember what I said at the beginning of the chapter, about how *acting on it* helps you fine tune your truth? If you don't try, if you don't go through that experience, how will you ever know it wasn't right? Better to try and learn and then move on to the next thing than to live a static life of regret and the haunting "what if?" in your head. When you do get to that point—when something re-ally isn't working and it isn't making you happy anymore—it's time to reconsider, to step back and look at the big picture. Think about why it's not making you happy. Maybe you'll come back to it later.

Maybe one day I'll do some acting again. Who knows? Changing course is not the same as giving up. When you hit a brick wall, you have to go a different direction. You walk away for a while until your head clears and you can make a new strategy. Don't torture yourself, running into the wall over and over again. Think about turning the wheel just a little, to change direction. It might not take all that much of a shift to turn toward the next big thing.

When I turned twenty-six, I decided enough was enough. I hadn't "made it," and my time was up. My acting career wasn't going to happen. I'd given myself every chance (in my mind), and now that I was "old" (in my mind), I had to act on what I'd finally realized about myself and move on.

And so I quit acting. I married Peter. And I got a real job—a job in event planning. And the next chapter of my life began.

My acting career, such as it was, had a purpose. I didn't realize it at the time, but everything I learned while living in Los Angeles would pay off later, some of it in event planning and some of it much later, even now, as I'm filming my own television show. I'm entertaining, and I'm comfortable in front of the camera as *me*. The experience I gained—learning poise and confidence, how not to be camera-shy, comic timing—has been invaluable for my life now. At the time, I felt like I'd wasted my time, but now I see that it wasn't a waste at all. Here's where attitude is everything—nothing is ever wasted on the fearlessly curious.

But even if acting hadn't really gotten me anywhere—and I'm not sure any job experience is ever truly worthless—I would still be glad I tried it, just because if I hadn't, I would always wonder if I should have tried. Acting on my desire to act was worth it, for where it took me.

And acting on my desire to change course was also worth it. Sometimes you have to be realistic and honest with yourself. You have to pay attention to whether you really are good at something or willing to pay the price for the dream you want.

At some point, your dream may change, like mine did. In fact, it probably will. Hardly anybody knows at nineteen what they will end up doing at forty. And sometimes your life situation will have to temper the pursuit of your dream, at least for a while. If you need to earn money and you are supporting a family, you can't necessarily quit your job and throw away all your security to go pursue your dream of making it big with your rock band. You can't be stupid or too rash, but there is a line between rash and risk. It's the line that rule #3 can help teach you to walk.

So get moving. It won't be easy. You'll have to work. You'll have to try. Most important, you'll have to *do*. Don't fall into the trap of thinking that good things are just going to happen to you. *You* have to happen. *Act on it.*

Taking action won't always result in a direct achievement of all your dreams, but it will get you moving in the right direction. If you've always wanted to be a writer, sit down and start writing. If you've always wanted to be an athlete, get out there and start training. If you've always wanted to be a singer, join a choir, get a videocamera and put yourself and your song up on YouTube or enter a contest. It's never too late—you could be the next Susan Boyle or Justin Bieber or Kelly Clarkson.

And when it happens for you, be ready.

Your dream might not turn out exactly the way you thought it would, but you'll be better because of it—and it might even lead to a better dream, the next stage, opening up opportunities you never would have believed could have happened to you. Because of my foray into acting, I know more, I'm braver, and I have a more precise understanding of where my skills are—and where they aren't. It took me to a new level, and that's what *acting on it* can do for you, too—because the bottom line is, you don't ever want to have to say, "I should have . . ."

Rule 4
• • • • • • • • • • • •

Everything's Your Business
Finding My Stride As an Entrepreneur

There's nothing like biting off more than you can chew, and then chewing anyway.

—*Mark Burnett, television producer*

The quote above defines me. It describes my life and how I approach everything—especially business.

I love to talk about business and write about business and be *in business*. In fact, I'm somewhat relieved to be done with the first three chapters in this book, chapters that chronicled so much struggle and pain in my past. When I went into business, my passion was truly ignited. This was the life for me, the role I was born to play. Filming my show, traveling, doing appearances, cooking, yoga, all of that is fun—but the bottom line is that I'm a businesswoman, and I live by rule #4: *Everything's your business.*

But *everything's your business* doesn't have to be about business *literally*. This rule is about anything you are trying to accomplish in your life. Rule #4, follows naturally out of rule #3, *act on it.* Once you begin to act and your life begins to change, you need to become more discerning about what you actually do, and you need to do whatever you choose to do to the absolute best of your ability. You see a path, you see options and opportunities, and you can begin to refine. That's when you employ rule #4.

Everything's your business doesn't mean you are a busybody, and it doesn't mean your life becomes all about work. When I say everything's your business, I mean treat everything you choose to do with as much importance as if your career depended on it. *Everything's your business* means that every job, person, and experience is worth your full attention. Whether you are at work or cooking dinner or cleaning your apartment or reading a book to your child, make what you do matter, and do it well. You never know who you are talking to, who is standing behind you in line or next to you in the elevator, who might notice the quality of your work, your attention to detail, your "I'm on it" attitude. You never know when a connection might matter, when an experience might prove relevant, or when a seemingly random event might lead to something significant. It could be about your work, but it applies to any part of your life.

You never know when hard work and dedication will result in a better life—all you know is that eventually, it *will*.

If you assume it's all important, from the way you clean your house to the way you run a meeting, then you have your radar up for opportunities, you're putting your best foot forward for everyone to see, and you'll actually enjoy your work, and your life, more. Quality can benefit you in the moment, too.

When I was an event planner, I once hired a coat-check girl for a birthday party for the late photographer Herb Ritts. Her name was Denise Valenzuela, and she didn't have a résumé or any experience, but I could tell she was one of those people who would do her best no matter what the job was. The event production company had taken a risk on me, so I decided to pay it forward and take a risk on this girl.

It paid off. She took coats like her life depended on it, and she did so much more than take coats! She helped with everything and she gave it everything. She took pride in her work and every word out of her mouth came from a place of yes: "I'm on it, I've got it, I'll do it, what else do you need me to do?" If I had told her to go clean the Dumpster, she would have done it with passion and pride. She made everything her business.

She once told me that doing this event felt like being on another planet for her. At one point, she was in the bathroom talking to Roseanne Barr and Brooke Shields. You never would have known that she was uncomfortable or in unfamiliar territory. There were other people working the event that night, guys screwing around and joking and laughing and slacking off, and as far as I know, they are still goofing off at some job they think is beneath them. Denise, on the other hand, scored a permanent job. I hired her to work for me at Merv Griffin Productions in the event productions department, and we did many huge events together after that, including some for Disney.

Because of her place-of-yes attitude, when I left that company and moved on to my next job, she moved right in and took over my position. She was always ready for a challenge. After that, she went on to manage events for Paul Allen and other notable Seattle-area billionaires. Today, she's event marketing manager for Red Bull North America.

A résumé might as well be written on a paper towel, for all it really matters. Let your job performance be your résumé, let your passion be your recommendation, and let the quality of your work shine through. You'll get farther than any slacker who only looks good on paper.

· ·

FROM MY IN-BOX
ᘓᐧᐧᘔ

This letter comes from event planner Denise Valenzuela,
a former employee of mine:

"I'm grateful that my entire life has been built on a place of yes.
If it hadn't been, I would not have accomplished what I have in
life or seen the amazing sights I've seen. By refusing to say no or to
accept no from others, I created a path of success, fun, friendship,
and fabulousness. And, I've done it my way.

"My family is a fun, crazy Mexican clan from the San Francisco
Bay Area with very humble beginnings. The youngest of five daughters, I was a pretty good teenager with a positive outlook who knew
she wanted to see the world and experience something special in life.
At one pivotal point in my teens, a guidance counselor told me not
to bother applying to a university and that I should go to a junior college first. Really? They won't accept me? Oh yes they will, I thought.
I applied, was accepted, and was the first of my parents' daughters to
leave San Lorenzo and go away to college. I was on my way.

"When I graduated college, I moved to Los Angeles with a
typical lack of knowledge about what I wanted to do in life. That's
where I discovered event production, and I discovered I was very
good at it. I started my career as a coat check girl and wound up,
fifteen years later, producing my own multimillion-dollar inter-
national events. When I started my career, I knew that my path
would be one of honesty, loyalty, and hard work without stepping
on other people to get ahead or losing my integrity. My family had
taught me those lessons and I wasn't about to stray from them. Los
Angeles didn't always make it easy to be a stand-up gal, but I never
relented. I always knew that things would work out for me if I kept
true to my roots.

"The 1999 death of my sister Monica from breast cancer at the way-too-young age of thirty-four cemented my views. We only get one chance at life. Live it remarkably and with no regrets. To me, that doesn't necessarily mean dancing on club tables in my bra (though I have done that once or twice). Instead, it means being a good friend, believing in myself, helping others when I can, soaking in the simple and beautiful experiences life has to offer, and always being grateful. Of course I've made mistakes and I'm not always Pollyanna, but I'm damn proud of the fact that I am where I am in life.

"By saying yes instead of no, I'm healthy, I'm strong, I've traveled the world, I've produced events I'm incredibly proud of, I've made my parents proud, my best friends in the world are still my best friends from high school, and I'm generally pretty happy. I do believe that one gets back what they give. By saying yes to life, I've been given great gifts in return. As I sit with my friends and family, sipping red wine and watching the sunset with good music in the background, I hear, smell, feel, and taste a resounding yes to life. Thank you, I'll take it!"

—Denise Valenzuela

. . . .

This rule has taken me far, and I know for a fact that it works. Many people write to me and ask about my personal life, or ask my advice about eating, cooking, and staying healthy. They ask about my childhood, they ask about Jason and Bryn, but the question people ask me the most is this: *How did you do it? How did you make it in business?* They want to know how I got here—how I created a brand, how I produce the Skinnygirl cocktails and film my shows and make the workout DVD and keep coming out with new products to help women; how I do all that and also write my books and do talk shows and other appearances and performances, how I juggle this complicated and multifaceted career with marriage and motherhood, all of it.

In other words, they want to know how I became successful.

Rule #4 is, in many ways, the reason for my success. I had to follow the first three rules first, but once I got out on my own and experimented with acting and then moved on, I learned rule #4: I treat everything I do as if it is an essential part of my business or an important step forward in my life.

Making everything my business helped me find *myself,* and when you do that, that's when it all begins to happen for you.

So this chapter is about "business," but it applies to anyone at all, in any situation. If your "business" is to be a good mom and homemaker, it applies. If your "business" is to graduate from college, it still applies. If your "business" is charity or creativity, entrepreneurial or supportive of someone else's business, the rule still applies. You never know where you might end up if you run your life this way. You could end up more successful in every area of your life than you ever dreamed.

Perfectionist Noise

You make it heaven, or you make it hell, by your actions.

—George Harrison, musician

Rule #4 carries a potential downside that you have to keep an eye out for. When *everything's your business,* when you commit to doing your very best at everything, there's the danger that you'll scatter your energy, or spread yourself too thin. You can kill yourself trying to go above and beyond what's realistic for you. This is perfectionist noise. I still fall into this trap. Making *everything your business* is not the same as *saying yes to everything,* or demanding extremes that will wear you down and break you. That's not a place of yes, that's a place of anxiety and dysfunctional multitasking. You can't do it all, whether you are running an office or running a home. You have to take responsibility, but you also have to have boundaries and know how to delegate. You have to know when you've done enough.

Perfectionist noise is the noise in your head that tries to convince you that you won't really ever be able to accomplish your dream unless you do it without making any mistakes. It makes you beat yourself up for not being good enough.

It might also tell you that what you are doing isn't good enough, so you shouldn't give it any effort at all. It's an all-or-nothing point of view. Life isn't always perfect. The people we love screw up sometimes, and we've got to deal with it. Houses get messy and you have to clean them. Things go wrong. Not every job will be your dream job, but that doesn't mean you shouldn't do your best at it anyway. If the job, the relationship, or the activity isn't perfect for you, the perfectionist noise can make you blow it off. Are you always looking out for something better instead of doing your best with what you have? But perfectionist noise is tricky—it can also paralyze you if you are successfully maintaining the status quo. It can, for example, keep you locked in the "golden handcuffs." This is a term for what keeps someone in an easy enough but unfulfilling job that makes good money. You become paralyzed to leave it because something else might be riskier or more difficult. The golden handcuffs are a form of perfectionist noise.

Sometimes you do need to take a job because you have to make money. I've been in that position many times. These days, when a lot of jobs don't pay as much but people still have the panicky feeling that they'd better hold on to *any* job, those handcuffs might be made of stainless steel. Even so, they keep you fed, they keep the bills paid, and they keep you tethered in your cubicle or office. I completely understand the need to stay in a job like this, when times are hard, but people also get stuck in jobs that are easy enough and make decent enough money, just because they don't require all that much hard work. But what happens when you wake up one morning ready to retire, with the realization that you never went for it? That you wasted your productive years doing something you never loved?

The need for money *now* should never eclipse your vision for your life. If you need to make money, think about finding a job that won't keep you stuck for the next decade. What could you do that will make it easy to move on when you get a good opportunity? Make the money you need, but don't get stuck. Hardship is better than regret. Perfectionist noise has another side, too: entitlement. Career noise can give you an inflated sense of yourself before you've earned it. You feel as if you are better than the job you have, so you don't actually have to try. Maybe it's a job in the mail room or slinging hash off-campus or typing memos or cleaning up after people. Maybe it's bartending to make extra cash, or managing the household while your husband works even if you would rather be out there working, too. Whatever it is, do what you need to do, but keep your eye on the prize. There is no shame in doing any job well.

This can be a hard lesson to learn, but it's crucial if you ever want to get ahead. Hard work in a seemingly lowly job can give you great perspective and appreciation for the money you might earn someday, but you'll never see it if you listen to perfectionist noise.

Most of the really successful, fulfilled people I know learned early how to work diligently at jobs some people would consider beneath them. They've had to get down and dirty. I've done it over and over, as you'll soon see when I tell you about the protracted, sweat-fueled spiral into hell that was my baking business. When you learn how to work hard and you remember where you came from, I think you try a lot harder and appreciate success more when it comes, compared to someone who's never had to try as hard to get what they want. This doesn't just apply to work—it applies to anything you are doing in your life.

You must find the line between high standards for yourself, and destructive perfectionist noise.

Setting Priorities

Decide what you want, and decide what you are will-
ing to exchange for it. Establish your priorities and go
to work.

—H. L. Hunt, entrepreneur and oil tycoon

Making everything your business helps you set your priorities as it helps you do your best. It is particularly helpful when you have to make a big decision. Should you do something or not? Ask yourself whether you truly want to do it, and whether you are willing to give it all you've got. Will it feed into your plan for your life, will it move you forward, is it in line with your goals and your values and who you are? Will you enjoy it? Do you think it will be worth your best effort? If it is, then commit to it fully. If not, then say no—because in that case, saying no will be coming from a place of yes.

Here's an example from my life. Recently, to my great surprise and pleasure, I was asked to be on *Skating with the Stars*. Ice-skating! I loved the idea, but my first thought was that I didn't have the time. In fact, I thought there was no possible way I could do it. I was just beginning to film the second season of my show, and we film four to five days a week. Bravo said there was no way I could fit it in—I was still finishing up this book, doing frequent appearances—it would be impossible. It would be insane. Plus, it really didn't have anything to do with my career. Would it be a ridiculous thing to do? I considered all the angles.

I knew it couldn't compromise more important things, like my family, and Jason would have to be on board with it. The show involved a lot of early-morning practices at the rink. Would that cut into our important family time? Would I be sacrificing time with Bryn? I knew it would put a lot more pressure and responsibility on Jason.

On the other hand, *I love to skate!* I thought it would be *fun*. I thought I could set a good example for Bryn, and for women every-where. If I could go on a show like that at the age of 40, when I couldn't even skate down the ramp on the first day, wouldn't that inspire women? Wouldn't they see they could do *anything,* if they want it enough? I wanted it enough.

Jason was behind me 100 percent. He came from a place of yes, and said, "You can do this. I'll get you through it." He could tell how much I wanted to do it, and to him, that meant we should make it work. Someday we could show Bryn the pictures of Mommy skating in the pretty costumes. It could actually be fun, even a bonding activity for our family.

I definitely wasn't free from doubts, not to mention perfection-ist noise. I love to roller-skate, but I hadn't really ice-skated since I was a kid, except for a few times at Rockefeller Center, maybe every five years or so on a date. Could I do it? What if I fell? What if I made a complete fool of myself? A lot of those skaters took ballet, and I didn't. I'm more athletic and not all that graceful, and ice-skating is ballet on ice. What if I looked ridiculous? What if, what if, what if?

But fear is a mindset, and so is the will to succeed. It's all in how you approach it. Don't think of all the ways you can't do some-thing. Think of all the ways you *can.* I could have focused on how hard this would be—many of the other people on the show are just doing the show, while I'm simultaneously filming my show, writing my book, managing my business, and at the same time, have a new husband and a new baby. Add to that commuting from New York to Los Angeles every week. I could focus on how hard it would be.

Or, I could focus on how much I wanted to do it.

It might even be great. I made something great for myself out of the *Real Housewives* experience, which could have been a career killer if I'd handled it the wrong way. Also, I'm a gambler and I like to be in on the ground floor of things. If Bravo asked me to join the *Real Housewives* franchise today, I would probably say no be-cause it's nothing new anymore. When I said yes to that show (more about that story in a later chapter), it was the beginning of a whole new era of television. The same applies to *Dancing with the Stars,* which just finished its eleventh season. I could have gone on that show, but I preferred the idea of doing a Season One, even if I was taking a risk on a show that might or might not even have a Season Two.

My agent said, "Why don't you wait to see if it's a success, and if it is, you can go on the second season?" I thought about that, but it's really not my style.

I also considered that my show is on a specialized cable channel, but *Skating with the Stars* is on network television. This would be a much wider audience, and that alone has a lot of potential in terms of getting my name and face out there and expanding my business and my message. It could take me to the next level. (In actuality, it also almost killed me! But that's the nature of risk.) So I could see benefits for my career. Ultimately, though, that is not why I did it.

My gut said to go for it.

So I said yes.

It was the most grueling, difficult, excruciating experience of my entire life. But once I decided to tackle it, I knew I had to go all the way with it. When you decide to do something that really stretches your limits, you have to stand by your decision, not do it begrudgingly or tell everybody you're too tired or it's too hard.

Even when it was hard and I was tired and stressed, I couldn't complain about it because it was my decision and nobody made me do it.

One day, Julie looked at me and said, "Hey—we did it." She was right. We were surgically efficient and maximized every minute to make it happen. I was never late for a rehearsal, and when I was there, I was totally there, not thinking about what I had to do next. Jason helped make it happen in every way he could, and I couldn't have done it without his help. I pushed my limits and embraced something that wasn't necessarily comfortable. In the end, I probably never should have done it. I've never done anything so difficult in my life. Everything's my business, but I had no business doing a show like this. It was just so grueling—sometimes I wanted to crawl into bed and never come back out. I probably cried every day.

But here's the thing: I said yes, so I honored my commitment, and I ended up making it to the finals. I improved so dramatically, it still amazes me. I went from amateur to actually knowing how to ice-skate. It was a true accomplishment for me.

I learned two important lessons from this experience. One: know your limits! Women tend to take on too much and spread themselves too thin. Perfectionist noise! You have to do what's good for you, girls. You don't have to say yes to everything! Two: When you do say yes, keep going. No matter how difficult it gets, plowing through and taking responsibility for what you decided to do can transform you. It builds character, and it helps you to push yourself to accomplish what you never dreamed you could.

Although truth be told, if I had to do it over again? I would say, "No, thank you."

Know What You Stand For

A brand is a living entity and it is enriched or under-mined cumulatively over time, the product of a thou-sand small gestures.

—Michael Eisner, former CEO
of the Walt Disney Company

The next important element that can help you understand how to make everything your business is to really decide what your business *is*. Whether your business is technically a business or not, you can't make everything your business unless you have a clear vision of what that means for you. Specifically, you need to have a message, and you must know what you stand for.

Even if you are a stay-at-home mom and you don't work for any-one, you can have a personal message, which is to say that you can have a mission statement or vision of what you are doing with your life and what it means for you.

Ask yourself: What is your purpose? What do you want to ac-complish? What's important to you? Try to frame it in terms of action. A mother's personal message might be, "My children will have a better life than I did," or "I will run the best-ever event at my daughter's school." An artist's mission might be, "I create beauti-ful things that inspire people." An emergency room nurse's mission might be, "I save lives." A weekend athlete's mission might be, "I'm going to run a marathon." Anyone's mission could be, "I do every-thing with complete commitment," or "I maximize my health." Or maybe your mission is simply, "I make as much money as possible" or "I have fun every day." It's your brand, your mission, and your decision. It might change tomorrow, but decide what it is *today*. I won't judge you. Just make it true to you.

Having your own personal mission statement focuses you in a very powerful way. It helps you see exactly how to make everything your business, because you see what fits with your mission. For me, my business evolved directly out of my own personal beliefs. I'm passionate about natural health, being fit, eating well, and solving problems. The Skinnygirl brand naturally grew from these things I stand for.

The purpose of the Skinnygirl brand is *my* purpose in my career— to solve problems and inspire and help women live healthier, better lives. Everything I do relates to that in some way. I have a clear pic-ture in my mind of who the Skinnygirl is: She's the girl we all want to be, whether size 2 or size 12, the girl who is comfortable with her-self, who feels good in her body and loves her life.

People often asked me how I came up with the Skinnygirl name. I first came up with the name when I created a simple recipe for my Skinnygirl Margarita. I was working on recipes for my first book, *Naturally Thin*, and I wanted a margarita without the guilt, something perfect for the health-conscious woman who still wants to have fun. The Skinnygirl Margarita is the drink I always order, or make at home. So I nailed down a formula and gave it that name.

I began ordering them, and telling bartenders how to make them, and then I mentioned the drink on my show. The term became a buzzword. Questions about how to make a Skinnygirl Margarita flooded Bravo network's website after the show on which it was mentioned.

Other people began making them and ordering them, and I got so much great feedback about the idea of a cocktail that was fun and easy but not loaded with sugar and calories that it occurred to me: Why not bottle it, to make life even easier?

I was solving a problem, and the brand was truly born.

It wasn't without obstacles, though. The Skinnygirl Margarita truly was the little cocktail that could. When I first took the Skinnygirl Margarita concept to several major liquor companies to develop as a product, no one bit. Liquor is a completely male-dominated business, and I encountered surprising resistance to the idea that I wanted to sell liquor. They told me that there wasn't room for this product in the ready-to-drink market. They didn't see the potential.

But I had a feeling this was a good idea. No matter how many people told me no, I knew that women buy most of the products for the home. Why shouldn't a woman sell liquor to women who want to drink it? Don't listen to the world tell you what is or isn't a good idea. Listen to your instincts. I really pounded the pavement with the Skinnygirl Margarita, and it was frustrating that nobody else could see what I saw, but I didn't give up because I believed in it.

Now they see it, and now, many of the same people who turned down the idea have offered to buy me out. What do you know. Every major liquor company in the world has some kind of knock-off. Little did I know that this idea would start a nationwide trend. Once people saw the idea working, they wanted to piggyback on it. Now it's all I can do to keep bottles on the shelves.

The best ideas are the simple ones that solve a problem. For example, I've always had trouble finding time to exercise, and I don't really like going to the gym. Why not make an exercise/yoga DVD people can do at home on their own time, as much or as little of it as they want? I believe in a moderate approach to exercise, one that can change according to your day and mood and energy level. You do what you can, when you can. That's the whole point behind the *Body by Bethenny* DVD—you do it in the privacy of your own home, at your own pace and level, no pressure. It's been popular because other women feel the same way. They just want an easy way to feel better and healthier.

Another common issue I've encountered in my own life, and something people often ask me about, is the best way to detox. I believe in a healthful, moderate approach to detoxing, which can be dangerous for your health if you take it to the extreme. That gave me the idea for a gentle, healthful supplement program that purifies subtly and gently at night with a green lemonade drink, and also contains supplements for better nutrition during the day. It's called Skinnygirl Daily because it fits into the whole Skinnygirl mission of simplifying life and helping women get healthy. It's a "cleanse and restore" product I always wished existed, so I thought surely other women would want something like that, too. It just makes sense to me that supplements and detoxing shouldn't be complicated or extreme, any more than eating or exercise should.

I've also had problems finding skin care products that work for me. What products lie to you more than skin care products? A face lotion isn't going to give you a face-lift in two days or make you look like Heidi Klum. Companies charge hundreds of dollars for little bottles that don't do anything but clean and moisturize. So, I thought it would be a good idea to create a product that simply does what it says. What a concept. It's straightforward and simple. The money put into the product goes into the product, not into fancy packaging. If you are consistent with it, it will do exactly what it says: help your skin be healthy and look good. When I was developing the product, I was told I should include all these fancy ingredients, but I said no.

Skin care shouldn't be a chemistry experiment. You just need to keep your face clean and moisturized.

And what about those dresses and tops you can never wear because nothing works underneath them? I hate that. Since everything's my business, I thought women would really love shape wear that fits under strapless dresses or plunged necklines or those other common wardrobe difficulties. And what about when you want to wear lingerie (or somebody else wants you to wear it), but you just don't feel like taking off all your clothes and putting on some fancy getup? Wouldn't it be great if you could wear something comfortable under your clothes that is also sexy enough to thrill your husband when you take your clothes off? Voila, you're in lingerie, without having to do anything. Simple. That is how I came up with Skinnygirl Smoothers & Shapers, a line of what I call "lazy lingerie."

I'm rattling on about some of my projects, just to explain why I chose to invest in these particular ideas. In my life, I want simple, I want clear, I want easy, streamlined, obvious. It's surprising to me that there aren't more products that fit that description. We all experience many of the same problems—finding the solutions is my business, and I wouldn't take on some product or project that had nothing to do with me. This is what I mean about making everything your business. Look at your life. Look at what you want to celebrate or improve or repair, and then think of ways to do that, even in the simplest way. Believe in what you believe in, and then make it your business by doing it well.

You might come up with the next great idea that changes the world, or you might just fix something annoying that has been bugging you for years. It might not have anything to do with creating a product—it might be more about how you organize your refrigerator or spend time with your kids or manage your busy schedule. It could be about your work or hobbies or your relationships—but solve problems, take your life seriously (but with a sense of humor), and make everything your business. Whatever you are doing, base it on your real life.

When you stay focused on your own message and mission, you never know what might happen. You might not make your passion into an actual business, but you can make it into your life's work. Making everything your business keeps you active and engaged in your own life, always analyzing your progress and tweaking your situation to improve it and keep it in line with your goals. It helps you to live with intention and it helps you to do everything better. It doesn't have to have anything to do with money. It just has to have something to do with your reality.

So know what you stand for, and make it matter, whether you work in the mail room or the boardroom or your own living room. You could be a dishwasher or a CEO, a seasoned author or artist; you could sell Christmas trees or deliver newspapers; you could be a personal trainer or a personal assistant or between jobs; newly married or a new parent. You could be anybody at all. No matter what you do, it reflects on who you are, so do it with integrity and honesty and quality, by investing yourself in your work. Do that, and any job can be a good one, or could lead to a better one. Every opportunity might be a golden one. And everything will be your business. *Life* will be your business, in the best possible way.

Be the Best: Event Production

*There are two types of people: The ones who give you
50 reasons it can't be done . . . and the ones who just
do it.*

—Hoda Kotb, host of *The Today Show*

It's taken me a while to get back to my story, but what happened
in my life next, once I moved on from acting and moved into event
production, is directly relevant to rule #4. Making everything my
business became my new mode, so let's pick up the story again. I'll
show you how I used this rule to my advantage, even though I still
had a long way to go before I figured out where it would all lead, or
even what I really wanted to be when I "grew up."

So there I was, done with acting, done with being single, and
ready for a new challenge. I would get a "real job," and I would get
serious about my life. I thought I would be good at event production, and when I heard an event production company needed to
hire someone, I convinced them to interview me.

They had no idea how green I was. Even I didn't know how
green I was. I got the job, based on the little experience I'd had
producing events in an unofficial capacity. I figured I could do it
because I had a knack, and I was highly motivated. I would jump in
and make it happen.

My very first assignment was to go to San Francisco and single-
handedly produce a movie premiere party for the movie *The Rock*,
for Disney, on the island of Alcatraz outside San Francisco. This
event had a seven-figure budget.

I didn't have the slightest idea what I was doing, and I was momentarily terrified, but I realized that if I could pull this off, the
payoff would be huge. And if I couldn't pull it off, well . . . what was
the worst that could happen? I'd lose the job? The upside was enormous, the downside was minimal, so I took it on.

You know that feeling, when someone is telling you something you have to do, and you just nod and smile and say "yes, yes," but inside you are having a panic attack because you don't even have the remotest idea how you are going to do it? I was coming from a place of yes all right, but my perfectionist noise was also screaming, "Holy shit balls!!"

I didn't even know how much I didn't know—and why would I know anything about the professional world of event planning? But they had taken a risk on me, so I decided I was going to make that risk pay off for all of us. When someone takes a risk on you, you don't want to let them down, or prove them wrong for believing in you. So, I just put one foot in front of the other and learned everything I could possibly learn as I went. I wouldn't think about how much I had to do all at once. I would just do one thing at a time.

In situations like this, you have to forget your insecurities—jump in, don't look to the left or the right, do what you need to do, and make it happen. Do your very best, and don't let perfectionist noise bog you down. I still believe that aside from brain surgery, you can figure out most jobs if you're motivated enough. Even those guys on Alcatraz figured out how to escape, so many years ago. There is always a way.

Producing an event of this magnitude was big—really big—and I had to organize the entire thing. That meant a to-do list miles long, keeping track of every aspect of this complex and high-profile event. It was hard-core. I had to manage every single detail, from menu creation down to the last piece of celery. I produced the hell out of that event, from conception to completion, from soup to nuts. I organized barges out to Alcatraz with electricity, plumbing, and every piece of equipment necessary. I managed the lighting, sound, staging, rentals, communication, food and beverages, entertainment, and every rider and permit was on file and in order. Those who know me can only imagine how this fed into my natural obsessive tendencies.

In a job like this, "good enough" *isn't* good enough. I had to be better than that, and fast, and efficient, and detail-oriented like I've never been detail-oriented before. The company also told me I had to make a 30 percent profit, which meant I had to negotiate deals with major vendors. I'd never done anything like that, but I pulled it off, and it was worth the extreme effort. I took a gamble and won—and the job was a true gift. I had found my calling.

This was trial by fire, but instead of letting myself get intimidated, I made it happen. I realized I had found something I could be great at. I loved event production. Never assume that everybody else knows more than you or is better or smarter than you are, because there were people at that company who had been doing the job for years, and I was lapping them. I had found a new passion and I was learning at an exponential rate.

The company noticed, and I moved on to do other events, like the premieres for *Con Air, Evita,* and *The Hunchback of Notre Dame,* as well as events for the Emmys and the Grammys. I learned so much, and it is knowledge I still use today. I was so relieved to be through with acting and doing *business.* It felt right to be in a job with a real salary, benefits, action, and tangible forward momentum. Once you get into your comfort zone in a job, you can really pick up speed, and that's what I did. Although event planning was nothing like acting, in many ways I was still putting on a show.

After a few years of doing event production for other people, I felt I was ready to move forward again. In almost every job, unless you own your own business (and even then), there comes a time when you've done all you can do and you get the feeling that it's time to move on. I've always had that itch because I love endings and I love beginnings and I always have to go bigger. It's hard for me to just settle down and stay somewhere. I always want more, so I decided to start my own event planning company.

I gave it a cute name: In Any Event. I found a business partner, and we started to plan events. They weren't as high-profile as the ones I was doing before, but they were still challenging and satisfying—corporate events and private parties, things like that.

However, I always say "know thyself," and during this time I realized that I'm really not cut out to have a business partner. I'm more of a go-it-alone businesswoman. I like having a team, and I do have business partners in some of my ventures now, but they are all involved in other businesses, too. They aren't working with me on a daily basis. I'm not someone who can keep checking in with someone. I need to be able to make decisions and move on, without having to negotiate every little thing. Some people are great team players and work best in a group setting, and others are more independent. Neither is better, it's just a matter of who you are. Our partnership ended amicably and we both moved on.

Owning my own business taught me a lot, although I still had a lot to learn. Although I was good at getting clients and producing quality events, I had no clue about taxes or accounting or any of the financial aspects that keep a back office humming. I had to learn those skills in the field, and I didn't always handle them as well as I could have. However, in the end, I don't think I ever really needed a complicated business plan. I learned from my mistakes, capitalized on my strengths, and just kept plowing through. It may have cost me more money that way, but I got something for all that money—experience.

. . . .

GRACEFUL ENDINGS

Having to end a business partnership, or any relationship, is simply part of life, and it's better to know how to do it and be brave enough to do it than to hold on to a bad situation because you are afraid to hurt somebody's feelings. Like in a breakup, it's best to be straightforward and honest, and do it gracefully and cleanly. Don't just cut someone out with no warning or be cruel about it—you do a lot more damage that way. Preserve your professional connections, don't foster bad feelings, and then move on.

. . . .

Quality Control

The quality of a person's life is in direct proportion to their commitment to excellence, regardless of their chosen field.

—*Vince Lombardi,*
former Green Bay Packers football coach

I learned something very important during this stage of my life. It was something I always understood at some level, but not as consciously as I did once I started working in event planning. I realized the supreme importance of producing high quality work, whether it's a product or a service. I learned to do everything well at this stage of my life, and I've carried that with me ever since. I don't just make a cocktail—I rim the glass with sugar. I don't just serve takeout—I put it on a fancy plate and add homemade garnishes. Every part of your life can benefit from attention to detail and a high standard for quality.

People don't succeed overnight by luck. They work their assess off and they stand out because of it. They demand only the best from themselves. They make everything their business. The truth is that most people don't exert very much effort. The ones who do are more likely to get noticed.

If you slack off, in work or in life, you won't know how you really feel about a job, either. You won't know if it's right for you. Of course a job you blow off and do half-assed is going to be terrible. If you give it everything and it still doesn't work, *then* you know. Don't hang around the middle. Be the cream that rises to the top. Get in there, get dirty, get noticed. No job done well is embarrassing. The only embarrassing thing is to have never worked a day in your life, and I don't just mean working at a job. I mean working on your life.

In the interest of full disclosure, I haven't always done this. I have had times in my life when I blew off a lame job.

For a short while, I worked at a PR company, but all we did was print out guest lists and invitations, and stuff envelopes. I sat in a room with no windows, in a little cubicle, spending the whole day licking and sealing and stamping envelopes. It was mind-numbing. On top of that, the company had a strict rule: no personal phone calls.

I thought that was completely absurd. Why couldn't I talk on the phone while I was stuffing envelopes? It wasn't like I couldn't multitask well enough to talk to a friend and seal an envelope at the same time. It wasn't rocket science. I probably would have been a thousand times better at that job if talking on the phone had been allowed. In my life now, I would never tell my assistant she can't use the phone. I don't care if she works part-time for 1-800-HOT-GIRLS as long as she is doing her job.

At this job, they didn't see it that way.

So I made my personal calls anyway. I remember the boss coming over while I was on the phone and saying, "Bethenny, no personal calls." I rolled my eyes and said to my friend, "Hold on a second," and put my hand over the receiver. "What?" My boss repeated, "No personal calls." "Okay," I said, then turned back to my envelopes and the phone and said to my friend: "So, what were you saying?"

Needless to say, that job didn't end well.

I remember another job as a temp at a different PR company. I was the receptionist, and one of the employees there was named Gina, and one was named Ina, pronounced like *eye-nah*. I would always get them mixed up. I called Gina Ina, and Ina Gina. One day, I said something to the one I thought was Gina, and she said, "I'm *Ina*," and I said, "You say va-geena, and I say va-gina." Then I kept going, singing to the tune of that old song: "Gina, Ina, Va-geena, Va-gina, let's call the whole thing off!"

That job didn't end well, either.

I wasn't making those jobs my business, or taking them seriously, or doing my best at them, but I also didn't feel that I learned anything, either. They weren't getting me anywhere and even though

I was interested in PR, the positions I had at those companies weren't useful or helpful or upwardly mobile. You don't always have to know exactly where you are going, but you should have some general idea of the direction so you don't waste your time. Those jobs felt like a waste of my time—but I should have either committed to them or moved on right away. If you commit to a job, you have to play by those rules. If you're not willing to do that, you shouldn't take the job.

You have to know yourself and what works for you. Have a sense of humor, and never take yourself too seriously, but also know what you can and can't tolerate. If you like light and windows, don't get a job stuck in a basement. If you don't like being around a lot of people all the time, don't get a big corporate job where you have to take clients out to lunch or drinks and schmooze everybody. If you like a lot of chaos and noise in your working environment, don't get a job like my assistant Julie, who works at the office here in my apartment with me and Cookie all day.

Even if you work for someone influential, even if there might be potential, if you really hate it, if it doesn't fit you, if you just don't click with the other employees, sometimes you just have to bust out.

The distinction I'm making here is the fine line between thinking you are too good for a job and having the life sucked out of you by a job you truly hate. It's the difference between laziness and a bad match—between perfectionist noise and finding your truth.

And sometimes, it's just time to move on. My former assistant always wanted a job in the music business. She worked for me and learned a lot, but after two years, she had to go in a direction that was more in keeping with her goals for herself. Working for me while I was on *Housewives* was not exactly a joyful experience for her. She found it embarrassing, which I can understand. We ended amicably, each in our own direction. She gave the job her all when she was in it, and then she moved on when it was time. She had to be true to herself, and I completely respected that.

So rule #4 isn't simple by any means. You have to customize it to *you*. It builds out of all the other rules—you figure out who you are and what you want, you act on it, and then you keep on refining, making everything your business until you find your stride.

It's your stride, nobody else's, so find your truth, and keep seeking it as it evolves. You also have to decide how much you are willing to do. What kind of life do you want? I absolutely murdered myself for over a decade before my career really took off. Be honest with yourself. There is nothing wrong with not wanting to torture yourself for a decade. Find the level of success that matters to you and the kind of job that makes you happy, whether it's being in charge or working behind the scenes, high-stress or low-stress. It took a long damn time for me to get somewhere great. Maybe you'll find a shorter path to a happy career. The point isn't necessarily to get famous or be the biggest or richest or most powerful. The point is to love what you do.

In my case, at this time in my life, I did love what I was doing. I loved event planning. However, you know me by now. You know that enough is never enough. So, not surprisingly, I always had one eye looking out for another opportunity. Sure enough, I found one.

JOB HOPPING

Job hopping can be productive, or it can be counterproductive. If you don't feel content where you are, if a job doesn't feel right to you, then you should act on that impulse and be open to change. But if you are job hopping because you don't like anything, you aren't interested in anything, or you just don't really like to work very much, then you aren't making everything your business. You aren't making *anything* your business.

Take Risks: Princess Pashmina

The defining factor in success is never resources, it's resourcefulness.

    —*Anthony Robbins, author and motivational speaker*

I was running my own little company, busy and happy, at least in my work life. Life was better than it had been, even though my marriage had failed and I was embroiled in my various relationship struggles. At least I was in business. It wasn't always easy, and I wasn't exactly filthy rich, but I was getting by, I was challenged, I was working.

Then I had an encounter with a pashmina.

I'd never seen a scarf quite like the one I saw that afternoon in Neiman Marcus. It was the softest cashmere I'd ever felt, with the most vibrant colors. It was gorgeous, it cost $500, and I had to have it. Necessity is the mother of invention, and I needed something like this, for times when a cardigan doesn't work. I saw a hole in my wardrobe I never knew existed and I wanted to fill it.

Unfortunately, I didn't have $500.

I checked out the scarf and saw that, according to the label, it was called a pashmina. I asked my assistant to search *pashmina* and see what she could find out. If you did that now, you'd get over a million results, but back then, there were only two: a company in Ohio, and a company in India. Obviously, somebody was buying them. I hadn't really heard much about them, but I figured if I could buy it online, I could have my pashmina without going into debt.

I called the source in Ohio, but they wouldn't sell me just one. The minimum order was ten, at $110 each. At this point, I still just wanted a pashmina, so my immediate goal was to figure out whether I could buy ten, keep one for myself, and find nine other people to buy the rest of them. It wasn't a business venture by any means.

I checked around with some people I knew who were more fashion-forward than I was, and I did a little research. There was interest—people were buying them. I started to realize that maybe I was on to something. Maybe I was hitting a moment in women's fashion. Could I possibly sell *more* than nine pashminas?

I contacted some friends with connections to celebrities, and got a great response. My next thought was that maybe I could get pashminas even cheaper from India.

I contacted the source in India and sure enough, if I ordered fifty, I could get them for $68 each. It was a better price but riskier—that's me, the gambler. Could I unload forty-nine pashminas? I had no idea about the quality of the pashminas from India, and the quality of cashmere varies a lot. I didn't know how the fabric would hold up, or whether the colors would be any good.

I decided to come from a place of yes and go for it. I realized that this could be a major opportunity. I trusted my intuitive ability to spot a trend and shelled out $3,400 that I didn't have, wiring the money to a total stranger in Bombay, in exchange for the promise of fifty pashminas. For all I knew, I was sending all the money I had in the world off to some scam artist, but I just had a feeling I was in on the ground floor of something. I was sweating my balls off and praying that I wasn't being completely idiotic. I called more friends—celebrity friends, agents, publicists, and friends who knew celebrities. I was very cool about it. I told them, confidentially, that they were getting in on a great opportunity, an exclusive deal. Thus began my next venture, Princess Pashmina.

I did receive those fifty pashminas a short time later, and they were gorgeous. Word got around, and I began selling them all over town, then ordering more. I decided to go bigger. I began hosting pashmina parties and selling them online. I was riding high on my success, making money hand over fist. So I went bigger still. On someone's suggestion, I invested in a booth at the MAGIC Market-place, a major fashion trade show in Vegas, one of the biggest shows in the country for textiles and clothing.

I paid a lot of money for the booth and set up a spectacular display. I bought cubicles at IKEA and organized the pashminas by color palette, stacking them up in graduated colors. Under each color, I put a big jar of jelly beans and other candy in the same color, which I had ordered online from a bulk candy supplier. So I had all the graduated shades of green pashminas, and a jar of green candy; all the graduated shades of purples, and a jar of purple candy. It was striking and garnered a lot of attention at the show. I took hundreds of orders.

Before I knew it, I was selling pashminas in showrooms all over Los Angeles and shipping them all over the world, to Japan and Paris. The money was rolling in. I was still running my event pro-duction company but more and more of my time was going toward Princess Pashmina, and I planned to milk it for everything it was worth.

I remember coming from one of my pashmina parties and meet-ing a few friends for lunch. I was wearing a pink pashmina tied like a halter top, a yellow pashmina tied as a skirt, and a green pashmina draped like an actual pashmina. I walked into the restaurant not even realizing how ridiculous I looked. I looked like an Easter bas-ket gone horribly wrong. My friends laughed so hard when they saw me that they practically spit out their food. I laughed, too—I *was* Princess Pashmina. I was owning it and making it my business.

I was so motivated to keep growing the business that I started to diversify to the point of absurdity. I couldn't leave well enough alone. I tried to make pashminas into everything—robes and hal-ters, skirts and ponchos, purses and pajamas. I spread myself too thin. Now that I have more business experience, I see that it would have made more sense to diversify gradually—get the line solid, then introduce one new product at a time and get each one on track before the next.

That's what I've done with my Skinnygirl line, having learned my lesson. When you have a successful product, it often makes sense to hold steady for a while. I waited out a good solid year of sales with the Skinnygirl Margarita before introducing new flavors and different-sized bottles, instead of coming out with four different flavors at the beginning. You have to build on what works, in a rational way.

But I didn't know that yet during Princess Pashmina. I was too excited by my quick success, and too big for my britches—which were also made out of a pashmina.

Part of the reason things went awry was that I had all this money, but I had no idea what to do with it. I didn't have an accountant and I didn't know how to do my taxes. I had passion and balls but I got cocky and started going in too many different directions. The brand wasn't focused.

The market wasn't cooperating, either. In fact, it froze. Pashminas were getting easier and easier to find. Now you can buy them on any street corner in Manhattan. I had cashed in on something that was no longer new, and I lost control of the business.

If I had done things differently, Princess Pashmina might still be a viable business. A brand is a brand, even if there are copycats. It doesn't matter what anybody else is doing. But it was not to be. Still, Princess Pashmina taught me more about myself and where my skills lay.

I realized that I loved being in a business full of action and I loved tapping into a hot trend, but I didn't love being in the clothing business. In the clothing business, you are constantly putting the money out and hoping to get it back—you pay, then you have to build something and sell it before you get paid. You are on this money treadmill, and for me, personally, I was always in fear that I wouldn't have the money to front the next order. I had too much money noise and too many cash-flow issues, and that made me uncomfortable.

In the end, I made a final misstep. I invested most of the money

I made from Princess Pashmina into an internet company on the advice of a friend, and I lost it all. From that, I learned that you should never gamble more than you are willing to lose, and if you are going to invest, never blindly buy a stock because someone told you to do it. *Make it your business* to understand the company you are investing in and where it might be headed.

I'm not about to give you investment advice—I know more about "investing" at the blackjack table than in the stock market. But for me, I now invest in myself, not in some company I know nothing about. I learned my lesson.

• •

FROM MY IN-BOX

"For a long time, I thought that yes was a word to use when you were surrendering and losing ground in a conversation or negotiation, but today I use yes with strength. At the height of an extremely tense moment, I'm always empowered by the word yes. It's a handshake, a peace agreement, and helps me gain the support and the trust of whom I'm dealing with, so that we can both get to the place we both want to be. Nobody wants to hear the word no. Removing it from your vocabulary is the first step towards success."
—Robert Verdi, celebrity stylist and television personality

• •

As for Princess Pashmina, I tell you this story because I turned something as simple as a fashion choice into a profitable business. Necessity is the mother of invention—I couldn't afford a pashmina, so I found a way to make it work, and then some. I made it my business, literally and figuratively. It took hard work and obviously I made some mistakes, but it was a great experience, and I learned lessons that have helped my Skinnygirl brand thrive in ways Princess Pashmina never could.

When everything's your business, then each new phase gets better than the one before because you learn and grow and keep pushing the envelope.

So what's your business? If you answered, "Everything!" then I think you've got it. No matter where you are in your life, take those calculated risks, jump on the opportunities, and never assume anything you do isn't relevant to where you're going. There will always be those moments when you have the opportunity to seize the day, and you never know when they might happen, so you have to be ready to jump.

Making everything your business and being the best at everything you do will take you far, professionally and personally. Get this rule into your head and start living it, and you'll be surprised to see that the next rule will happen almost by itself.

All Roads Lead to Rome
The Rise and Fall of BethennyBakes

*You've got to jump off cliffs, all the time, and build
your wings on the way down.*

—Ray Bradbury, author

There's no getting around it. Sometimes, in life, if you take risks,
if you go big, you're going to screw up. You're going to do the wrong
thing. And the beauty is that sometimes, the wrong thing can lead
you straight to what's right, even when you think there's no hope,
or that you're going completely in the wrong direction. Of course,
hindsight is 20/20, and objects in the mirror are larger than they
appear. You won't know this at the time, but you will be able to see
it later.

This chapter is about a great mistake—and a great success. It's
a story that led out of rule #4, and straight into rule #5. This is the
rule to apply when you don't know what to do, or have hit that wall
of frustration so hard, you don't know which way to turn to get yourself up and going again. Remember this rule and you'll know how to
come from a place of yes again, because this rule reminds you that

no matter what you've done, even if you regret it, even if you don't know what the hell to do next, every single thing that happens to you has the potential to open new doors. It happened for a reason— and it's still taking you somewhere, even if you can't see it right now.

Life is a mystery sometimes, and not knowing all the answers is exactly why you can stumble right into the life that's meant for you in a way you could never have planned out in a million years. Yet, somehow, you got there. This is due to Rule #5: *All roads lead to Rome.*

All roads lead to Rome means that as long as you are working hard and doing your best—when you are following your truth, acting on it, and making everything your business—then everything you do will eventually get you where you want to go—or someplace even better. You don't need to know how it will happen. You just need to trust that if you are following the previous rules, it will happen. If you forget the earlier rules, this rule won't necessarily work. Cheating, lying, taking shortcuts or the easy way out—those might lead you to, say . . . the Vegas version of Rome. Or worse. But hard work and integrity will take you to the real thing every time, one way or another, even if the path isn't always a straight one.

You'll still need to use your common sense, know when to stick with something and when it's time to bail, but if you've got your head on straight and you're coming from a place of yes, then *yes*— you will get there, even if it looks like you're headed straight into the pit of doom.

I've seen this rule play out many times in my life. Just when I thought I'd gone the wrong way or messed it all up beyond repair, something happened that made me see it was all for a reason.

Money Noise

Don't make money your goal. Instead, pursue the things you love doing, and then do them so well that people can't take their eyes off you.

—*Maya Angelou, poet and author*

I've talked a lot about money noise in this book, and I'll talk about it more, because it's one of the most pervasive and damaging kinds of noise that people experience today. However, I want to talk specifically about money noise now because this chapter is, in many ways, about taking a leap of faith. When you have to remember that all roads lead to Rome, that's usually because things aren't going so well, and often, when things aren't going so well, it's about money.

Money noise is the noise in your head that makes money emotional rather than factual. In reality, you either have as much money as you want or need, or you don't. However, money noise fills you with fear when you don't have enough, or greed when you do. Or it makes you spend more when you don't have enough, racking up credit card debt in a desperate attempt to soothe your anxiety. Of course, you're just making it worse. Believe me, I've been there. It can also make you vain or miserly, when you make it too important.

Money noise also makes you associate your self-worth with what's in your bank account. When you're solvent and have something in the bank, you feel as if you can do no wrong. When you're broke, you feel like a worthless loser. Money noise is incredibly stressful. Just look at what it's probably done to many people you know—it breaks up marriages, it tears apart families, it makes people do evil things. It's powerful.

When you have money noise, it can take over your entire brain and make you believe that money is all that matters and the lack of it is a matter of life and death. The problem with getting past money noise is that sometimes, a lack of money really is practically a matter of life and death. You need money to live. You need money to buy food and pay for a place to live. You need to pay for heat and water. You need to get by. That complicates things.

Not having money can make you feel so angry, depressed, and inferior. How are you supposed to just trust that everything happens for a reason, that everything will eventually be fine, and that your path really will lead to Rome at some point, when you can't even afford to meet your friends for dinner? (Been there, done that.)

Getting over money noise isn't easy, and some people never conquer it completely. Money noise is one of the main reasons I had so much trouble finding the right relationship. I kept looking for the easy fix to my money noise, and it took me years to realize that the only way to conquer my money noise was to make my own money, rather than relying on someone else to give it to me. It was a tough lesson. I still have money noise, but now it's more about preserving what I have and not wasting it. I can't stand to pay too much for something, and I often worry about losing it all. I've seen what can happen to people who think they can spend whatever they want.

But this story isn't about my money noise now. It's about what happened after my years in event planning—what happened after I moved back to New York, and rejected yet another wealthy fiancé, and tried to do something new and great with my life.

This story is about how all roads, even the long hard torturous ones, lead to Rome. It's about money noise, and the hard lessons I had to learn.

And this story is also about cookies . . .

Becoming a Chef

Cooking is like love. It should be entered into with
abandon, or not at all.

—Harriet Van Horne, newspaper columnist

Fast-forward a few years: Event planning and I had had a good run,
but I had hit one of those times in my life when I just wanted to
be married, and frankly, I had begun to feel like I was spinning my
wheels. That's when I met Jimmy, and agreed to marry him, and
quit my job, thinking (you remember chapter 2 . . .) that I would
be happy doing nothing while he supported me. I moved my life
to Chicago, and then I convinced Jimmy to move us to New York
temporarily.

You've already heard the story—I was in a bad place. I needed
to be doing something, but I just didn't know what. So I enrolled
in the chef's training program at the Natural Gourmet Institute for
Health & Culinary Arts.

This was a very in-the-moment time for me. I didn't have a plan,
and I had certainly never thought of myself as a professional chef,
but I've always loved cooking and I've always been interested in
health. I discovered the Natural Gourmet Institute in New York by
seeing the ads in health magazines and by looking around on the Internet (as I do with everything), and I found that they had a unique
program that combines culinary arts and health. That fascinated
me, so I decided to give it a try.

And, at the time, it seemed like a better option than driving off a
cliff to avoid my impending wedding.

Little did I know how important this would prove to be for my
future. I was headed to Rome without realizing it. You just never
know when a seemingly random decision will reset the course of
your life. On the first day of class, when we were all asked why we
were there, I told them I was engaged but . . . I wasn't sure where it

was going, or where I was going. "Who knows," I remember joking, "maybe I'll start a cookie business!"

It was a prophetic statement—or maybe it was a self-fulfilling prophecy—but at the time, I had no idea I really would soon start a cookie company called BethennyBakes. It wasn't on my radar yet.

Even though it wasn't part of any long-term plan, I gave cooking school all my energy and attention. I made it my business. I did my best, and the experience ignited a passion in me. I hadn't been truly challenged for a while, the way I had been in my early years as an event planner, and this was an entirely new subject. I was in my element, learning about the art and skill of cooking and health.

In my classes I emerged as a leader, and I discovered that I had a talent for making healthful food taste really good. I loved it just as much as event planning, probably in part because it was such a relief to be back to some kind of work. I felt like I was beginning to find myself again as I learned more and more about food and health and how they relate to each other.

Culinary school had its challenges. I've never been one to play by the (cook)book. I frustrated my teachers because I would make some incredible dish but I couldn't tell them how I did it. I never wrote down my recipes. I was a fly-by-the-seat-of-my-pants kind of chef, resistant to measuring and always eyeballing portions and amounts. I wasn't the best at keeping my area clean or keeping my knives perfectly sharpened, but I always had a knack for making the food taste great, and that trumped my maverick methods in a way that worked for me, if not for them.

It took me years to change my ways—when I wrote *Naturally Thin* and *The Skinnygirl Dish*, I was forced to start measuring and writing down recipes. I realized that if I was going to share what I knew, I had to buckle down and be more precise. Now, every time I cook something new and delicious, I try to write it down so I can post it on my blog or in my newsletter, but I still tend to eyeball things. I'm trying to be better about it, but at the time, I was almost rebellious about using those little measuring cups and spoons. I loved to improvise, and although it didn't always work, I had many more successes than failures.

Actually, what turned out to be a liability in cooking school became the whole point behind my second book, *The Skinnygirl Dish*. I don't like to measure, and neither do a lot of women. So why not create a whole cookbook about cooking intuitively, using what you have instead of a set list of ingredients? Of course, when you write a cookbook, you do need to be precise and supply guidelines, but this was just one more example of how all roads lead to Rome. Not measuring worked for me, so I knew it could work for others.

For our final project, the class was divided into two teams, and we had to make dinner for 100 people. I was chosen to be a team leader, and it felt so natural for me to organize the group and make that dinner happen. I graduated with flying colors. I had a sense of accomplishment and a new direction.

• •

FROM MY IN-BOX

"The restaurant business is trying on a daily basis. You must be committed to facing challenges that seem impossible. But when it's the moment of truth, I just tell my team 'Yes, we can make this happen.' That's how you separate yourself from the pack."

—Bobby Flay, celebrity chef, restaurateur,
Iron Chef, and cookbook author

• •

The Beginning of a Business

The important thing is not being afraid to take a chance. Remember, the greatest failure is to not try. Once you find something you love to do, be the best at doing it.

—Debbi Fields, founder of Mrs. Fields

After graduating from cooking school, I got a job managing a small chain of vegan restaurants called Blanche's. I was finally back to work and back to making money, even if it wasn't a lot. What a relief.

I really enjoyed this job. I baked healthy cookies and muffins for Blanche's, and made sandwiches, salads, and soup. I cultivated a small celebrity clientele who loved my food. It was fun, but I didn't really know where I was headed, until I had a stroke of luck, disguised as an obstacle: Blanche's was going out of business.

When I first heard that Blanche's was closing, I was disappointed that I would be out of a job. So what was I going to do about it? I could have sat around waiting for my last paycheck, but then I had an idea. Instead of fretting about my future, what if I came from a place of yes and used this chance to start a business of my own? I'd done it before—maybe this was my chance to do it again, but bigger and better.

I realized that every day for the next few months before the store closed, I had access to a full restaurant kitchen and ingredients to make baked goods. I love baking cookies, cupcakes, and muffins, and I was already making healthful vegan versions. What if I developed a few of my own, original recipes, then tested them out on Blanche's clientele?

Blanche's became my test kitchen, and I got to work; inventing cookie and muffin recipes without wheat, eggs, or dairy products. I courted the vegan crowd I was already in touch with as well as the wheat-allergy and low-fat crowd. I baked and tasted, gave out samples and asked for opinions: "What do you think of this one?" "Here, try a bite of this. Do you like it? Would you buy it?"

I tried a lot of different recipes during those months, and finally, I had a few core recipes that everybody loved. They didn't just taste good as vegan or wheat-free cookies. I didn't want them to be just pretty good health-food-restaurant cookies. I wanted them to be low-fat, healthy cookies that could stand up to any fattening cookies. As I worked on the recipes, I used the concept of take it or leave it—keeping the elements in each recipe that worked, and changing the ones that didn't—tweaking every batch until they were perfect. In fact, that's where my whole passion was born for renovating recipes for health without sacrificing flavor. I realized I could be on to something.

And oh, did I have visions—visions of something big. I wouldn't just be a cookie baker. I would be *the* cookie baker. I would start a business, it would take off, I'd go national, and everyone around the world would be in love with my cookies. I would be the next Mrs. Fields, the next Famous Amos, but the healthy version— people would think "cookie" and they would say my name—they would say "BethennyBakes."

I felt like a door had opened, and in typical Bethenny style, I would go big or go home.

Looking back, I can see that a lot of my ideas were unrealistic. I didn't really know how to do this kind of business, but that's never held me back. I figured I could jump in again, and learn as I went. I'd learned a lot from running my own event planning business and from Princess Pashmina, and I had learned from past mistakes.

Of course, I had no idea about the many mistakes that were still in store for me, mistakes that are obvious to me now, in retrospect.

But this business was true to me. I knew I was on the right track because food and baking (especially sweets) are so important to me. Anybody that knows me knows I have a sweet tooth. I would kill a man for a spoonful of frosting. My goal was to figure out how I could align that desire and natural affinity with my passion for health, and turn both interests into a business. I could take what I learned in cooking school and turn it into a venture that would finally launch my career.

When Blanche's finally closed, I was ready to launch.

The first step was to secure a space. I needed a kitchen. I found one in a restaurant next to my house that was open just for dinner. I went in and plied them with cookies and begged and pleaded and finally convinced them to let me use their kitchen in the morning. As long as I was out by 4:00 p.m. every day, we had a deal.

When I first stepped into that kitchen, I had such a feeling of lift-off. It was a new beginning and I imagined the limitless possibilities. I looked around at the ovens and counters and mixers and utensils and it was such a thrill. Then the real work began. Like so many things, I had absolutely no idea what I was in for. Work is hard—you may enjoy it, but I'm just telling you, guys—it's hard. This was brutal.

Visualize this: Me, in an apron, my hair pinned up, mixing huge bowls of cookie dough and then scooping the dough by hand with an ice cream scoop onto tray after tray. Into the oven and out of the oven. I baked 400 cookies a day, the absolute maximum number of cookies I could produce in the time I had. It was like a math problem: if it takes 1 minute to scoop each cookie, so many minutes to bake a batch, so many minutes to seal and label each cookie, then 400 was the answer. It was all I could do. I was operating at maximum capacity with the resources I had, and hanging on by my fingernails.

It was no way to run a business. When 4:00 p.m. approached, I would put all the trays of cookies onto a massive metal rolling rack. I cleaned everything until it was spotless. Then I rolled that big rack of 400 cookies out the door and down the street to my building, up the handicap ramp, and into my studio apartment. I have to give a shout-out to my doorman, Frank. He thought I was crazy for running this business out of my apartment, but he was always supportive and he even pitched in—I put him to work sealing and labeling cookies. I was employing the doorman—this was how desperate I was for help.

In fact, I have to add a big thank-you to all the doormen in all the buildings in which I've ever lived. I don't just make everything my business, I make my business everyone else's business. Whenever I've had a doorman who is sitting with nothing to do, I tend to hand them boxes to assemble or labels to stick on, and they've always been generous and kind enough to rally around me and help me. So here's to the doormen!

As the sun was setting, I used a blow-dryer and an industrial sealing machine to seal every single cookie into a package and shrink-wrap it. Then I stuck on the labels I had printed at Kinko's.

By this time, it was late—after-midnight late. This is when I loaded the cookies into the back of my car . . . if you could call it a car. Actually, it was a green Ford Bronco with a cracked windshield that I had bought for $500 from a construction worker who was unloading it because it was such a piece of crap. I had the crack fixed and spent $100 to get this disgusting vehicle "detailed" so it would be at least remotely respectable (it still wasn't). Once, driving out to the Hamptons in this car, I ran into a guy I had had a date with—he was a wealthy trader, a big shot in a fancy Mercedes. You should have seen the horrified look on his face when he saw my car.

In fact, all my friends used to laugh at that car. They used to shake their heads at me like they couldn't believe what I was doing. I say, never be embarrassed if you're working hard and doing what you need to do. Never care what people think, as long as you feel that what you are doing is right. I remember once, my ex-boyfriend Larry let me use his car when I was in a bind. This was a white Ford Blazer totally shrink-wrapped in a Fanta advertisement—completely covered in multicolored fruit, with all the words in Spanish. He had a business that shrink-wrapped cars. I drove that car all around the Hamptons. I could write a whole book about my relationship with crappy cars.

Now I drive my Skinnygirl car all around, too. So what? I like my Skinnygirl car, and it's business. Did you see the episode of *House-wives* when I drove the Skinnygirl car to the Hamptons for lunch? I pulled it up outside the restaurant and went in to meet Luann. She saw it out the window, and she told me, "Darling, I wouldn't drive that car around if I were you." Well, of course she wouldn't. But me? I'll drive it around, all right, and be proud. There ain't no shame in my game.

But this green vehicle was definitely several steps below my Skinnygirl car. It barely held together. I would spend the whole night driving this rattletrap to dozens of bodegas and delis in Manhattan, hand-delivering cookies before the sun came up. Each store would get about thirty cookies, and I'd take back the ones that hadn't sold—on a typical day, at a typical bodega, that would be over half of them—eighteen crumbled, broken, open cookie packages. I just didn't have the packaging capability to do it better. Defeated, I'd head home with a broken-down car full of broken cookies. And one week later, I'd do it all over again.

One of my business fatal flaws, I soon realized, was that my cookies had no preservatives. This was one of my major selling points, of course, from a health standpoint, and the cookies were great fresh out of the oven, but they just didn't hold up well and didn't have a very long shelf life, especially when the weather was humid—they didn't just crumble, they got moldy. So I'd take them back and throw them away, half my efforts wasted.

I was surviving on no sleep and working like a dog. It was hell. The business was bleeding money, but I was stubborn and determined. I couldn't give up after investing so much time and energy. My pride kept me going, even though, in the back of my mind, I could see the cookie was crumbling.

· ·

FOOD IS THE HARDEST BUSINESS IN THE WORLD

Food is the hardest business in the world because of perishability. Recently I saw mold on something in a bakery display case and if I had never had the experiences I've had, I probably would have been disgusted. Instead, I politely and discreetly told them about it. It was a sweltering August day in New York City. I felt their pain.

· ·

The Beginning of the End

If at first you don't succeed, try, try again. Then quit. There's no use being a damn fool about it.

—W. C. Fields, actor

My business limped along like this for a while. I moved to a catering kitchen that supplied a food court and was open only for lunch, in an office building on Third Avenue. They let me in at 3:00 p.m., and I had to be out by 6:00 a.m. I thought that maybe this was my chance to really step it up. This kitchen was better equipped, with more space. I thought this would help me increase my production.

I hired anybody I could find who was willing to work, and I mean anybody. A more motley crew you've never seen, some who didn't speak English, mixing cookie dough and scooping it with an ice cream scoop. A second crew sealed and labeled until 6:00 a.m. The cookies were all different sizes, because they were scooped by hand and the recipes produced different results. The almond cookies rose more than the banana chocolate chip. Some types spread more than others, so the cookies were never uniform. I was losing control of consistency, but I kept going. I refused to see that the business wasn't working. I refused to see that maybe it was time to call it quits.

Every week I "rewarded" one of the members of my crew by letting them choose the "quote of the week" that went on the cookie label. Yeah, what a reward. The quote was supposed to inspire or amuse, but what the quote should have been was: "You are a schmuck for working here because nobody is ever going to buy these cookies!" Or, "Confucius say: This business will soon swirl down the toilet."

We worked all night and by 6:00 a.m., my assistant, Damona, and I would be in tears, trying to get the cookies out in time. Then we loaded up that $500 car and headed out to all the bodegas and delis again, not having slept for twenty-four hours. Being a prostitute would have been a lot easier, more dignified, more lucrative, and frankly, more glamorous.

I went on like this for six months and it was truly a comedy of errors, but I was crying, not laughing. I had to keep moving the business because each new bakery had some disaster—one flooded, destroying product and equipment. One was robbed, one didn't have any equipment, one had a machine that pulverized the cookies, one was so hot that the cookies got moldy before I could even deliver them.

Something was always going wrong. I was a mom-and-pop baker, so I was selling to mom-and-pop stores, and there was no potential to become profitable. I couldn't manage to take it to the next level because there were so many barriers. I couldn't generate enough capital to go bigger. I was stuck in the small time and I didn't know how to change my situation.

The problem was, I never really had a plan, and the train had already left the station. I had no budget, so I never had enough money for what I really needed. It was like going to the mall to buy a dress to wear to a wedding, then buying sunglasses, lipstick, jeans, earrings—finally realizing you have no money left for the dress. Ironically, I was too small to afford or have the volume for a kitchen with the machines to make everything uniform and consistent, but I needed those machines to be able to get to the next level. Growth became impossible.

I had some opportunities along the way, but I just wasn't in a position to capitalize on them. I met with QVC to discuss the potential of going on TV, but thank goodness I never did it, because I didn't have the resources to get enough product prepared. To be on QVC, I would have had to be holding thousands of cookies the minute I went on the air, to be able to ship to meet the demand. There was no way I could make thousands of cookies that would be fresh and ready on the day I might happen to get a spot. It just couldn't be done, and I knew it. Sadly, I had to pass. If you can't do something well, don't do it at all.

I also fell into an opportunity to get my cookies into Whole Foods, and my product would have been perfect for that market. Again, I didn't have the consistency, the uniformity, the shelf life, or the volume. Because of another connection, I could have had my cookies in Target for a Valentine's Day promotion, but when I found out how many cookies they needed, I knew it wasn't going to happen. My cookies were not lasting long enough on the shelf and I didn't have any way to meet their minimum requirement. I would have lost my shirt on that deal, and ruined a potential relationship.

I also lacked the confidence for projects of this scope, and I never regretted that I didn't get in over my head trying to do these projects. I would go big when I was ready—all roads lead to Rome. When I wrote my second book, *The Skinnygirl Dish*, which has recipes for some of those same cookies, I was able to take the book on QVC. I had plenty of books at the ready and sold thousands of copies in the first few minutes. Now I have a great relationship with QVC. My books and DVDs have sold in Target, and who knows, maybe someday I'll have a product in Whole Foods, too. If I had disappointed any of those outlets by making a deal I couldn't execute, maybe they wouldn't be so interested in carrying my products now.

Everything happens for a reason. I ended up getting to Rome eventually, just a little later, but in a much bigger and oh-so-much-better way.

And BethennyBakes? In the end, it was an epic failure, but a great learning experience. I wasn't well organized and I didn't know enough to run it the way I probably should have—still, what I learned then helps me run my current business better.

Sometimes I think back on what I could have done differently. I should have had a budget. If I had invested money up front to start out with a professional setup and the automation the business required to grow, I would have done much better. Instead, I started on a shoestring and spent as I went, throwing good money after bad to put out all the fires. That is a no-no! I probably lost $100,000 all told with that venture because my ego wouldn't let me shut it down. I couldn't accept that it was time to fold, and my money noise was so loud that I kept hanging on to the idea that this was my one chance to make my millions and I shouldn't give up. But in many cases, you only get one chance. Better to do your homework and do it right the first time.

Of course, you can't predict the future, and it can be hard to know when it's foolish to give up and when it's smart. However, if you don't know when to hold 'em and when to fold 'em, you can waste a lot of time and money. I finally came to realize that BethennyBakes wasn't going to make it, and I had to call it quits, with no other prospects, and no other bright idea in the works. Sometimes you have to close one door before you can open another one. It's like ending a relationship before you've got another one, with the faith that you will find someone or something better.

And I did.

In fact, it was my commitment to BethennyBakes that led to the next big thing, before I had any idea what it would mean. It was my road to Rome.

You see, I was truly passionate about those cookies. I thought I was doing the greatest, bravest, best thing ever when I started that business, and in many ways, I was. I believed in those cookies with such fervor that even as the business was dying a slow and painful death, I decided to take my cookies to a big natural foods trade show.

That was the same week I heard about the deadline for applications to a new show called *The Apprentice*—a show that required an audition on videotape. Because of my passion for BethennyBakes, I just happened to be perfectly positioned to make that videotape. I'll tell you that story in the next chapter, but suffice it to say that in a roundabout way, I can thank poor, downtrodden, put-upon BethennyBakes for my television career. I probably would have arrived there one way or the other—because all roads lead you-know-where—but this was my path, and BethennyBakes gave me the opportunity to show my entrepreneurial spirit in a way that enabled me to take my career to the next level. If you believe in fate, the failure of BethennyBakes really was a success . . . in the end.

Truth be told, I could do that business now effortlessly, and one day I probably will have a company like this again. If I do, however, I guarantee that I will do it right. Those many mistakes weren't lost on me. People say, "If only I knew then what I know now." When you learn from your mistakes, you just might have the opportunity for a redo. You never know.

Or maybe your next move will be to something entirely different that grows out of your past experience. Everything you do can lead to something else if you are ready for it, and you may have only one chance to knock it out of the park, so go with your passions and do your best until it just doesn't make sense anymore.

And when you have to change course, change course—because of your hard work and dedication, your future is already shaping up, even when you can't see it yet. Persistence can be blind, but it can also result in a big payout. So have faith in yourself, your passions, your talents, and go big. Or go home.

. . . .

FROM MY IN-BOX
~∞∞~

This email comes from my PR and marketing
associate for the Skinnygirl brand, Maggie Gallant,
who has also become a close friend.

"*The tragic events on 9/11 took the life of a larger than life guy I had met in college. He had big dreams to work on Wall Street and that dream job took his life that day. I, like so many others, was haunted by the picture of a young person who woke up, went into work one day only to never be heard from again.*

"*I was tempted to pack myself up and fly south like a bird where I felt safe. Instead, I found strength from my family and friends and from somewhere within and decided to say 'yes' to staying in a city I could just feel held a future for me. Armed with a little bit of perhaps misguided confidence and a belief in my own abilities, likely instilled by my doting parents, I decided at twenty-one to open my own PR shop. Next thing I knew I was going after some of the country's most prestigious companies and somehow talked them into hiring me to get their word out. What did I know about running a business besides watching* Working Girl*?! But this working girl found so much joy in a career that was born out of such a dark day. My real 'Place of Yes' moment came seven years later when I was approached with the opportunity of Rogers & Cowan buying what I had always seen as my little PR shop. A million negative 'What Ifs?' popped into my head. It all seemed too good to be true. But, it was true and it was so good.*

"*Now two years after that 'Place of Yes' moment, I sit in my of-fice in midtown Manhattan and look out my window that faces south. I think of the doubts and fears that haunted me, and I take a moment to remember how I got here.*

"When people ask me what it's like to work with Bethenny, I sum it up by sharing my favorite part of her which is that she never forgets to laugh, I mean really laugh till she cries, at how funny life can be. She dreams big, but unlike many celebrities you may admire on the red carpet, she makes her dreams happen by buckling down and saying yes even when she is tempted to say no and stay in her pajamas. If I knew her back when I was tempted to move home where it was safe, I know exactly what she would say, 'Maggie, make it happen. You are staying here and you are going to go for it. End of story!' I am so thankful that I did."

—Maggie Gallant, senior VP, Rogers & Cowan

. . . .

A Detective Story

Winning isn't everything, but the will to win is everything.

— Vince Lombardi, football coach

Let me tell you one more story, about persistence and taking responsibility for your own situation, even if the odds are against you. This story is also about how all roads lead to Rome—but only if you insist on continuing down the road, despite the obstacles that might be in your way.

This is the story about something that happened to me, back while I was struggling to make BethennyBakes work. During this time, I was barely getting by. I had a lot of money noise and I often felt desperate. However, I always have a few irons in the fire, and often in my life when things have been tough, I'll sell something I own that is worth some money. It was one of those times, and I had an idea of how I might keep my business limping along a little bit longer.

I still had an engagement ring from my former fiancé. It was a 5-carat radiant-cut diamond ring that I had held as my security blanket. (I've returned engagement rings before, but when I had first agreed to marry Jimmy, when I quit my job and moved my whole life to Chicago, he told me that if it didn't work out, he would make it right and make sure I was okay. When we first broke up, he told me I could keep that ring—although, believe me, he did regret that later.) This ring had been my backup plan for a while, and as my resources dwindled, I decided it was finally time to sell it.

I had only recently discovered the existence of eBay, and I was (and still am) a big fan. It didn't have all of the safety and security aspects it has now, but at the time I thought it would be the perfect opportunity to sell something valuable.

I took a photograph of the ring and opened an eBay account and posted the item. Then I waited anxiously to see who would buy it and send me a great big check so that I could finally have some financial breathing room.

It didn't take long to find a buyer—someone willing to pay $42,000, which was a pretty high price for that ring. I was so pleased and relieved, since honestly, I was flat broke at the time. Now, I thought to myself, all I have to do is get the money.

But this was a lot of money, and online money transaction services weren't the simple and safe programs they are today. The buyer suggested we use an escrow company called Safe Exchange. I asked a lawyer about it; he looked into Safe Exchange and said it looked fine. Once the transaction was done, I paid the escrow company and sent the ring to the address the buyer provided. I still remember it: 500 S. Maryland Drive in Pennsylvania.

But with the ring out of my hands and no check in my hands, I began to get nervous. Two days later, I called to make sure the buyer had received the ring, and to check on the status of my payment.

This was my first inkling that something was wrong. When I called, I realized that the package had been delivered to a Federal Express location, not someone's home or personal business. Sirens started going off in my head. The buyer had strategically chosen a location that had sounded like a street address. Why would he have me send the ring to a Federal Express location? This was all the money in the world to me at the time, and I got a chill—you know that icy feeling that you've made a huge mistake? Frantically, I started searching online to find out everything I possibly could about Safe Exchange, and to my horror, I found a website that contained a list of look-alike scam sites to avoid. I saw that there was a site called SafeXchange.com, spelled differently from the legitimate Safe Exchange. That's when I really panicked.

I'd been scammed, and this wasn't money I could afford to lose. This was my entire life savings, my only backup plan. Immediately, I called the cops. I called eBay. I called my online provider, and anyone else I could think of. I called the police again, thinking it was their *job* to help me.

Nobody would return my calls. The cops said there was nothing they could do. I realized that those TV cop shows with high-tech computers and detectives who will stop at nothing to solve a case of injustice are just a fantasy. They didn't have a fax machine. They didn't even have email, which is ridiculous because this was an Internet crime.

My boyfriend at the time hired a private detective in New York, someone who was well known for being the best in his field, but he turned out to be worthless, too. He told me to fax him everything because he didn't have email either.

Nobody would help me. I was desperate, and I didn't leave my tiny studio apartment for days. I was glued to my little computer screen. I felt as if I was in a black hole and nobody was coming in after me.

That's when I realized that I had got myself into this, and I was the only one who was going to get myself out of it.

I realized that I had to come from a place of yes and make this happen. Whoever said you are only as good as your best client was wise—nobody will ever care about your problems as much as you do, and nobody will ever be as motivated to solve them as you are, so take control and do what has to be done. Don't wait around for someone else to fix your problems.

I began to formulate a plan. With just my crappy little computer in my apartment, I vowed to succeed where the cops had failed.

First, I instant-messaged the buyer, not letting on that I knew I was being scammed. I kept messaging him, collecting clues that could help me prove the buyer was engaged in illegal activity. His messages made him sound young and inexperienced. Whenever I went to his scam site and sent an email to it, I wouldn't get any response. Then I would instant-message the crook again, saying I wasn't getting a response from what I now knew was the scam site, and suddenly I would get a response through the site. It became obvious to me that he was manipulating the bogus site—and communicating with me only through instant messages, which aren't traceable the way emails are.

Through our conversations, the scammer wrote that he had to get the ring appraised at Tiffany on Jeweler's Row in Philly. More red flags—there is no Tiffany on Jeweler's Row. But I didn't dare reveal that I was on to him. I wanted to keep the lines of communication open so that I could collect as much evidence as possible—evidence that could finally help me force the police to get involved.

I investigated further. I looked into the buyer's eBay profile—his name was Corvette 20Z and he used "Corvette" in his email address. I saw that all his feedback (where buyers and sellers get to comment on their experiences with those eBay users they have done business with) was positive and full of glowing reports, but all the comments were "coincidentally" from other users with car names, like Bronco 47, Ferrari 78, and so on. Either those people were all the same guy, or he had his friends in on his game.

They always say criminals work close to home, so I decided to go back to the scene of the crime. Maybe this guy was so obvious that he would actually turn around and try to sell my ring on eBay.

I searched for five-carat diamond rings, and sure enough, I saw my ring, listed right there on eBay! I checked the GIA (Gemological Institute of America) certificate, and they were using a scam certificate that was almost identical, with tiny changes, so they could get away with it. But they didn't change it so much that I couldn't recognize it. Instead of a GIA certificate, it said "Certified by a GIA Graduate Gemologist." The wording was close, but it wasn't right. If you didn't know about diamonds, why wouldn't you believe it? I printed out the information and sent it to GIA, and they confirmed it was likely the same ring. Thank goodness for eBay, or I probably never would have found it. I called the number on the listing and discovered that the ring was now being sold at one of those booths on 47th Street in Manhattan, in the Diamond District.

All right, I thought. Two can play at this game.

I called the store, pretending to be a potential buyer, and I said I was looking for a five carat diamond ring but I tried not to be too specific, so that I wouldn't arouse any suspicion. They told me to come into the store and they would show me what they had.

At the same time, just to distract the scammer who had provided the jeweler with the ring, I kept messaging him, inquiring politely about why I hadn't received my payment yet. He kept putting me off, just as politely.

But I needed backup. I felt a real sense of urgency about getting into that store *that day*, before somebody else bought the ring or the diamond was cut down and rendered unrecognizable. The jeweler had obviously just received it, so I knew I had little time. Diamonds are like snowflakes and every diamond is unique—any alteration and I would never get it back. Who could help me *now*?

I called Fox News Problem Solvers and told them that they should meet me at the store and we could catch these guys in their scam. They were interested, and wanted to set up a sting for the next day, but I thought that might be too late. I also called the one person I knew at *The New York Post,* but couldn't get anywhere with them, either—they also said they could follow up the next day. I convinced my assistant to play along because, as brave as I felt, I didn't want to go there alone.

So we went there, just the two of us, with no news team or reporter or even any law enforcement to back us up. Together we tracked down the storefront, in one of the busiest areas of the city, packed with booths and people and hustle and bustle, full of noise and chaos and crowds. We walked into the booth, and I said I was looking for a 5-carat engagement ring. I said I was serious and ready to buy. What did they have to show me?

Just as I had hoped, the creepy guy working the counter took out a bunch of rings and one of them was *my exact ring.* He handed it right over to me to try on! My heart leapt. You can imagine how much I wanted to lunge over that counter and strangle him, or just run for it, ring on my finger, but I knew I had to play by the book or I could lose it forever. I couldn't afford to make a mistake.

I examined the ring on my hand—there was no doubt it was my ring, in my exact size, with the unique setting that I had designed, and the bent prong I knew so well, not to mention the certificate I had seen on eBay.

I held out my hand and admired the ring, not letting on that I was anything other than a random interested girl trying on a random 5-carat diamond ring. Hey, what do you know, it fit perfectly. Like it was made for me! I asked about the price. The guy said I could have it for the low price of $18,000. This was another big clue that this guy was crooked—with the legitimate GIA certificate, he could have sold the ring for twice as much, but they probably didn't want it traced or traceable in case it was stolen—it was that kind of place. I knew how much less than its value this was—and how much it really was a "steal." (Pun intended.) I pretended to show even more interest, as if I was really going to buy it, just to get him more engaged and off guard. If people think they are about to get a lot of money, they lose focus. They make mistakes.

. . . .

BEFORE YOU BUY

If you are in the market for a diamond ring, take my advice: Choose one with great color, that you fall in love with, and make sure the GIA certificate is genuine! And if the price seems too good to be true, there is probably a reason.

. . . .

So there I was, my ring on my finger, the crooks standing there in front of me . . . and no law enforcement in sight. I knew I had to maintain my cover or they would be gone, and my ring with them. Thinking quickly, I told them I was really interested, and that my boyfriend would pay cash for it. I told him we would come back by 5:00 p.m.

I rushed home with my assistant and that fake certificate in hand. I finally had the proof I needed. I called the police one more time. I told them this was it. I was going back there by 5:00 p.m. I told them I was going to get my ring, and if they wanted things to proceed legally, if they wanted to get their man, then they should meet me at the address I gave them.

Maybe it was my less-than-charming attitude, but they refused! I was furious. I told them that if they didn't meet me at the store, I was going to have Fox News so far up their asses, they wouldn't know what hit them. I was not going to leave that store again without that ring. I was beyond tenacious. Even if I had to steal it back, I was taking what was mine, but I wanted the police there because I wanted to end it, get justice, and *get my ring*. I knew it was risky, I knew these crooks were probably dangerous, but I also knew that I deserved to have the law on my side, and the clock was ticking.

I was on a mission. I was single-minded, a dog with a bone who was not about to give up or give in, but I was also nervous as hell. I took a deep breath, and went for it. By the way, when this happened, Cookie was waiting in the car—Cookie was part of the caper!

The cops showed up to meet me a few minutes before 5:00, thank goodness. The store was just getting ready to close. I walked into that store with its dozens of jewelry counters. I asked to try on the ring again. I slipped it on my finger, raised my hand, and the cops moved in.

This time it *was* like one of those cop shows. It really was a sting operation. They confiscated the ring and took over the scene. In the end, I found out that I had helped to uncover a major Russian crime organization that had been scamming people for years. Because the crime crossed state lines, the FBI was involved, and my ring was in "jail" for more than a year because it was evidence. When the case was finally solved, I was able to sell it legitimately for $30,000. I lived on that money for several years, until I got my first deal with Pepperidge Farm to be their spokesperson.

It would have been so easy to have given up and had a sob story to tell. The police told me there was probably less than a one in a million chance of getting my ring back, given the circumstances. Did that faze me? No, statistics mean nothing to me. The odds mean nothing. Beyond the obvious fact that you never want to screw me over in business, the moral of this story is that you should always bet on yourself. People often bet against themselves—don't do that. Don't let anyone reduce you or your passion to a number. The horses picked as the favorites hardly ever actually win the Kentucky Derby. Odds are nothing. Instead, follow your gut, because it knows better than the odds. What if you're the long shot? If you want something, you have to go for it. If it goes badly, you'll learn from it. If it goes well, then you win, odds be damned.

It's worth taking some risks in your life, because when you come from a place of yes and go for what's rightfully yours, for what you really really want, then you stack the odds in your favor. If I had listened to the odds, I would have given up and let it go and hated myself for years. Instead, I acted on it. I made it my business.

By the way, let's also just establish that I was a *moron* for shipping a five-carat diamond ring to some guy I didn't even know. I definitely learned my lesson.

Anything is possible if you want it enough. Not everyone would have gone to the extremes I did to get back a diamond ring, but because I wouldn't stop, because I was relentless about what was rightfully mine, I won that round. My road led to Rome, in the end.

You won't always get the proverbial ring back. Your business won't always earn millions. You won't always get what you think you deserve. But if you always give it your all, if you always go for it with everything you've got, you won't ever have to have any regrets.

At the end of the day, you can look back on what you've done and say, "Maybe I got burned, but I did everything I could have done. Now, what's next?"

My takeaway from this whole period of my life is that every experience leads somewhere, and your life will be what you make of it. Sometimes the worst experiences have the best results, hidden just around the bend. If you can have a little perspective when things aren't going well, you will see that it's not always about what you are getting right now, it's often more about where you are going and what *right now* will grow into, later.

The reward isn't always immediate, but it's always out there. As long as you are working toward something with integrity and passion, you'll be getting closer and closer to your big moment, your launch, your flight. Your Rome.

Go for Yours

The Apprentice, Martha, and Me

Hell is the place for people who did not live their lives according to the best of what was in them.

—Harriet Rubin, author and media consultant

You could follow just the first five rules for a long time and do pretty well. You could even be very successful. Sometimes, however, you discover something you *really want*—something you want beyond a mere goal. It could be something like an injustice you need to right (like my diamond ring story), it could be some rare opportunity that you just know you have to go for, no matter how much of a longshot it seems.

When that happens, you need rule #6: *Go for yours.*

This is the rule of the driven. It embodies ambition in high gear. This is the rule I've always used when I wanted something big and difficult, and wanted it badly, yet had no idea how to get it. It kept me going until I got my engagement ring back from those crooks, and just a few years ago, it triggered the next stage of my career, in a surprising turn of events that took me in a completely new direction from the one in which I was headed. This is the rule that got me on television.

You can apply this rule to anything you really want, whether it seems big or small. Maybe you want to get married, or elected to office, or graduate from college, or become a mother, or get a job you know will be competitive. You might want to lose fifty pounds or finally get in shape or make a lot of money before you turn thirty. When you apply rule #6, don't worry about the exact nature of what you want, or whether it's "right" or "wrong," or even what will happen once you get it. If you are already following the first five rules, you can have faith that your desire is genuine for you and worth achieving. Let rule #6 take over now. This is the rule of focus, determination, tenacity. It will get you there—one way or another. This is a rule that can help you *get* to Rome (rule #5) when you're not getting there fast enough.

Going for yours is about pursuing something with such a singular focus that you put all your energy into getting there. You'll have to sacrifice some things. It might be tough, tiring, the hardest thing you've ever had to do. But if you keep rule #6 in front of you like the proverbial carrot in front of the horse, you'll be developing a valuable skill—a skill that can bring you success. You won't need rule #6 every day, but when you do need it, you'll be awfully glad you've got it under your belt.

The bottom line for rule #6 is that it allows you to take control of your life to a degree you may not have done before. Surprisingly, most people never really do this. They live their whole lives wanting things yet letting those dreams pass them by because they think it will be too hard to go for it, or they might fail. It's incredible to me how people don't believe they can actually have what they want— how often, as I mentioned in the last chapter, they bet against themselves. I don't get it. You *can* have what you want. I don't know if people are afraid of effort or failure or are embarrassed if they say they want something and don't end up getting it. But I do understand. Whatever barriers prevent you from reaching what you want, rule #6 can help you break through them.

It's time to stop wanting and start getting. It may sound greedy or a little selfish, but going for yours has nothing to do with greed. It's not about being ruthless or cruel or stepping on others to get ahead. It's about being your own greatest advocate and about making the most of all your abilities to achieve your goal. This is no time to be a martyr. I'm talking about raising yourself up and using your personal resources—your knowledge and skill and personality—to put yourself in the position where you can get what you need to have the life you really want.

And so what if it takes a while? What's the hurry? Great things take time, and your life is a project. You will probably make some mistakes, like everybody does, and you might even end up doing some backtracking, but fearing those missteps won't get you anywhere. Nothing's going to happen if you don't *go for yours.*

This rule both pushed me ahead and saved me from self-destruction during the next phase of my career. I've lived my life by it, and it's always paid off eventually. But it also has a dark side.

Desperation Noise

I must govern the clock, not be governed by it.

—Golda Meir, former Prime Minister of Israel

Every rule has its noise, and the noise I associate with *going for yours* is the noise common to so many people who want something very badly. People can smell desperation and it will color everything you do in a negative light—desperation noise.

This noise confuses your ambition, frazzles your energy, and makes your efforts feel grasping and scattered. Desperation makes you come across as something less than you really are. It drains your confidence and urges you to make rash decisions rather than smart, carefully considered decisions. It can make you think that you are running out of time for whatever it is you want or need. It can scare you into believing you have to take drastic measures. It can even tempt you to cheat or put down others to get ahead. When you go for yours, you are in control, whereas, when you start listening to desperation noise, you lose all control. When being driven turns into being desperate, you've got to take a step back.

Desperation noise can launch you into a panic, thinking you're going to die childless and alone, or never realize your dreams, or be stuck in a dead-end job, or married to someone you can't stand, or living a life of drudgery and frustration. I've had moments, alone in bed at night, where I wallowed in misery and self-pity, thinking I've wasted my life and it's too late for everything I've always wanted to happen. Desperation noise is going to a bar, and instead of just relaxing and being yourself, you hope and pray Mr. Right is going to give you his number. You look every guy in the eye with that look that says, "Please, please, please pick me! Aren't I worth *anything?*" I can almost guarantee that when you "go for yours" with that attitude, with desperation noise, regardless of how great you look, Mr. Right is going to run the other way.

The thought "it's too late unless I quickly do X, Y, or Z" is a sure sign of desperation noise.

You do have to be realistic. Before you pursue something with too much energy, you should take a good hard look at what it is and whether it really makes sense for you. Chances are, though, that if you are already following the first five rules, and you are willing to put in the energy, you can have whatever it is you really want. At any age and any stage of your life, you can still get fitter, get more organized, get a better job, learn a new hobby, travel, fall in love. You could still start a band or lose excess weight or learn how to sew or speak French or paint. Some of those things might be challenging, but they aren't out of reach if you really want them, and you can take some of them further than you might think. Where there's a will—and rule #6 is the will—there is usually a way.

As long as you keep your desperation noise under control.

As I realized BethennyBakes wasn't going to make it as the business I'd believed it could be, I was suffering from desperation noise. I was over thirty, I had no good relationship prospect, I had no good employment prospect, and I was drifting. It was a frustrating time—I still believed that I had great potential to do something amazing with my life, but nothing I was doing was working. Nothing was launching my career or taking my personal life to the next level. I didn't know what to do and my fear about my age wasn't helping. Desperately, I kept wondering who was going to take care of me, and how I was going to be okay.

At the same time, I always had my eyes open for the thing that would finally shatter my uncertainty about both my present and my future. Part of me was still coming from a place of yes, and I was ready to jump, even if it was a long way to jump, up and out of the pit I felt I had dug for myself.

And then I just happened to be with a particular group of people having a particular conversation.

The Apprentice

I don't have to be enemies with someone to be competitors with them.

—Jackie Joyner-Kersee, Olympic gold medalist

The night I first heard about a television show called *The Apprentice,* some friends and I were having dinner at a restaurant. Sometimes I would go out with my friends just in case I might meet someone, but it was always stressful because I couldn't really afford it at the time. I was always terrified when I tried to do the gracious thing and offer to chip in, because what if they actually took me up on my offer? If I had to split the huge bill, even if I didn't order anything, I'd be cash-strapped for weeks. I'd go home paralyzed by anxiety and money noise. That's one of the most liberating things about my life now, in fact. I can go out to dinner without panicking about the check. That is a feat in and of itself.

That evening, someone at the table mentioned that he had seen a new show on television called *The Apprentice.* It was a competition where contestants would vie with one another to win a job working for Donald Trump. The guy who mentioned this went on to explain that the point of the show was to measure the entrepreneurial potential of each contestant through various silly tasks, like running a lemonade stand. Contestants would be eliminated, one by one, until the end, when Donald Trump chose the winner. (Incidentally, the tasks I had to do were a lot more difficult and complicated than running a lemonade stand, but more about that later.)

I've always loved a scavenger hunt–type challenge, and I've always been competitive. I listened with interest, and then I threw in my two cents. I said I thought I would be great on that show, because I was a natural for a competition like that. I liked the concept, everyone starting out on an equal footing and each person having to prove that they were the best. I loved the idea that something a fifth grader could do, like running a lemonade stand, could take on this much significance and actually be judged by The Donald. If a lemonade stand could get you a job with Donald Trump, then how you make coffee, take out the garbage, or even check coats means everything, too—it represents how you will do any job you ever get. The show seemed to stand for everything I had always believed about business.

But this guy at the dinner, who had mentioned the show, scoffed at me. He said I would be a terrible contestant on *The Apprentice,* and I could never do it. He went so far as to say that *he* would get on the show, but I wouldn't. He had connections in the world of real estate, and he knew people who knew Donald Trump. He said he was perfect for it.

To me, that was the ultimate challenge. If you want to get me to do something, then tell me I can't do it. Make it a contest and I'm in. He said, "Mark my words, I'll be on that show." I said, "No, mark *my* words, *I'll* be on that show." And that's all it took. I was officially obsessed. (Incidentally, he never made it on the show.)

Back then, reality television was much less pervasive than it is today. I had no idea how reality TV worked. I had no idea what I was in for, and I certainly didn't have the slightest hint that this was something that could change my future. Today, people are much more tuned in to the possibilities these shows offer. *The Apprentice, The Bachelor, Survivor, Jersey Shore, Big Brother, Amazing Race,* the whole *Housewives* franchise—all these shows offer their fifteen minutes of fame (more often than not, people on reality TV shows fade into obscurity when the shows end), but be careful what you wish for. I had something to prove . . . little did I know what that would eventually require.

A few weeks later, someone who had been at the dinner happened to mention to me that the deadline to apply as a contestant for season two of *The Apprentice* was approaching fast. The deadline happened to be on the day I was at the Natural Products Expo, in my BethennyBakes booth. I realized it was the last day and I panicked momentarily, but then I decided to come from a place of yes and go for what I knew could be mine.

I sent my business partner off in search of a video camera, something reasonably priced, lightweight, and easy to acquire. He filmed me in my booth, selling my cookies, then I sent him off to a local place that could edit the footage down so I could get it in the mail *that day.* I filled out all the paperwork, and somehow, while still working the expo, I got that application in the mail.

After I sent the tape, I stored the whole thing in the back of my mind and pretty much forgot about it for a couple of months. Then I got the call: They were interested in me! Suddenly, I was convinced that this was the beginning of a whole new phase of my life. I was sure of it. I was instructed to go to the Trump Hotel in New York to meet the casting directors. They had narrowed the field down to approximately 250 people nationwide—including yours truly.

As I prepared, physically and mentally, for this seminal meeting, I had this idea in my head about what they wanted. I thought about it as if it were an interview for a real job, rather than an audition to get on a TV show. I imagined that they wanted to find someone who could work for Donald Trump, but also someone with a distinct personality—a *business* personality. I set to work tweaking my own personality to fit the mold I thought existed—accentuating some parts of myself, stifling others. I remember exactly what I wore: A Moschino skirt with hearts on it (a heart is my logo to this day), and a red jacket, because red is a power color. It was all carefully calculated. I spent a lot of money on that outfit—money I couldn't afford to spend. I had my hair and makeup done professionally before the meeting, too, because I just knew this was my ticket. These were odds I thought were worth the gamble.

During the meeting, I was my most outgoing self. However, because I didn't understand the nature of reality TV, I didn't realize they wanted unusual characters as much as they wanted business-people. I kept my more eccentric side to myself and showed them my business side. It was me, but it wasn't the whole me. There are so many situations in life where, although it sounds like a cliché, it's really just best to be completely yourself. I would live that reality eventually.

The interview went well, so I had hope and even confidence. Then, all I had to do was hurry up and wait. I waited for about a month, and then I got the news: they liked me. They wanted to see more. I had made it to the next level.

The producers sent me a fifty-page background check document and a lengthy contract. If I passed the background check, they would fly me to Los Angeles and I would enter into what I didn't yet realize was a grueling, mind-numbing, insanity-inducing selection process. All I knew was that I would have to be sequestered in a hotel for a week. So be it. Whatever it took, I was willing to do it.

I filled out every page of that contract. I sent it in, and the obsessing began again. I checked my messages every day. I thought about it all the time. I had to have it. I was driven. I was a dog with a bone, even though there was nothing I could do but gnaw. I was going for it, in every way. But I was also filled with desperation noise, two forces at war within me, both racing for the same goal.

Then I got another call—and just like that, I was on a plane to Los Angeles.

On the plane ride over, I decided that not only would I get on the show, I would win. I would win it all. I believed that everything was riding on this one opportunity. I felt so much pressure, but also so much hope. Getting onto *The Apprentice* became my one-pointed reality.

Passion is great. Obsession can even be productive. But desperation is fatal.

Of course, you couldn't tell me that at the time. (Nevertheless, I hope you'll listen to me now, so I can save you some pain.) Once I arrived in Los Angeles, I checked into the Doubletree Hotel, which became my prison for the next week. I got to my room and I began to strategize in earnest. For me, the game had begun.

It was going to be a tough one, I could tell from the first day. Mark Burnett, the producer, doesn't mess around. He had the casting process worked out to the last detail. It was a military operation. I was locked in my room and I wasn't allowed any contact with the outside world. None of the potential contestants was allowed to speak to or know anything about one another. We had twenty-minute meal breaks, where we eyed one another in silence—no talking. Everyone there had to drop everything in their lives and go through it, and I know I wasn't the only one driven to make it on that show. But since none of the potential contestants could even acknowledge one another during that brutal week, I could only wonder about them.

And wonder, I did. I came up with theories and preconceived notions about who would probably make it and who obviously wouldn't, who were the ones to beat and whom I'd already trumped (so to speak).

Every potential contestant had to take psych tests and IQ tests and meet with doctors and psychiatrists. They wanted to know everything about us, not just who we were and what we'd done but how we might be or what we might do if we made it on the show and were thrown into that intense environment. At every meeting, during every test, I tried to be the person I *thought* they wanted to cast on the show. I was the model contestant in every way—or so I believed. But what did I know about what they wanted?

I'm not the most religious person on the planet, but I prayed and dreamed and begged God to make sure I would be chosen. It was extremely stressful. I felt totally alone, isolated, and desperation noise kept me from sleeping all week.

Day by day, people left. I suppose people were sent home as they didn't measure up to the increasing scrutiny and evaluation. All I knew was that they were paring us down to a final eighteen contestants. And I was still there.

At every opportunity, I tried to count how many people remained each day. Because the meals were in shifts, there were people I never saw. I was never sure how accurate the count was. I had one trusted friend I called, obsessing about whether I would make it, and on the sixth day, I told her that I thought I could count approximately eighteen people. This was it, I thought—I got it. I got this. The week is almost over. I'm still here. *I must have made it because I have to make it. I did everything they want. I'm in.*

I was wrong.

One of the producers came to my room that day to break the news: I was chosen as a "first alternate." What? How's that for a kick in the balls?

It took me a few minutes to process what that meant—and to realize that my dreams were shattered. I was so sure I had made it, so sure I'd actually win the whole season—and I wasn't even going to be on the show? I was *so close.* They chose eighteen people, plus one male and one female alternate. The male alternate actually made it on the show because on the last day, one of the contestants was cut. I, on the other hand, had to go back home.

To say I was devastated is a gross understatement. To go through that horrible week and get that close and not make it was like a punch in the stomach.

But what else could I do? I went home. Sometimes, going for it doesn't work. Or . . . that's what I thought at the time. I was feeling angry and defeated, but somewhere in my subconscious, I remembered rule #5: *All roads lead to Rome.*

Afterward I thought (obsessed) about it, dissecting every moment of the experience, trying to figure out what I did wrong. This doesn't always work. You won't always know what you did wrong. Maybe you didn't do anything wrong. However, I began to figure out that I hadn't let those producers see the real me. I'd let them see parts of the real me, the parts I had already decided would be suitable for the show. I had focused on the business part, not the whole package that is Bethenny Frankel. Why did I think I knew so much about what they wanted?

And then, there was my desperation noise. I don't think this was a big factor in terms of the producers not choosing me, because I think I hid it pretty well, but it was a big factor for me, mentally. And it was getting worse because I felt like I'd missed my one and only chance. It was all over for me. I would die alone in miserable poverty and no one would ever remember me.

This all sounds ridiculous, but it's how I felt at the time. After I recovered from the initial disappointment and anger, I realized that I still had to come from a place of yes, even if the producers of *The Apprentice* had said *no.* So I took a deep breath and made a plan.

I would stay in touch with the people I met who worked on the show. I would keep connected . . . because you *never know.* I wasn't sure they would remember who I was, but I kept everything—all the names, cards, emails. The world is smaller than you think, and people are often more accessible than you think. I had imagined the show had hundreds of producers, but there were actually only five, and they all remembered me. And that turned out to be very important. I know a lot of the other people who were cut just stayed angry or gave up and never stayed in touch, but I vowed to keep going for it. I decided that they had said no, but that didn't mean I had to say no. So, every few months, I touched base. I wasn't going to give up. All that I had gone through just had to come to *something*. Maybe next season?

Next season was not to be, either. They passed me by for the next season (which, incidentally, bombed in the ratings). It was tempting to give it all up, go another route—but I still had a feeling, just a feeling, that I wasn't done with this adventure yet.

And I was right. Months upon months later, I got another call. They were doing a spin-off of *The Apprentice*.

A *Martha Stewart version*.

And they wanted me to try out for it.

Martha Stewart? Can I begin to express how excited I was? How completely mind-blown I was? *Martha Stewart!* She was one of my all-time idols, a strong, powerful woman, one of the first female self-made billionaires. I really admired her brand and her business sense, and I understood what she did—her audience was women, she was a cook and gave lifestyle advice, and her whole empire was built around things I understood. I wasn't interested in real estate—I was interested in *this*. Obviously, this show was way more fitting for me.

I was terrified of being heartbroken again. Yet I just had a feeling this was right. And it all became clear to me: *this* was why I didn't make it on *The Apprentice*. I thought not getting on *The Apprentice* was the most devastating thing in the whole world, but if I had gotten onto that show, I never would have been a candidate for Martha's version. I was meant to be on this show, instead.

I don't mean that to sound mystical—in fact, recently someone from that show told me one of the reasons they didn't choose me for *The Apprentice* was that they were already planning on doing the Martha Stewart version down the road, and they were saving me for that one. I don't know if it's true or not, but that's exactly how it worked out. Sometimes the thing you've been waiting for pops up right in front of you and you have to be ready to jump on it. I was so ready.

And then I realized what was involved, and it was: Here we go again!

Even when I learned I would have to do that whole devastating week all over again, I didn't care. I had a whole new attitude. I would be *Bethenny Frankel,* not *Bethenny Frankel's idea of the perfect* Apprentice *contestant.* I would be myself in every way. I wouldn't try to please anyone. I would let the full force of my personality shine through. This was a new beginning for me.

So I flew to Los Angeles, again. I checked into the Doubletree hotel, again. And I repeated the whole sequestered nightmare. But this time, my new attitude helped me feel less obsessive and calmer. It was different than before. In part, I knew what to expect, but I also felt powerful, not desperate. I had finally conquered my desperation noise. I was actually able to sleep at night. I knew I could do it. Sometimes you just feel it, you just know.

At the end of the week, when it was down to the last few potential candidates for Martha Stewart's show, Mark Burnett, the producer, gathered us in a group and told us that this was going to be the biggest TV show in history. Martha Stewart had just been released from prison, and this was supposed to be her coming-out party.

He said 40 million people were going to watch each episode, and the PR person said we were going to beat out *Desperate Housewives* in the ratings. That didn't turn out to be true—the show didn't actually get the ratings they had hoped for—but Mark got us all fired up about the show's potential. We all knew this was something big, and hit or not, the opportunity really was something big for me.

At the time, I had no idea how much this experience would

change my life. All I knew was that I wasn't going to screw it up. This was everything, my final shot, the chance that was meant for me. I was damn well going to get it. I was going for mine.

During a simulated meeting, where they put some of the potential castmates together in a room to see how we would interact, Mark Burnett asked me why the other people shouldn't be on the show, and I was my ball-busting, one-liner-slinging self. "*She* shouldn't be on this show because she's carrying a knockoff Marc Jacobs bag," I said, pointing at one of the other candidates. Not that I've never worn a knockoff, but I knew it would be funny, and it was.

I could feel it in the room—I was a lock. I was in. I didn't just will it. I felt it, and I knew it. They kept pairing me with different people to see the dynamic, and I went for it with everything I had— the whole me.

And I got it.

The invitation to join the cast on *The Apprentice: Martha Stewart* was a great moment for me. It made me realize that there is no point in regret. When you regret something, what you aren't seeing is that someday, later, or maybe sooner, you're going to see why you didn't get the thing you wanted. So often, something better is just around the corner.

So be where you are and keep looking out for what's next—you don't have to stress out if you have a master's degree and you find yourself working at Starbucks or sweeping floors or washing dishes because you didn't get the job you thought would be yours—or because there aren't any jobs. There will be. Just keep going for yours, and as long as you are aware and awake and ready to move when you get the chance, you'll keep rolling toward your goal.

YOUR BIG IDEA: WORTH ABOUT A NICKEL

I am the queen of the brilliant idea. I have had a million and five great ideas, and I mean really great ideas, moneymaking, revolutionary, billion-dollar ideas. But guess what? A great, moneymaking, revolutionary idea is worth about a nickel.

Having an idea is easy. Making an idea work is *hard*. It takes guts. It's expensive. And it's a hell of a lot of work. It's also risky.

So don't get pompous and think you are Einstein because you are full of great ideas. (And I can only say this because sometimes I think I'm Einstein because of my own great idea.) If you want credit for your idea, you have to make it happen. Actualize it.

Sometimes this takes some research and consulting with others who know the field. Don't be so secretive about your ideas that you never make them happen because you're afraid someone will steal them. Executing ideas takes a lot of work, research, and often a lot of manpower. You may not be able to do it alone. Bounce ideas off people who can give you advice.

That doesn't mean you should yell about it to everybody on the street. You have to be discerning, but do what you need to do to follow through. Otherwise, your great ideas offer no evidence that you are a genius. I can tell you 500 great ideas right now, but the idea is only 1 percent of what matters.

So get up and start making your ideas happen. Just pick one. One single billion-dollar idea, fully realized, is worth more than a billion unrealized ideas. And who knows, it could result in . . . what? A billion dollars? I think that sounds like something worth getting off the couch for.

Martha's World

I've got a theory that if you give 100 percent all of the time, somehow things will work out in the end.

—*Larry Bird, former NBA basketball player*

I went onto Martha Stewart's show with a clear plan: I would win, and I would be Martha's successor. I knew she was getting older, and I thought she was seeking someone appropriate to take over her empire. I would eventually democratize health the way she democratized style. I thought that Martha, like Oprah, would want to pass the baton and empower other women.

Oh, how naïve I was. I didn't realize at the time that Martha had no intention of giving any of us a real job. And I don't think that Martha will ever really retire.

But I don't regret my attitude. Part of going for yours is to go for it, heart and soul. People say, "Don't get your hopes up," or, "Manage your expectations." I don't agree with that at all. I think it's great to get excited, to pour all your hopes and dreams into something you really want, even to be overly optimistic. If you don't get it, at least you had fun immersing yourself in the possibilities. And what if you do get it? You were right! If you don't believe in yourself, you might actually sabotage your chances. Any other attitude besides total commitment and the highest of hopes defeats the purpose of going for what you really want.

I was always surprised, talking to some of the other contestants on *Martha Stewart,* how many of my fellow contestants made a big deal of saying that they didn't really want to be on the show. Some said their friends signed them up, or they did it because they were bored.

Yeah, right.

Getting onto a show like that is absolutely grueling and if you don't want it more than you want anything, you would never put yourself through that experience. It's not something you do because you're bored. Saying you don't care may feel safer, but I don't think it helps you win. I think it helps you lose.

What if those other people lost because they didn't channel their enthusiasm, their passion, their desire to win? Let your true feelings show. Wear your heart on your sleeve. Why not? It won't hurt any less if you lose, and if you win, you deserve it. It might even help you win.

That was the way I played it—but to me, it wasn't a game. It was my life.

This was such an exciting time for me, full of potential and promise. After being chosen, I flew back to New York and waited for the show to begin taping. It would be filmed in New York, centered on the offices of Martha's company, so when it was time, I didn't have far to go. The contestants all had to stay sequestered in a residential apartment in New York, to prepare for the show. We called it the Ponderosa. (By the way, Cookie stayed with friends during this time, in a house with several other dogs. That freaked her out, and this was probably the start of some of her issues.)

Each day we were prepped. We were allowed to see one another, but we weren't allowed to speak. We were all in a room, but nobody could say a word because the game didn't start until the cameras were rolling.

Of course, we all formed judgments and made assumptions about one another during this preshow period, but it's really true that you can't judge a book by its cover. The one guy I was sure would win was cut on the second day. Another guy I thought looked promising to win was the first one to go home. Don't ever assume you know everything. I can guarantee you don't.

We met with a series of people who prepared us for some of the ins and outs of the intense experience to come. They lectured us on how to handle the press. They gave us "safe sex" lessons (seriously). We had to meet with a therapist who told us that we would return to see her when we got "fired." They were preparing us for the psychological meltdown of getting cut from the show.

When you get fired or cut from a reality show like this one, you don't usually get to go back home to your old life. You have to stay at the residential apartment where you started, and remain sequestered again for weeks or even months, until the show finishes filming. They do this so there aren't any information leaks. People have breakdowns. It's brutal.

When the therapist told me, "When you come back, you can talk to us," I said, "I won't be coming back here." I had no intention of getting "fired." Of course the odds were that I would, but I was determined to stay positive. I expected nothing less than total success. (Incidentally, I was right about never going back there. I didn't get hired, but I also never got fired.)

That first day, as we all entered a loft where we would be living, and eyed one another and waited to meet Martha, I knew I really did have my chance, my golden opportunity. We were all equal on this show, like horses coming out of the gate, and may the best horse win. There was no favoritism. No built-in advantage. It was a level playing field.

And a crazy, insane playing field. The best way I can describe the show is as a freak, sleep-deprivation business experiment. Until I was breast-feeding my baby, being on that show was the single most exhausting experience of my life. I slept two hours a night for two months until the finale.

In the loft there are no ceilings, very few walls, and lights on twenty-four hours a day. If you get up to go to the refrigerator for a glass of orange juice without a microphone on, you will be yelled at. Every moment must be captured. Nobody is allowed newspapers, cell phones, or credit cards. It really is sick and brilliant, and I wouldn't give back the experience for anything in the world.

Each day, we would meet with Martha, get our task, and work like crazy to make it happen, competing against one another individually or in teams. We were able to do things you would never get to do if we were out there working on our own, like design a car dealership showroom, produce a television commercial, pick out and sell a product on QVC, build a three-bedroom hotel room from nothing in a single day. After each task, we were called in to see Martha, and somebody would get the axe.

Right from the start, I could tell what the other contestants were made of. Intense situations bring out true character. Some of them came out of the gate at 150 mph, but couldn't sustain the pace and burned out fast. Others came out slowly, worked steadily, and stayed under the radar. The competition helped me see what I was made of, too. I discovered parts of myself I didn't know I had, and have been able to use them since. I endured exhaustion, irritation, frustration, desperation—every emotion you can imagine. Looking back on it now, I don't doubt that this intense experience prepared me for some of my future on-screen encounters and experiences.

One of the smartest things I did on that show was to protect myself physically. Reality shows are so extreme, they can be completely draining. I ate well, while the others were eating junk food or living on energy bars. I slept as much as I could, and I tried to get along with the other contestants (though not at the expense of doing the job or sacrificing my own position). It's important to know yourself in situations like this—to know what you can and can't do, and what you need, so you can maintain your endurance.

I protected myself emotionally, too. I did my best to stay a little bit distant, so I wouldn't get so close to someone that I would be hurt if they left. I got along with everyone, for the most part. There was this one guy who was just a very unusual character. Nobody else could get along with him, but I thought he was hilarious and I became friends with him. That ended up helping me in the competition. In corporate America, if you are the kind of person who can deal with anybody, that's coming from a place of yes.

Humor really helped me through the competition, too. I never took myself too seriously, and I laughed a lot. That diffused some of the pressure.

Every challenge was a new adventure on that show, and I took full advantage of the situation to learn everything I could. With every task, I played a key role—I always stepped up to be a leader or the person with the out-of-the-box idea, someone integral to the team, never playing it safe in the background. I made some mistakes and did some stupid things, but I was always in the front row. I knew that presence would be important. We also knew what we accomplished would be judged pretty closely. For one task, we created a commercial for Song Airlines, and our team won. The airline said they were actually going to use the commercial.

But there was one responsibility I had avoided for much of the show—that was to be the accountant on any of the projects. I still had money noise and my bad experiences with the financial aspects of my past businesses made me shy away from taking this on. I didn't want to get fired from the show because of a stupid money mistake.

As more and more people were eliminated and fewer people worked on the challenges, I really hit my stride. There had been rocky moments in the beginning, but I was really getting the hang of this. We were given a team challenge to design a showroom for Buick. We had twenty-four hours. I decided I would be the accountant. I went outside my comfort zone because I didn't want to look back on the experience and know that I avoided something or missed out on any aspect of what I could learn.

I also had a great idea. What if we designed the car showroom like an art gallery? The team liked the idea. We created this beautiful gallery and turned it into a very VIP experience. Buick loved it, too, and told us that they were going to use the concept in their showrooms nationwide. The project manager took credit for the idea but at that point, I didn't even care. I wanted our team to win and I wanted to do a good job with the accounting. I did it! We won the challenge and I faced my fears about the budget and came out ahead.

And as we went through all of these highs and lows, the crazy schedules and impossible challenges, we always had to please Martha Stewart at the end of the day. I have to say that Martha Stewart is brilliant, and is someone whose career I respect immensely. But be careful when you actually get to meet your heroes. Martha was my idol and I really wanted the job as her apprentice, but now that I know her a little better, I think it wouldn't have worked out very well. Martha Stewart was not the mentor I imagined she would be. I remember after one of the challenges, I made a random comment about how I was so embarrassed, I wanted to cry. I remember just what she said: "Cry and you are out of here. Women in business don't cry." To me, this represents one of our greatest differences. I say to Martha: I am in big business, and I cry all the time. I don't think it's hurt me one bit.

As women, we need to do things our own way, and our emotions are part of who we are.

Most of the other contestants didn't think I would go all the way because I was abrasive and inappropriate half the time. I might have acted like a goofball, but I was being myself. I was also determined to win, so I wasn't going to let myself get waylaid or sidetracked or distracted by what other people were doing. I was going for mine.

The Finale

Losing is the price we pay for living. It is also the source of much of our growth and gain.

—Judith Viorst, author

I went the distance. The very last task was to host a party that would raise money for charity. Our team had to put on a circus. After my success as the accountant on the Buick showroom project, I became focused on the money and obsessed about our team raising enough of it. The other team put on a good party, but we raised significantly more money than they did, and our party was a great success—in fact, most people who watched the show said it was the clear winner. All my crazy compulsiveness felt worth it. We won the challenge, and I thought I was a shoe-in to win the entire competition, which was supposedly based on that final challenge.

As the show neared its conclusion, my ex-boyfriend Larry, who was still a good friend, sent me two packages. One included a card that said, "If you win," and the other included a card that said, "If you lose." I wanted so badly to be able to open the package with the "If you win" card!

On the other hand, I was already having some doubts. The show wasn't getting very good ratings, and Martha had disassociated herself from it midseason. She was very clearly unhappy to be part of the show, and had even been quoted in the press, as the finale neared, as saying, "We're getting close to which of those inappropriate contestants we are actually going to have to hire." At first, she had said she would handpick the winner, but she didn't really seem interested in the show at all anymore. I was no longer sure I wanted the job, even though I could have really used that $250,000 employment contract and new car.

I actually considered respectfully declining the job on live television if I won. I thought about it for a long time, and tried to see the big picture. I realized, though, that if I were to do this, it might be a big scandal when it happened and immediately afterward, but it would have lasted for about a minute. The brouhaha would soon be forgotten and wouldn't do anything to help my career. I also decided it would be disrespectful, no matter how I did it. Even if I didn't want to work for Martha, turning down the job would not have been a strategic big-picture move. It wouldn't have been worth the consequences.

But when Martha announced the winner . . . it wasn't me after all.

I was the runner-up. I'll never know what really happened behind closed doors as Martha and the producers picked the winner, although there was a lot of speculation about that in the press. All

I knew was that I was very disappointed, even though I was also a little bit relieved. Even if I really didn't want to work for Martha, I hate to lose.

I was also hurt because Martha dismissed me in such an unkind way. As I recall, her exact words were, "Bethenny, you're spunky, you're a show-off, and you feel the need to make a physical impression, which is really not entirely necessary here." That definitely hurt my feelings, and I felt it was an unfair summary of my efforts on the show, but I controlled myself. I was gracious. I congratulated the winner, blah blah blah.

I have to give props to Donald Trump, however. At the end of *The Apprentice,* he is generous and congratulatory, he tells each person what a great job they did, he always says it was hard to choose a winner, and he makes everyone feel as if they gave up months of their lives for *something,* even if they didn't win. They feel appreciated and elevated. It wasn't like that on this show. Martha wasn't nice, and I felt as if I'd given up those months for no appreciation in return.

When I got home, I opened both packages from Larry. The one that said "If you lose" had a check for $15,000 (thank God, because I was broke—he understood how badly I had needed to win, financially) and a funny note about how Martha obviously didn't know what she was doing. The one that said "If you win" contained a sweet congratulatory letter about how I deserved all this and more, and a pretty cashmere hoodie sweater.

I didn't win . . . but Larry let me keep the sweater.

And I was proud of myself. I endured a lot, I learned a lot, and I gave it everything. I really went for it. And it didn't take me long to step back and realize how relieved I was that I did *not* have to go on to work for Martha Stewart.

In the end, coming in second was the greatest gift I could have received. Second place opened so many doors for me. What seemed like an abysmal failure in the moment actually turned out to be a success. If I had won and been Martha's assistant, we would have clashed and I probably would have faded away into oblivion. Or, she would have ignored me completely and I would be out as soon as my "prize" contract was over, which is in effect what happened with the winner.

But I still think you always have to fight for first.

Do each thing you do to the best of your ability. Be passionate and committed, and *go for yours*. It's the only way to get your life moving. It's how I popped out of obscurity and into the life I wanted.

Truthfully, I thought the show would be big for my career, but nobody really cared that I was on it, ultimately. However, the real pay-off was in the reality TV experience I gained on the show, and what I learned I could do when I want something enough. I found a new direction that changed my life—and I found out I could be the best, or pretty damn close.

I once read a quote in a book called *Competition*, that said, "Your opponent, in the end, is never really the player on the other side of the net, or the swimmer in the next lane, or the team on the other side of the field, or even the bar you must high-jump. Your opponent is yourself, your negative internal voices, your level of determination."

That's exactly right. You have to stay in your lane. If you keep looking to the left and to the right to see what everyone else is doing, you slow down and lose your momentum. In any kind of competition, if you keep your mind on you and not on anybody else, you stay focused and efficient. It's a psychological game and you can psych yourself out if you make it all about the other. It's all about you.

I wasn't cast on the original *Apprentice* because I was fighting myself. Once I became centered and focused and figured out how to go for mine, my opponents were nothing. I do owe Martha a debt of gratitude. I don't know how she would feel about the fact that she helped me to get where I am, but that is certainly the case. Because of that show, I learned how to be on television. I learned that I could take a lot of stress and still thrive. I learned a hell of a lot about how to run a business. I learned that when I really go for what I want, I win . . . even when I lose. And I learned what kind of business woman I really wanted to be—not the heir to someone else's great empire after all, but a businesswoman on my own terms, and of my own making.

Rule 7

· · · · · · · · · · · ·

Separate from the Pack
My Life as a "Housewife"

In order to be irreplaceable, one must always be different.

—Coco Chanel, French fashion designer

When you put everything on the line, it's exhilarating, and sometimes it's disappointing, but it's always an adventure. And then what? You go back to your old life?

Never! Every step as well as every leap along the road to your success should change you because you're in a different place than you were one step before. And each step is a decision, and matters for your future. Whether you win or lose, when you follow the first six rules, you are *moving*. You are active, engaged, and making your life happen, instead of waiting for your life to happen *to* you.

Now what?

The more you evolve in your life, the more you will begin to realize that your own sense of control over your destiny isn't an accident. You are who you are because of you, not because of anyone else. Others may influence you, but now I'd like you to think about how much you might want to consider limiting that influence.

You are your own person, you are unique, and although you may or may not feel like you "fit in" all the time, you know when you look inside yourself that you aren't like anyone else. What separates you from the crowd might be your looks, your beliefs, your heritage, your opinions, or you might not even know what exactly it is.

Now is the time to be proud of it. Now is the time to embrace rule #7: *Separate from the pack.*

When I was a child, I wanted more than anything to be named Jennifer because I thought it was a "normal" name. Now I'm so glad I have a more unusual name, and the unusual personality to go with it. My unique qualities may have made my life difficult at times in the past, but they have always made my life my own. They are what distinguish me and give me confidence. Your unique qualities distinguish you, too—are you taking advantage of that?

If you are wasting time and energy trying to be as much like everyone else as you can, you are throwing away something precious: your individuality. When you embrace your difference, your DNA, your look or heritage or religion or your unusual name, that's when you start to shine.

Your mother should have told you when you were a child that you were something amazing and wonderful (and shame on her if she didn't) and you can and should tell your own children how amazing and wonderful *they* are. Your friends know it's true, and you should be the first one, not the last one, to recognize and celebrate what makes you different from every other person on the planet.

Your individuality is your strength. The qualities about you that are common will help you blend in when you don't want to call attention to yourself. However, what makes you *you* will help you rise up and be different and stand out from the crowd.

Separating from the Pack

It takes courage to grow up and become who you really are.

—e. e. cummings, poet

Standing out is hard. Sometimes it's even painful. Something about people makes them want to fit in, and punish those who don't. It starts in childhood. The kid who is different gets left out of the group, or bullied. As a young child, being different is isolating, and as a teenager it's humiliating.

I wish I had been able to stand out with more confidence when I was a child, and especially when I was a teenager. I was different, but it wasn't always a conscious choice, and it often made me miserable.

But I'm all grown up now, and so are you. Today, difference is your strength, your power, and your trademark. It's your signature. It can still be difficult to be different—sometimes even harder than it used to be. Even so, it's time to embrace being yourself. It's time to be authentic. You have no more excuses *not* to explore the many ways that being exactly who you are really can be your biggest asset. It's time to see the beauty in your difference.

If you are deeply entrenched in a group, it can be hard to see what your personal strengths and weaknesses are, and when you move with a group all the time, you can't always see where your next steps should be. How will you know what your path is, if you've never struck out on your own? How do you see where you are going from the middle of a crowd?

This is why anyone who wants to live a fulfilling life has to, at some point, in some way, practice rule #7. Separating from the pack isn't about being different just for the sake of being different, outrageous, or controversial. Establishing your value and place as an individual isn't about getting attention just for the sake of attention.

Instead, I want to see you be exactly who you are, in spite of what everybody else expects.

Don't be afraid to stand apart when doing so distinguishes you. You still have to be practicing the other rules up to this point— finding your truth and acting on it and going for yours—but when those things necessitate the refusal to blend in, that's a good thing. Your differences are exactly the things you want to underline, not hide. In times like these, many companies want people who stand out, who have their own ideas and their own style. It's the twenty- first century. Difference is chic, difference is powerful, difference is your edge. Difference is also sexy and attractive to others. Who wants to hire or date or hang out with someone boring and forget- table? Be yourself, because I can guarantee that the *real you* is nei- ther boring nor forgettable, and there is nobody else quite like you.

But it's not just a matter of throwing up your hands and saying, "Okay, I'll disregard what everyone thinks. Forget societal pressure, I'll just do whatever I want." When I was in my twenties and mar- ried to Peter, and then later when I was engaged to Jimmy, I felt enormous pressure to be at the same place my peers were, not to rock the boat. None of my friends were divorced. Divorce was enor- mous, and breaking an engagement was a scandal. In both those situations, if I had known other people who were getting divorced or ending an engagement, I might have been able to do it sooner. It definitely would have been less painful for all involved. I would have had more of a context to understand what I was going through. Difference was painful.

I felt like a lone wolf who wrecked everybody's plans and dashed their expectations. I felt I was doing something wrong, because I wasn't doing what was expected of me. Maybe I was doing some- thing wrong in some ways (although in many ways, I was doing something right), but believe me when I tell you that what is ex- pected of you has nothing to do with the rightness or wrongness of a decision.

When you focus on what other people think, or what your family or your social network or your society expects of you, the idea of separating from the pack seems terrifying. Over time, however, those voices fade away and are replaced by new ones. In a few years you won't remember the pain, but if you act contrary to your sense of integrity, if you go along with the crowd against your own inclinations because it's easier, I can *guarantee* that compromise or pain won't fade away. You'll be married to the wrong person, living in the wrong city, working at the wrong job, or ponying up to the bar to forget about the fact that you hate your life because it's just a giant compromise—a deal struck out of fear. And if you already feel like you are going along with a life that doesn't make you happy or proud, you may need to act on finding your truth in other ways—through friendships or your work or parenting. There are always ways to express your unique nature.

Going against the status quo isn't always about major life decisions—it's not always that dramatic. You can exercise your individuality all the time, so when it really counts, you'll be more comfortable in your own skin. I have social acquaintances who only go to the same places in Manhattan that everyone else goes. Wherever your hometown is, you probably know which places are in or hip or cool. I like to go to those places sometimes, and work takes me to a lot of them, but some of the best and most interesting places aren't on that A-list. Jason and I love to research new, little restaurants where "nobody" goes. We even make an effort to order things we've never tried, just for something different. It's more fun because we have no one to impress and we get to experience something out of the ordinary. That's what I'm looking for. There's a lot to discover off the beaten path. It's just one more way to practice being unique.

Image Noise

The image is one thing and the human being is another. It's very hard to live up to an image, put it that way.

—Elvis Presley, legendary musician

Of course, every rule has its noise, and this one is no exception. There is a specific kind of noise that can get in your way and make it extremely difficult to *separate from the pack:* it's *image noise,* that terrifying static that fills your brain when you don't fit in with any of the cliques in high school and you feel desperately alone. At the same time, it's that pointless rebellion that led you to be different just for the sake of shunning others in the first place. Whether you were a freak or a geek or totally chic, image noise leads you to act in ways that are not motivated by who you truly are. Instead, you act in anticipation of the reaction from others. You are concerned about your image, rather than yourself. You forget that your image is *not you.* This is not the path you want to take, trust me.

No one is immune to image noise. Think about celebrities like Elvis or Michael Jackson, or even Lindsay Lohan and Britney Spears. Think about the terrible pressure to be who society decided each of those people were or are. People crack under that pressure. They turn to drugs and other destructive behavior, just to escape the image noise that has taken over their lives.

The real Elvis, the real Michael Jackson, the real person behind any celebrity is surely much different than the image society constructs, but nobody has to believe in anyone else's notion of who they are. Instead, they can separate from the pack. Think of the actor typecast as a comedian who gets paid $20 million to do a blockbuster comedy movie, then goes off to do theater for no pay at all, just because he really wants to do it. That's an example of thwarting image noise.

Image noise can manifest in other ways, too. It can keep you quiet and out of sight, never drawing any attention to yourself, just because it's easier or safer or because you are afraid of anyone challenging you or bothering you. If everyone thinks you are uninteresting, they'll leave you alone—and after a while, even you come to believe you are uninteresting. The fact is that sometimes being different is just plain annoying. Maybe you are constantly explaining yourself or having to take an extra step in certain situations just because you don't look or sound like what people expected. It's understandable to want a break from that.

Image noise can also convince you that you really are better than everyone else, just because the world believes it. (Or you think they do—or they do today, but tomorrow, who knows?) Think of the celebrities who act like divas, like the world owes them a living, like they are entitled to special treatment. Some of them take themselves so seriously—they have become completely fooled by image noise, thinking their popular image is the same as who they are. Don't do it. Don't drink your own Kool-Aid. It's a hard road back from that place. Nobody is worthless, but nobody is better than everyone else, either. We're all just people. Image noise can convince you to forget that. Image noise lies.

The existence of image noise isn't really so surprising. People encourage it all the time. We all tend to gravitate toward people who are like us and do the things we do. It's human nature. However, sometimes the right thing to do is to exceed your nature. I think it's a real virtue, not just to be yourself despite how everyone else acts, but to appreciate and be kind to people who are not like you. Teach this to your children, too, and the world will start to become a better place. What do you lose when you don't speak up on behalf of someone else, or even on behalf of yourself? What do you compromise? Maybe it's just a group at a dinner table saying something you find offensive or prejudiced or mean. To separate from the pack is to say something about it.

In other words, image noise keeps you lost in the crowd. You might rise through the ranks on a tide of popular opinion, but you'll never be one of those few who really reaches the top of her game by taking a step forward and saying, "I'm like *this*, even if you are not." You have to feel comfortable in your own skin to do it, but that's what the first few rules are about. Now you know who you are, so step up and be that person, despite the crowd, and foster that same courage in your children. Think of people from Lady Gaga to Madonna, from Gandhi to Martin Luther King, who were always themselves, who never blended in, and who built whole careers out of their ability to separate from the pack.

Maybe I sound like your mother talking, but your real friends will love you for who you are, not your ability to mimic them. Being brave enough to be yourself, whether you blend in or not, is the best way to separate the people who matter from the people who won't be important in your life. (Can you tell I'm practicing this speech for when Bryn gets older? Because teenage girls are the *worst,* and I remember what it was like to feel different and alone as a kid and victimized by the other girls in my class.)

I'm not perfect—I still have some image noise. I still gossip and I wish I didn't. But the older I get, and especially as a mother, I've gained perspective and try to keep my eye on this rule and adhere to it. My daughter will be watching me as she gets older, for cues on how to act. I can see now more than ever how important it is to be compassionate and kind to people. In a way, it's also easy *not* to laugh, *not* to make fun, just to choose not to participate in what the crowd is doing. Sometimes, separating from the pack means simply not doing anything at all—abstaining from the behavior you don't condone. *Not* chiming in with the snarky comment (easier for me to say than do, I'm still working on this!). Not being bothered by the snarky comments from others.

The bottom line is, if you want to live your life making other people happy, you're likely to lose touch with what makes you happy. At some point, or at many points during your life, you may be faced with a choice. You may have to decide: Do I go with the crowd, or do I separate from the pack, to be myself? Rule #7 helps you to keep from getting lost in the crowd. I hope I can inspire you to see this, so you can stand up for who you really are, but not just for the sake of being different—but for the sake of being yourself.

· ·

SEPARATING FROM THE PACK IN YOGA CLASS

Most yoga classes end with a pose called *savasana,* where everyone lies on the floor and completely relaxes after the strenuous workout. When I go to yoga class, sometimes I'll start my *savasana* early. When I can tell that I've had enough and I need to rest, I'll just lie down on my mat, even though the class is still going. I used to feel a tiny bit self-conscious, lying there as everyone else is still doing poses. People might think it's strange, but it's my journey and my yoga practice. I don't let what the rest of the class is doing influence what I know I need to do for me.

· ·

"Manhattan Moms"

Always be a first-rate version of yourself, instead of a second-rate version of somebody else.

—*Judy Garland, actress*

Rule #7 was the key rule I practiced at this next critical juncture in my life. *The Apprentice: Martha Stewart* aired in the fall of 2005. My experience taping the show was over, but the world was just getting to see it for the first time. It was a strange moment for me—I was done, but there I was on television, and it became very clear that I was standing out from the group. In fact, some said that was the reason I didn't win the show—I didn't blend in with Martha's empire. I wasn't a Martha clone, that's for sure. Now I see it as fitting that, while Donald Trump told people they were fired on his show, Martha's words were: "You don't fit in."

Now, however, I was floating. I hadn't won the competition, but I had recognized that perhaps I could leverage the show's exposure to help nudge my career in a good direction. I was beginning to understand that there was a potentially new path to the career I wanted. I wanted to take the lemons and make lemonade, but I wasn't completely sure how to do it. I was open to what would happen next, and it was very clear to me that being myself would have to be a crucial part of the next step in my journey.

As I recovered from the whirlwind of my first reality show, I got by on hustling. I still had money noise and I still wasn't financially secure, so I often sold things on a kind of ad hoc basis when I could, like selling one of my expensive purses when I needed some fast cash. BethennyBakes continued to limp along, never quite paying the bills. Occasionally, I cooked for celebrities in their homes or on location, or I catered small events to build my reputation as a natural foods chef, and I had a healthy meal delivery service.

But I was a different person than I had been before. I was coming into my own. My experience on *Martha Stewart* had matured me, and although the show wasn't a success, I was trying to make it into something. I wasn't famous by any means, but my name and face were out there.

About a year later, I was dating Kevin, my celebrity photographer boyfriend, so there were opportunities to brush elbows with celebrities and influential people, and I used that to try to rescue BethennyBakes and to get other jobs. I cooked for Denis Leary in his trailer on the set of *Rescue Me,* which paid pretty well, although I still wasn't making enough to pay the bills. I did my best to get in front of the public to see what else might happen, and Kevin helped with that, too. I felt it was my time to shine, and I began to recognize how important it was to network, meet people, pass out my card, and get my name and face out there.

Because you just never know what might happen.

I had also started writing my first book, because I had a message I really wanted to share. I put a lot of irons in the fire, and I waited to see which one would ignite.

Little by little over the next couple of years, I raised my profile and I finally managed to get a publicist. Slowly but surely, as I kept making connections and getting out there and being seen and talking to people, I started to get small "hits"—placements in the media here and there. I made an appearance on the *Today Show*, I scored a small column in *Health* magazine, and there was a great story in *Life & Style* magazine about me.

Then my publicist got me a great gig: an offer to be a spokesperson for Pepperidge Farm! This job felt like everything to me. I was going to create recipes for and promote their crackers, crisps, and pretzels. Acceptance from a national brand like Pepperidge Farm was a huge step forward, and it was perfectly in line with the career I was trying to create. Despite all the stupid mistakes I'd made before, I felt as if my career was about to take off.

If you've ever surfed, you know the feeling as wave after wave passes you by and you just don't seem to be able to catch the right one. Then all of a sudden, you feel a swell under you and you know a good one is coming, that it's *your wave*. You have a gut feeling that it's going to work this time, even if you haven't caught a single wave yet. You're going to stand up on the board and ride that little wave. It feels like the beginning of something. You're learning to surf, and when the big wave comes, you'll be ready. I was feeling like that. I could feel the momentum gathering beneath me. It was happening. I felt I had a shot at something greater.

Then, in 2007, I went to Polo in the Hamptons on a sunny Saturday, and everything changed forever.

By this time, Kevin and I had parted ways and I was dating the first Jason.

That day, I really didn't feel like networking. It was hot outside, I had a headache, and I just couldn't muster the energy. Jason #1 pushed me to go. Jill Zarin had been an acquaintance I sometimes saw at premieres and other events. She was always a connector of people. When I arrived, she saw me and called out, in her usual way, in that Jill Zarin voice: "Hey *Skinny!* How did you get into the VIP area? Come over and *taaawk* to me!"

She told us that she was going to be on a new TV show for the Bravo network, and it was going to be called *Manhattan Moms*. She seemed very excited about it. Then she got distracted and went off to talk with someone else. Her husband, Bobby, brought the producers over to meet me, and I didn't really know who they were or what the show was about, but they told me that they were short one cast member and needed someone right away. The producers, who had come to Polo specifically to find a fifth cast member, wanted someone married, someone who was a mom—a *Manhattan Mom*.

Someone who clearly was not me.

I wasn't married. I wasn't even close to being engaged, let alone having children. My boyfriend had three children, but he didn't want to have any more. As if that all wasn't enough, the producers also wanted an unknown. I'd been on *Martha Stewart Apprentice* and even if I wasn't a household name, my name was out there and I already had a TV profile.

And yet, for some reason, they seemed interested in me. I talked to them for a while, and one Bravo exec knew me from *Apprentice* and already liked me. She started pushing Bravo to get me on the show. Soon enough, the other producers liked me, too. This is one of many instances in my life that has convinced me that fate really does exist. I didn't run in the same circles as any of the women on that show, and if I hadn't gone to Polo that day, I probably never would have heard anything about the show and then I probably wouldn't be where I am today. It was fate.

They asked if they could tape me for a sort of unofficial screen test. For some reason, I was very relaxed when we did this. I was chill. It felt like a new me in some ways—I wasn't sure if I was even interested, so I was calm and cool and I kept it all in perspective.

Then they asked me officially: Would I join the cast of *Manhattan Moms*?

I said no at first. In some ways, the whole idea seemed ridiculous, just because I wasn't a Manhattan Mom. Jason #1 was completely against it, and I understood why. When he met the other women who were cast alongside me on the show, his gut reaction was: *no way*. He thought they were all crazy and he couldn't imagine I would want to get mixed up in that group. He thought it was a bad idea, and honestly, it was—or could have been. It was a big risk.

But I also thought: What if I could turn it into a good idea?

We talked about it a lot. Would I look ridiculous? Would I ruin all the hard work I'd been putting into my career for the last few years? Would *Health* magazine and Pepperidge Farm drop me? He made many sensible arguments.

In fact, almost everyone in my life was against it, and intellectually, I agreed. A part of me could not deny that it was probably a bad career move. The show would be a train wreck, and I'd crash and burn right along with it because I'd be a passenger on that train.

And yet . . .

That evening, I didn't tell anyone, but I just *had this feeling*. It's a feeling I've learned to pay attention to because it always signals something big. It was a warm, excited feeling, scary like a roller coaster—risky and emotional. This was a moment in time that I knew I'd remember—it was a strong feeling of being present in the moment, instinctual, like when the hairs on your arms stand up and all your senses go on high alert. Something was *happening*.

Secretly, I was thinking that maybe I ought to say yes.

A few months into filming, during which I still kept saying no, I was sitting in an airport and I thought, You know what? It's not that easy to get on television, especially on a respected network like Bravo.

I reasoned the opportunity out. I thought about how outlandish the other cast members seemed, and I knew this was a high-risk but high-reward situation. I had the most to lose, as a struggling young businesswoman. The other women were already doing what they were doing and I didn't imagine their image on the show would impact that to any great degree. I was still trying to succeed at something. I could still be ruined, and I was the only one without a husband to support me if it all went to hell.

On the other hand, what if I could make something out of this weird new show? The payoff could be huge, if I did it the right way. What if *Manhattan Moms* was my next golden ticket? If I could capitalize on the experience and make it part of my business, maybe it would raise my profile to a more national level. Maybe it would start a chain reaction of good things in my life. Did I want to miss that? Should I roll the dice?

If the show was a total failure, I thought, then nobody would really watch it or know about it and it would go away. If it was a total success, and I managed to be myself and put it all out there, then maybe the show could bring me success, too. Maybe I didn't need to worry about my image so much. I began to see that part of what was holding me back was actually image noise—I didn't want to be associated with the preconceived notions people would have about someone on a show like that.

But what if I could just be myself?

It would be obvious to viewers that I wasn't really a "Manhattan Mom," and I wouldn't pretend to be one. I would just be me. If the producers really wanted me on the show, then surely they must want *me*, not me pretending to be something else. I was an unpretentious, self-deprecating single girl among rich housewives, trying to make it work in the Big Apple. I believe they invited me on the show to be the question-mark character, the one whose story hadn't yet unfolded. I could do that. It was true—my story *hadn't* unfolded.

I considered the big picture, the upside and the downside. I thought about who I was and whether I could do this. And I decided to say yes.

Besides marrying Jason, having Bryn, and writing *Naturally Thin*, it was the best decision I ever made.

. . . .

FROM MY IN-BOX
✎

This email comes from my trusted agent and confidant, Brian Dow:

"People sometimes sneer at the fact that a lot of my clients are on reality television, and many of them started out as underdogs. They've laughed that I represent people like Kim Kardashian and Kendra Wilkinson, but my reality show clients have appeared in multiple television series, including their own self-titled series with record-breaking ratings. They've become producers of other television series, appeared in features films, written New York Times *bestselling books, developed successful product lines, and built themselves into true brands—a lot of actors never make it that far.*

"In my career, I've always taken big risks. I don't believe in fate or luck. I believe your reality is what you make it and you have to make things happen for yourself. I don't worry about what other people are doing. I concentrate on what I'm doing, and I think that's why I've been successful as an agent. Bethenny and I are a lot alike in that way. When we achieve something, we don't stop going. We both keep looking to the future to see what we can achieve next.

"I'm lucky to be doing something I'm truly passionate about. I think when you find that thing, that's where you get the energy and the drive to take it all the way. I also believe you have to trust your gut. If I decide to do something, I'll make it happen, even if I'm not completely sure how. It's another trait Bethenny and I have in

common, and one of the reasons why she chose me to be her agent. We work well together.

"Bethenny, we knew it could happen, we lived as though it would happen, and therefore we made it happen—that's been our place of yes."

—Brian Dow, Branded Lifestyle department head,
APA Talent and Literary Agency

. . . .

The Real Housewives of New York City

Be your authentic self. Your authentic self is who you are when you have no fear of judgment, or before the world starts pushing you around and telling you who you're supposed to be.

—Dr. Phil, television personality and psychologist

So there I was, a cast member on a show that was now to be called *The Real Housewives of New York City,* the second installment in the franchise following *The Real Housewives of Orange County.* I still wasn't a housewife, or even close to married, but I was part of the cast. I joined the filming, already in progress, and I vowed to stay true to myself, my business, and my nature—I wouldn't be mistaken for a rich bored housewife, I wouldn't be someone I'm not. I wouldn't get sucked in to the drama, ha-ha.

That last one is easier said than done, of course.

But I was a tree with fruit ready to be picked. I had written my book and struck a two-book deal with one of the big publishing companies. My branding was established, and I was working with a business partner to put the finishing touches on my Skinnygirl cocktail. I would create an opportunity out of this show—that was my first priority. During season one, in the midst of all the drama, while the other Housewives were worrying about wardrobe, makeup, hair, and shopping, I was building my business foundation. As the seasons progressed, I was on a mission, writing books and launching the Skinnygirl brand.

I was so determined to stay in my own lane and do what I needed to do, that I didn't get distracted by what the other housewives were doing. By staying focused and true to my own goals in this way, instead of latching on to the goals of the other housewives or even of the network, I was able to put a kind of jujitsu move on *Real Housewives* and redirect the energy into something that would truly work for me.

Everything is what you make of it, and what I see as blue, someone else might see as black. What some might see as a train wreck, I decided to see as the fast track. One person might be on a show to get famous. Another might decide to build a business. I needed a bigger reason than fame, and I found one: I found a way to create a career that means everything to me, that gives me the opportunity to share my life with others and help them find solutions to the problems we all face.

At the same time, as we began filming season one, I still struggled with image noise. Even though I wasn't a real housewife at all, I was still embarrassed to be a "Real Housewife." What other women took pride in and put forward was the glitz and the materialism—the *stuff*. That's what Bravo wanted for that show—people who could drop thousands of dollars on a handbag or a pair of shoes without giving it a second thought. I had experienced the glitz via rich boyfriends—the trips, the boats, the planes, the luxury—but it had never been my own. Now I was at a place in my life where I only wanted what was really my own—what I had built or earned for myself. I never acted rich. I never claimed to be happy about being single. I lived within my means. I wasn't a Housewife in so many ways.

Here's the thing about image noise—sometimes it can seem

pretty valid. A lot of people *did* assume I was just another rich socialite, simply because I was on the show. I remember seeing articles in the press about it—"rich socialite Bethenny Frankel," etc.—even though that couldn't have been further from the truth. I hated that—I am not someone who aspires to be any kind of socialite. When I first began filming *Real Housewives,* I had $8,000 to my name. I couldn't pay my rent, I only shopped on eBay, and glitz and glam just weren't my world. I didn't spend my day getting facials and buying diamonds and lingerie (and by the way, I still don't). I wasn't living in a big house or on a boat or flying around in my private plane. Don't get me wrong, I love diamonds, and there have been times in my life when I identified myself with my possessions, especially during my most unhappy times. But by the time I got onto the show, that wasn't me anymore.

I was a single girl in Manhattan, living in a one-bedroom apartment on the East Side and trying to make something out of my life. During our tapings of the episodes, I really began to separate from the pack in a productive way. Because of my conscious decision not to get sucked into the "way" of the Housewives, and to be sure I maintained my integrity by not adapting my style to fit theirs, I was free to be exactly who I am. I thought about how, on *The Apprentice: Martha Stewart,* fellow competitors had believed it was better to stay under the radar and be as much like Martha as they could, thinking she would hire them if they were her mirror image. I didn't do that then, and I wasn't going to do it on *Housewives.* I had to be myself, even though I was everything the Housewives weren't. That distinction was exactly the advantage I needed, and why I think I ended up being perceived by viewers as someone more relatable to than the other housewives, or at least, that's what people have told me. Eventually, Andy Cohen would call me the Greek chorus of the show.

I've never been the best one at holding my tongue, and if I had something to say, I said it; if I had an opinion about something, I expressed it. Sometimes this got me in trouble, but if someone called me out on something true, I was also equally willing to take my licks in front of people in living rooms across the country, and I never tried to hide my mistakes.

Being myself on camera was (and still is) actually kind of terrifying. During season one, at Alex's surprise birthday party on the boat, I drank several margaritas—it was a lot of tequila. Mind you, I've got a two-drink rule and my advice is to never have more than that, but there I was, boozing it up after my big breakup with Jason #1.

When I got home that night, I was panicked—I'm a natural foods chef, and I was drinking, *on television*. How stupid was that? I wanted to be honest, but was I taking it too far? Shouldn't I at least pretend to have a little more self-control than that?

But the next day, a friend said to me, "Just own it." She was right, because guess what? I *am* a natural foods chef, and I *was* drinking too many margaritas. It was the truth. In my book *Naturally Thin*, I talk about how life is not "cookie-cutter," and every day is different. That was *that* day. It was a bad day. (Although those margaritas did help.) But it was reality, so I wasn't going to pretend it was something else. We all have those days, and that episode was a game-changer for me.

After that episode, I had a flood of communication from viewers. They related. They knew exactly what I was going through. Suddenly I realized that if I showed it all, flaws and mistakes and the black circles under my eyes when I can't sleep, I could be doing a real service to people. They wanted to see that someone on that show was like them. They wanted to understand, and I had a rare opportunity to reach out of that television and give people a hand by saying, "Hey, I'm not perfect, look at what I did now! But I can move on from this." I am who I am. And here's a news flash: I'm no stranger to tequila.

The other seminal episode was the one when I asked Jason #1 about moving in together. That episode was actually a life-changer for me. During the episode, he refused to talk about it on camera. I kept trying to get a commitment out of him, but on camera, he just kept saying, "We'll talk about it later."

That night, I was so embarrassed. I felt I must have looked desperate. Humiliating! It felt like when someone breaks up with you, but you want everyone to think *you* were the one who broke up with *him*. And yet, after that episode, I got this amazing outpouring of sympathy and, in particular, other women (and even a few men) saying they knew what that's like, to be embarrassed like that, to make yourself vulnerable and exposed and have it thrown in your face. We've all been through it, and a light went on after that—I realized that being vulnerable and exposed on television, having things thrown in my face like that, could actually be something very important and empowering, something the viewers could really use in their lives. It truly was the beginning of a new stage in my life, a stage in which I committed to honesty in front of the camera, no matter what. I would be myself, and fess up to whatever I did or said, because other people would see it and say, "I'm not alone!"

Here's another funny little story about not caring what people think. I'm not a big spender. In fact, I can be kind of a penny pincher, probably because of my years of having to watch every penny. This wasn't on the show, but during this same time, I was in Los Angeles in a cheap store, and I saw a dress I loved. It looked like an expensive Hervé Léger dress, and it was Fashion Week, and I had been invited to a low-key fashion event party for a new designer, so I thought I would wear this dress. As I was getting ready, I giggled to think what my castmates would have said to me about wearing a cheap knockoff out in public. But to me, it didn't matter that it was a knockoff. I can't resist a great deal on a cute dress. Once I was out, someone invited me to the launch of a fashion stylist's TV show premiere party. It was full of celebrities, including fashion celebrities like Diane von Furstenberg and Kate Hudson. Did I run back to my hotel in shame? What do you think?

That's right, I had the balls to walk into that party in my knockoff Leger dress. I owned it, loud and proud. People were saying (in that L.A. way) "Darling, you look *amazing!*" When a reporter asked who I was wearing, I said, with a straight face, "*Faux-ger.*" Little did I realize, I was wearing an exact replica of a Leger dress that Posh Spice wore a few years before. I ended up in a magazine next to a picture of her, in one of those "Who wore it better" polls. And I won! Hilarious. (Never one to miss an opportunity, I had my assistant at the time, Molly, call up the store, find out every location that had the dress, and buy them all. I put them on eBay and we made $4,000—I gave Molly $500 of it.)

So that was me, season one.

. . . .

"ACTING" ON REALITY TV

Being myself has been such a different experience than acting was for me. It feels authentic in a way that acting never did. Playing someone else and reciting lines memorized from a script wasn't me at the time. I didn't know myself well enough to play someone else. However, my training helped me not to be nervous or stilted on camera and during interviews and appearances, and it also helped me to be better able to access who I really am. All that experience in L.A. has paid off, but I'm simply more comfortable as Bethenny Frankel than as anyone else.

For a lot of people, being on a reality show means acting over-the-top. People like to speculate about whether people on reality TV are actually "acting." When I was on Regis and Kelly's show recently, Regis insisted that reality shows must be scripted, that we are all acting. I can't speak for other shows, but on the shows I've been on, there is no script, and though we are usually aware of the cameras and some people may act to the camera a little in order to appear a certain way, on reality TV, you really are yourself. There are plenty of moments when everybody forgets the cameras are rolling and gets taken over by emotion, or a little too much tequila or pinot grigio. Real personalities always come out eventually.

•••

Seasons Two and Three

If the career you have chosen has some unexpected inconvenience, console yourself by reflecting that no career is without them.

—Jane Fonda, actress

After season one, when the show was a huge hit and I was suddenly launched into the spotlight, I realized my life really had changed. I was operating in a whole new sphere, and I had to get used to it fast. But this transformation also called for some adjustments. Separating from the pack had the effect of getting me in the press a lot, and not always for the reasons I would have liked. Some people say there is no bad press. I must respectfully and wholeheartedly disagree with that.

It was time for some soul-searching at this point. I'd spent the previous few years trying to get any press exposure at all, but the more press I got, the more I realized that I wanted press for good reasons, not for ridiculous ones. I wanted press when I had something to say or something to sell. Otherwise, I was afraid the potentially endless snark was going to drag me down. I didn't want the idiotic kind of publicity that's just about celebrity spotting. I realized that being in a magazine just because you showed your ass or said something mean about somebody isn't helpful or positive or coming from a place of yes. Who cares where I had dinner or who I fought with or whether I was or wasn't invited to a party? I didn't want that anymore.

I had to learn how to reach what I felt was my true audience: YOU. People who struggle to find a balance in their lives, with issues like mine, for whom I can provide practical solutions. So I had to make some changes. I had to start being more selective.

Taking it to the next level always requires a shift, if you're going to start actually living at that next level. I also required an infusion of fresh confidence. Going into season two, I felt my career and my brand evolving, and I felt like I was really crafting my career. When I negotiated season two with the network, I recognized that the show was hot and we were all in a good position. At times like these, you have to know your worth and take advantage of the high points.

This was the I-am-woman-hear-me-roar season. I was alone, no boyfriend, no prospect of ever becoming an actual housewife, and I was okay with that. I had so much else going for me that I no longer felt I needed a man to be comfortable in my own skin. I could see the future: I could see success.

During this season, I was able to forge a strong relationship with the Bravo network. I stayed sane. I kept my head. Nobody ever had to escort me off an island or off-camera; I was treating the show like a business. Everything was my business. I knew if I could benefit Bravo, they could help me. And they did. They gave me the ultimate compliment: my own show.

Season two rolled along and when season two wrapped, we were still on a high, but when it came time for season three, things had begun to change.

The show was no longer so unique. Now there were *The Real Housewives of Atlanta* and *New Jersey*, with *Washington, D.C.*, and *Beverly Hills* in the queue. Suddenly, I realized we were replaceable. We were like jelly beans in a jar, and the network didn't need us like they needed us individually before. When it came time to talk about season three, I recognized that it was time to be agreeable. Not everybody in the cast understood that—some of them thought they were irreplaceable. Nobody's irreplaceable, never forget that. I recognized that I had to take it easy on the negotiations. It wasn't time to go to the mat, or worry about getting a bunch of perks. It was a time to find the balance and make it work for me. So I made my deal and signed on for season three. It was a business decision.

The emotional aspect of season three was a completely different matter. As season three of *Real Housewives* opened, I was beginning to have serious doubts about continuing. *Housewives* was beginning to feel like an insane roller coaster, lurching forward from the gate for its third run around the track, and I was ready to get off . . . even though I had already agreed to remain and the bar had already come down and there was no turning back. I had that sick, nauseous feeling, like . . . *oh* . . . *no* . . .

So many things were happening that season. I was just beginning to film my own show. I had two successful books under my belt and I was working on this one. Things were finally taking off in my career, and that's when I felt like my castmates turned on me.

I had a feeling there was going to be some animosity regarding my career, and particularly the fact that I had my own show. There was. My show was the elephant in the room—nobody *ever* mentioned it, except for Simon, in an email. Nobody congratulated me. Nobody said anything at all.

It was weird. I could feel the tension all the time. Relationships started to crumble. Season three was the most tense, anxiety-producing, aggressive, insane season yet. There were some truly nasty moments on that show, heartbreaking moments, pack-of-wolves moments of cruelty and betrayal. I had my moments, too—I wasn't always the nicest person, and I wasn't proud of some of the things I said, but when I was angry or indifferent or hurt, I didn't hide it.

Throughout the entire *Housewives* experience, I had to focus on not getting sidetracked by everyone else's drama, but this was never more relevant than in season three. Sometimes, I inadvertently allowed myself to get sucked in when I was carried by my emotions. I did my best to keep coming from a place of yes, but it wasn't enjoyable. In fact, it was miserable, and I didn't hide the fact that it wasn't fun anymore. I didn't pretend that we were "just creating drama for the cameras." It was excruciating, painful, sheer torture, and frankly, scary.

Plus, it was a traumatic year for me in many other ways. So much happened to me that year. My father died, I got engaged, I got pregnant, I had a dangerous blood clot during pregnancy and I was on bed rest, and I was filming my own show. That on top of the mean-spirited and unhealthy nature of season three, and it became too much for me.

Agreeing to do three seasons of *Real Housewives* was a business decision, but deciding not to do season four was a personal decision. I wasn't in that place anymore. But overall, without a shadow of a doubt, being on *Housewives* was one of the best decisions of my life.

Ultimately, however, I decided, along with my husband, that it wasn't a healthy environment for our new family. I got to a place where I no longer wanted to see women being rewarded for bad behavior.

Through my own show, my books, and whatever is coming next, I *will* still be out there, for you, committed to being honest and helping you solve your problems.

People ask me if I'm still friends with anyone on the show, and I do still have relationships with a few of them, but in general, as a whole, that social circle isn't where I am now. I enjoyed it in the beginning, when it was a new adventure, but I've got different things to do now. They have chosen to go on with the show and I haven't. So, we're all going in our own directions. I've realized that as I've increasingly prioritized my family, my social circle has evolved. I think that's natural and normal.

My whole life has been a series of steps, and I'm taking the next one. It's just one more way I'm separating from the pack so I can see where to go next.

But *Housewives* was a great run, and I'm grateful to everyone involved for the experience. I literally laughed and cried and broke up and fell in love and got married and had a baby, all in the company of the Bravo network and *The Real Housewives* franchise.

Sometimes moving on can give you growing pains, but you have to be ready for the moment when you realize it's time to go forward again.

Go Outside Your Comfort Zone

Move out of your comfort zone. You can only grow if you are willing to feel awkward and uncomfortable when you try something new.

—Brian Tracy, author and business consultant

There is one more reason that, despite how much the network wanted me to do it, I said no to season four: I really was ready to start pushing the envelope again. I've always believed that when you operate just a little outside your comfort zone, that's where you grow. *Housewives* had become not just uncomfortable and painful, but too familiar. I was ready for the next thing.

My own show has certainly been a new frontier in that regard, and one of the greatest challenges of my life. However, I've also been pushing myself to try even more different experiences that aren't so easy or comfortable, where I'm not sure what to expect. I think it's healthy. I've appeared a few times on the political show *Hannity,* and I've been on the family game show *Are You Smarter Than a 5th Grader?* and of course there was the ultimate envelope-busting experience, *Skating with the Stars.* All of these, in different ways, were outside my comfort zone, and they helped me grow.

When you operate just outside your comfort zone—whether it's taking on a new responsibility at work, or a whole new job, or saying yes to a date you might not normally have accepted, or signing up for a class you know nothing about—you force yourself to keep firing on all cylinders. You wake up and pay more attention to your life. And you grow. Just push the envelope of your own experience until you feel slight discomfort. That's when you separate from the pack. That's when the magic happens.

I believe that separating from the pack is the reason why my career has been so precisely *my* career. Each person's life unfolds in a unique way, but the best way to let that happen naturally is to take your own path, not anyone else's. It's your career, your health, your relationships, your journey, your blueprint, your *life*, so why should you ever act like anybody else and miss out on what could happen for *you*?

· ·

FROM MY IN-BOX

"Life is too short, and too fun, to not live it to the fullest with optimism and a smile. 'Yes' sounds so much better than 'No,' doesn't it? (And TV isn't exactly brain surgery.)"

—Andy Cohen, senior VP of Programming and
Development for Bravo network and host of Bravo's
reunion shows and weekly *Watch What Happens Live*

· ·

Rule 8

. . . .

Own It

Bethenny Getting Married?

Integrity is telling myself the truth. And honesty is telling the truth to other people.

—Spencer Johnson, business author

This next rule is one of those rules that applies at any stage of life—as much when you're first starting out as when you're at the peak of your success. It's a rule I've always lived by, and it really came to fruition at the next stage in my life. It will be your ally and your greatest defender, no matter what you've done. Rule #8 is your touchstone: *Own it.*

Owning it is about honesty, and copping to what you've done or said—no matter what. Some people say I take it too far. I am the queen of TMI. I sometimes overshare or say inappropriate things in part to entertain people, in part to entertain myself—it's my strange sense of humor. In some way, it makes me feel more real, like I'm really here with my two feet on the ground, running my own show and not under anybody's thumb. It's my way of being myself.

But no matter what I reveal, on my show, in my books, in my

appearances, or anywhere else, I will always follow rule #8. I will never deny something I really said or did.

When you break the chain, take responsibility for your life, find your truth, act on it, have faith that all roads lead to Rome, go for yours with passion and dedication, and separate from the pack, you'll absolutely have to own it. You've set yourself up to live with integrity, and this rule is the key to practicing that integrity.

If you do it, say it, think it—then own it, and you'll never have to scramble to cover your tracks or remember your lies or make up any excuses. Owning it means taking that final step toward fully acknowledging who you really are.

At every stage of my life, I've owned it, and owned it big. Sometimes it stung in the moment, but it was always better in the end. I've never pretended to be somebody else, denied anything I've done, or refused to admit to something I actually said, even when it might have benefited me in the short term to do otherwise. Sometimes, I've even felt as if my life depended on owning it. I live by all the rules in this book, but in many ways, this rule defines me. I've thought a lot about why owning it is so important to me, and I think I know why. It's because of rule #1, breaking the chain.

I told you all about my mother in the beginning of this book, including how, last year, after an article appeared in *People* magazine and I talked about my childhood, my mother came forward and talked to the tabloids, and sold my childhood pictures to the press. I knew she would do this at some point, and, oddly, I understood why. She felt exposed and uncomfortable about what I've said about her, and she wanted to tell her side of the story.

But I never felt like my mother was able to own her own life, and I think that's why I've always been overzealously committed to owning mine.

In writing this book, I never wanted to hurt her or anybody. I wish when this book comes out so she wouldn't have to see it or know about it. However, *my* conflict was that if I can't tell the truth about the past, I can't move on from it. I can't break the chain. Also, I can't help people, or even ask them to live a certain way, unless I can stand up and do it first. I have to tell my story. I have to let you under the hood of my life, so I can lead by example and help other people with their own struggles. I have to do it for myself, for my husband, for my daughter . . . and for *you*. I'm sorry if she's uncomfortable with how I remember my past, but I have to own it, and I can't be responsible for her inability to own what she's done or who she is.

She might be angry with me, or maybe she's not anymore. I don't know. All I know is that I'm not angry with her about the past. I'm deeply hurt by her recent actions, but not surprised. I believe people shouldn't complain or explain. At some point, you have to let it go. Every time I've ever talked to my mother, she's full of negativity. The last time I talked to her, I told her I was breastfeeding, and she said, "I didn't breastfeed you. Maybe *that's* what I did wrong!" Then she told me my husband must be from New York because my accent was horrible. (He's not, by the way.) When it comes to my mother, there is always a dig.

All I can do is stand up for myself and own my own life, and do everything I can to protect my daughter. That's the whole point of rule #8. The truth sets you free, so own it.

This book is about me. And it's about *you*. Maybe I take it too far by wearing my heart (and all my other body parts) on my sleeve, but I do it to defeat my own childhood noise. It's my coping mechanism. It's the way I own it, and it works for me. It helps me be lighter and not take myself too seriously.

If you want to have integrity, if you want to feel right and good and strong about what you are doing and where you are going with your life, you have to own it. Do you feel it? Did you say it? Did you do it? Did you really mean it? Is it who you really are? Then *own it*.

Rule #8 is about taking responsibility for who you are, what you do, what you stand for. It's about being truthful, not just to other people but to yourself—even if your friends aren't or your family isn't. It's about seeing the reality of a situation, accepting it, and working with it.

Perhaps I've chosen an extreme solution to making my life, my mistakes and successes, transparent—by putting it all on television. Some people might think my career and life are too public, and would never want to bare themselves in public the way I do, and I understand that. This is my way to do it, not yours. You'll have your own path for owning what you do and what has happened to you in your life.

Personally, I feel so fortunate to have this forum for voicing my ideas and sharing my experiences. When I think of something great, sometimes it doesn't seem truly great until I can tell people about it, and I've got a way to do that. But it's not for everyone, and when Bryn is old enough to be aware that she's on television, Jason and I will have to have a serious heart-to-heart about whether to keep her in front of the camera. A lot of that will depend on her. If there is any negative effect at all, of course it will end immediately, and who knows, I will probably be doing something else by then, anyway. My goal isn't to be on reality TV forever. It's to have a longer and more in-depth dialogue with my fans through a different outlet, such as a talk show.

But even though I'm guessing your life isn't on camera the way mine is, it's still your life and it's real and it's happening to you right now, and you can make it into anything you want. Owning your words and actions is the way. You don't have to be on camera having your life dissected by viewers in their living rooms to take responsibility for that life. You just have to own it.

Truth Noise

*The truth is incontrovertible. Malice may attack it,
ignorance may deride it, but in the end, there it is.*

—*Winston Churchill,
former prime minister of the U.K.*

The noise associated with rule #8 is a pretty direct response to the sometimes painful reality of owning it. How many people do you know who would crumble if they had to sit quietly and look in the mirror for an hour? The truth can be painful, it can be like opening a door to a dark, scary place. Of course, you won't always want to go there. And that's when you can be subject to *truth noise*.

This is the noise in your head that tries to justify anything other than owning it. It makes excuses for your behavior. It thinks of reasons why you shouldn't have to admit to something. It convinces you that you can get away with being someone other than who you really are.

You've probably seen this play out on reality TV, where people say, "Oh, the editing made me look like this, I'm not really like that," or, "But it's television, I was just trying to put on a good show." It happens all the time in real life, too. It's the "I meant to do that" syndrome. It's the "I've never seen that person in my life," syndrome. It's covering your ears and shouting "Blah blah blah" rather than admit to what's really going on.

Truth noise is common because owning it is so hard, but here's what you have to realize: owning it is always easier in the long run than the alternative, even if it doesn't seem like that in those first moments of coming clean. Everything comes out in the wash, and the truth will always come out eventually.

You don't have to scream your problems from the rooftops, but don't pretend you are something that you are not, or that you don't have issues. We all have issues.

Especially when you've done something you wish you hadn't, truth noise can hijack your brain. When you've done something idiotic, of course you will do just about anything to keep from admitting it. It may be natural and understandable, but it's not in your best interest. By owning what you do, you'll always be able to maintain your integrity. It's the pinch in the arm that hurts in the moment but is actually a vaccination against a much worse disease. It's totally liberating.

The best part about owning it is that when you accept what really *is,* you stop living in the past or in some dream world and start living in the real world, where you can actually do something about what's wrong. It enables action and change, whereas when you deny the reality of your situation, you stagnate. You can't get to the breakthrough place where you see what's true and recognize what you need to change. Owning it is a way to release your demons and come out on the other side.

A common example of this is infidelity. We've all seen it, if not done it, and anyone who is married is probably afraid of it, at some level. Infidelity is truth noise. When a marriage isn't working, it's easier to cheat to make yourself feel better, to get what you think you need from someone else, without actually confronting the problems in your marriage. However, eventually, it will always be worse for you. Cheating is a poison and it will rot you from the inside out. Yes, there are a few exceptions, but naming them to justify what you are doing is truth noise, too.

If you want someone else, own it. Come clean, at least to yourself, and either fix the marriage or end it and then move on to someone else. If you're already cheating, own it. Make it right. It's harder in the moment but it's better in the end, for everyone, and most of all, for yourself.

Here's another example—a friend of mine went to a great college but never actually graduated, leaving school a few credits shy. She hadn't told her boyfriend that she didn't have a college degree, and this truth noise tormented her for years. She was so afraid that he would think she was a liar, but she couldn't be happy in the relationship because she wasn't being honest with him. When she finally copped, it turned out to be fine. He didn't care. The pressure was lifted and she could finally breathe.

Of course, sometimes the person *will* care. Sometimes it will be bad. But just remember that it's the lesser evil. Truth noise is always worse than any repercussions from the actual truth.

Getting Ready to Own It . . . On Camera

In times like these, men should utter nothing for which they would not be willingly responsible through time and in eternity.

—*Abraham Lincoln, former U.S. president*

What better way to own it than to put my life on reality television?

Being on *Real Housewives* was certainly a roller coaster, but I was just one of the cars on the track. When the camera rolled, I was not always the one being filmed. I was part of a complicated story. I was one of a group of cast members. Some of the most important moments in my life were captured on the show, like when Jason said he wanted us to move in together, my positive pregnancy test and sharing that news—all of it was there on display, but it wasn't a show about *me*. That all changed with *Bethenny Getting Married?*.

This show *was* about me. My name was in the title, for goodness sake. The opportunity was wonderful but strange, and I had to spend some time wrapping my head around the idea. It would be my life, on camera—private moments, personal stuff, work and love and pregnancy and hormones and all of it. I was getting married and having a baby, my career was going full throttle. And I was going to let the world see it—anybody who wanted to tune in Bravo and watch.

I knew it was going to be great television—apparently I'm fairly entertaining—but more important, this was my chance to let it all hang out and to share what I have to go through every day. The glitz, the glamour, the shopping, the diamonds, all those *Real Housewives* trappings were gone, and although my life is crazy in some ways that people may not relate to, in most ways my show is about me, a regular person, going through the things that regular people experience every day. It's real. It's true. It's like *your* life.

Also, I liked the idea of this show because when I have a talk show someday, people who watched my show will know where I'm coming from. They will have seen my life. My intention was to let people see exactly who I am and how I live, the ups and the downs, the fights and the love, all of it. I want you to know me. I don't keep secrets from you, and your responses get me through my rough times, too. It's give-and-take.

But as we filmed the first season of *Bethenny Getting Married?*, I began to realize that this wasn't going to be easy. If I hadn't really been sure, or willing to share my private life, I wouldn't have agreed to the show, but I also knew that if some of those *Real Housewives* scenes were embarrassing, they were probably nothing compared to what was ahead. If I was going to embrace the experience, I really had to embrace it. I had to be willing to be exactly who I was, bridezilla moments and dog maulings and labor pains and postpartum freak-outs and all.

• •

FROM MY IN-BOX
∾o∾

"I believe in me. If I don't, nobody else will."
—Charles Barkley, former NBA basketball player

• •

Being the sole focus of a reality show has meant owning it to the extreme. I knew people would probably judge me, but I also felt a lot of people would relate, and maybe I could help them by going through all of this in front of them. People would see they weren't alone when fighting with their boyfriends, being overwhelmed by the stress of planning a big event, getting exasperated by work (me burning the first draft of this book!), dealing with their in-laws, wrangling with differences in religion, or reveling in the sweet things in life, like the smell of a baby, the taste of a really good meal or an excellent piece of red velvet cake. The show is about creating a family, and all that it entails. To me, it was something I had to do for myself, but also something I could do for other people. It's just me and my family; and all I have going for me is the truth.

As we prepared for the show, and even while we filmed the first few episodes, it took the producers a while to get this about me and what I wanted the show to be. They would ask me things like, "What's the story for this show? What's going to happen?"

My answer is always, "Let's do real." Reality is going to happen. Because it's reality TV, and ironically, most reality TV isn't really very real.

But the pressure was on. On *Housewives*, I wasn't responsible for anyone else and I couldn't control it when other people lied or misrepresented themselves, their actions, or the things that happened. On my show, I'm an executive producer, so I'm responsible for the content. I know that Jason and Julie are truthful and have integrity.

Bryn and Cookie can't help being truthful. Anyone on my show who isn't truthful probably won't be on my show for very long.

So I knew what it was, what it had to be. Now, I just had to do it.

The Question Mark

Our doubts are traitors and make us lose the good we
oft might win, by fearing to attempt.

—William Shakespeare, playwright

Then, there was the question of the question mark in the title: *Bethenny Getting Married?*

This question mark was large, and it applied to so many things I was gambling on when I agreed to do this show. The immense pressure of every great thing in life happening to me at once felt almost impossible to deal with and I had huge terrifying thoughts: What if I fell apart on camera? What if I couldn't do it? What if I couldn't carry a show on my own? And, what if I couldn't go through with the wedding? What if I ran?

Before the show started filming, Jason and I were fighting a lot. I honestly didn't know if we would make it to the altar. I was scared. Nobody knew for sure, when we started out, if it would really happen . . . least of all me.

I was terrified of failing. With just about everything caught on film, if I couldn't go through with things, everyone would get to see every gory detail. I figured my fans would hate me for screwing up the most perfect relationship with the most perfect guy ever. I knew viewers would *love* Jason, and if I did the Runaway Bride again, I would definitely be the bad guy. As if signing on to my own show and planning a wedding weren't enough, I had major pregnancy hormones coursing through my system. Those made my truth noise even harder to deal with.

Again, I started to think about my old idea that the man has to totally take care of the woman, and that even though I was making plenty of money now, I should only marry a man who could support me over the long haul. After all I've been through, you would think I would be over that by now, but the stress of this experience brought it back to the surface again, like a fossil come back to life. There was no logic to it, it was just something I'd believed for so long, it didn't want to die.

Every time we had a fight—when we were moving and Jason didn't want to hire movers because he thought he could do it all himself, and then he moved one coffee table and smashed it, or the time he wanted to paint the apartment himself—I started freaking out again that these were sure signs that it wasn't working. Absurd, ridiculous, I know, but that was my noise—and his. Jason hadn't ever really been able to commit to anyone, either. We both went through the same experience, thinking we would never really be able to do it. Every fight escalated that noise. Even having found the right person, we both still struggled at first.

We had issues about friends, family, religion, and we were dealing with being new roommates who were also about to get married and have a baby, all practically at the same time. No wonder we had truth noise. Even under the best of circumstances, we were in a stressful environment. It was all just overwhelming.

Before we officially began filming, I grappled with this every day: What if I really couldn't do it? I knew I loved Jason. He's one in a million, the best thing that ever happened to me, but what if there was something wrong with *me*, what if *I* was the problem, what if I was going to leave him at the altar in spite of myself . . . and *on camera?* What if he was going to leave me someday?

Jason was concerned, too, as anyone in their right mind would be. He knew my history. He knew I was scared. He was so sure that we were right for each other, and if he ever had any doubts, he didn't say so. I was the embattled one. A baby on the way, a wedding, writing this book, traveling the country, it was all overwhelming. Sometimes I wanted to curl up in bed and hide under the covers and never come out.

There were times when I really did think I was going to lose it, and Jason's just wanting it all to be easy didn't make it any easier on *me*. I had so much good in my life in those weeks before I began filming my show, but it was almost too much at once, and I didn't quite believe it. I felt like a rat in a cage. All the noise from my past relationships came crashing down. I hadn't been able to do it before, with perfectly nice men. What made me think I could do it now? How would I face the camera, the viewers, Jason's parents? I'd lost a family once, when I divorced Peter. How could I do it again?

Obviously, I was freaking out.

We both decided that we had to be sure we could handle all the pressure and responsibility before we agreed to begin filming. We knew our base had to be settled and strong. Both of us had to be ready, so that's what we did. We made sure—we talked and soul-searched until we became sure, both of us.

The great thing about Jason is that he is a constant, a solid. He doesn't give up. He comes from a place of yes, and he says yes to me and to us. How could I do anything but say yes to him?

When we were still dating, long before we started filming the show, we were attending a party at an art gallery after a magazine cover shoot. Jason noticed a sweet, lovely painting called *Follow Me* by the artist Romero Britto. It is a picture of a girl holding flowers and running away with a smile, and a man chasing her, his lips puckered for a kiss. He said, "That's so us." I felt this recognition was such a testament to his confidence, that he knew I would run, that he would always chase me, and that I didn't really want to get away this time—not from him.

It was one of those little moments when I became even more sure that he was the one for me. Months later, I gave him that painting as a wedding gift.

I finally realized that this struggle I was having was the whole point of the show. *This* was the story: Being who you are and figuring out how to make it work. *Bethenny Getting Married?* is about owning it, and life is about owning it.

Maybe for the first time, I could stay put. Maybe Jason wouldn't ever *let* me go.

So . . . roll film!

Bethenny Getting Married?

It's not easy for me to let people in, but this time, there is no turning back.

—Me, from the opening credits of
Bethenny Getting Married?

Filming *Bethenny Getting Married?* was a constant but quiet adventure. I think that the best scenes on my show are about nothing (with all credit to Seinfeld for the concept)—Jason and I standing in the kitchen eating cereal, or trying to figure out how to put a baby seat into a car, or arguing and then recognizing that we don't want to do that anymore, or just laughing until we cry. Life isn't usually grandiose. It's just life. If it's sincere and meaningful and you own it, it's interesting enough.

The show is just about me and the people in my life: Jason, Julie, Cookie, Gina, and of course, Bryn. It shows my life, from pajamas-on-the-couch to the red carpet. Whether I'm doing a fashion show, like the one in episode one of the first season, or doing a book signing, like during the Costco episode, where nobody showed up and Jason just fed me samples from the grocery section and I bought bulk containers of baby wipes and cashews (Costco is my church), or just trying to figure out how to work a stroller, my life is just my life. It's still crazy but now I've got Jason there with me, and we're working it out.

I like the fact that with my own show I can pull in some of the people in my life and have them with me, so I'd like to tell you just a little bit about some of them, and how they, too, know how to own it.

Julie

In my life, coming from a place of yes means never thinking a task is too big or too small or unimportant. Treat all things equally. The person who answers the phone is just as important as the person who signs the checks (I happen to do both). The way you cut tomatoes is just as important as the way you conduct yourself in a business meeting. For me, this does not only apply in my life as an assistant to Bethenny, but in my personal life. Every experience is unique and can be a building block for your future. Just look at where cutting tomatoes got me!

—*Julie Plake*

I first met Julie, my assistant, when I did a catering job for a party *Hamptons Magazine* was throwing for its advertisers. The editors weren't paying me, but I cooked for them on the weekends sometimes, for free, in return for a small column in their magazine.

Julie worked for the magazine and when I needed extra help in the kitchen, they sent Julie to be my sous-chef. I was immediately impressed with her. She had such a positive attitude and she was willing to do anything I asked. She didn't know anything about cooking, but she made it work. Whatever I threw her way— "Slice me some tomatoes," "Move these plates," "Chop this," or "Arrange that"—she was always right there. I call it the "I'm on it" approach. I remember saying to myself, I'm going to hire this girl someday.

After the job, Julie kept in touch. She sent me notes, dropped by, and always asked me if she could help with whatever I was doing. A few years later, when my assistant was moving on to a new job, and Julie was ready to move forward in her own career, she told me she was ready—I snapped her up.

It really was trial by fire. When Julie first started working for me, she didn't know anything about my business. Sometimes she would forget things or not follow through, but she always copped to it and totally owned it. She would say, "I'm sorry. I'm going to do better. I'm going to get it."

And she did. In fact, she would get so upset with herself, even more than was warranted by the situation, that I sometimes worried about her.

She went from being replaceable to being my most valuable business ally and friend and Bryn's godmother. Julie comes from a place of yes. She handles everything and if she doesn't know how to do it, she figures it out. She's been an important part of *Bethenny Getting Married?* Who knows, maybe someday she'll have a career in television.

My Dog, Cookie

Mommy is my first priority. When you find someone who takes care of you and is loyal to you and supports you, then you fight for her life. Daddy is my best pal. I love him because he takes care of Mommy, he walks me, and he lets me sleep behind his knees. Bryn is my little sister and I will protect her from the world, no matter what. Nobody can hurt my family with me there to guard them. I would do anything for them. Dogs understand the meaning of loyalty.

—Cookie

Cookie is like Lindsay Lohan—she's cute, but she's always getting into trouble. I think she's the most famous character on the show. She stole the show. She's been on *The Ellen DeGeneres Show,* she's been on Rachael Ray, and she has her own Twitter account. I'm sure she has more fans than I do. When I was on Ellen's show, Ellen said she was worried about Cookie, knowing how she can be a little bit scrappy, and how well she would get along with the baby. I said I was very glad they get along so well, because it would have been very hard to have to give up the baby. (Ha-ha.)

Not that Cookie doesn't have her issues. In the first season, I hired a trainer—Cookie's therapist—to come help me manage her because I was concerned about the way she kept attacking people and barking. I felt she was out of control. She's had to deal with all these new changes, and she's already a dog of a certain age . . . she's not interested in learning any new tricks. But when the trainer told me, "This particular dog, Cookie, doesn't particularly like people," it sounded uncomfortably familiar.

Cookie is protective, territorial, a little bit abrasive, and private. She doesn't care what anybody thinks of her. She's very loyal, and she guards her inner circle. She's suspicious of everybody else. Cookie is part Lhasa Apso, an ancient breed that once guarded the Buddhist temples in Tibet. Like all Lhasas, Cookie is a guardian at heart, and she can snap at people if she doesn't want them around. In fact, she prefers it when nobody is around but our immediate family.

Yes . . . Cookie is me.

But Cookie is also her own girl, and what I love so much about her is that she is incapable of pretending to be anybody else, of lying, of refusing to see anything other than what is. Seeing myself reflected in her behavior helps me to *own it,* too.

It makes me sad sometimes to think that Cookie is already ten. She was my first child, my furry child, and I love her so much. It seems that no matter what she does or whose ankles she nips, her fans still love her. She's an indispensable cast member on the show.

Jason

It's not easy being married to such a strong, talented, amazing woman. She has so many demands on her time, which can be stressful, annoying, and frustrating to a relationship. But I wouldn't change my life for anything. I show my love and support for Bethenny, Bryn, and Cookie every day by simply saying the word "Yes!" I love my girls!

—*Jason Hoppy*

Everybody loves Jason. He didn't ask to become a celebrity but now that he's been on the show, that's what happened. He gets mentioned in the press now, and the female fans adore him. Of course they do. He's charming, handsome, sensitive, and athletic. What's not to love?

But I also love how much he gets me, and I think that really comes across on the show. When I woke up each morning with my huge pregnant belly, Jason still thought I was beautiful.

I'm sure it's not easy to live with me, and Jason initially felt like I didn't always respect him. My apartment had to become our house, not my house. It had to become our life, not my life. This is easier for me to manage now, but at first, I was so accustomed to making every decision myself because I was single. It was a big transition for me.

We continue to have some issues; what couple doesn't? I can be a curmudgeon sometimes, and I recognize this, but I'm around people all the time because of what I do for a living. When we're filming, there are typically twelve people in the house, in addition to Jason, Bryn, Julie, Cookie, and me. Is it any surprise I'm not always up for socializing? We work out many of our issues on camera, and many more the normal way—in private. Maybe you remember when I said yes to the housewarming party he wanted so badly when we were filming *BGM?*. Then Jason got stuck in Florida, and I had to throw the damn thing myself. In a tutu. With a huge pregnant belly. And heels. It was kind of fun, I admit—but I never would have volunteered to do it. I did it for Jason. I'm learning.

For his part, he's had to adjust to my crazy life too, and he's come to understand more about what that's like. But during season one, most of my energy, my focus, was concentrated on getting down that aisle. Even my therapist asked if I was going to leave Jason at the altar. No . . . no, no, no . . . I already knew in my heart that it was right to marry Jason, and I would do it, but there were a few critical moments that were caught on film during the early episodes, moments when my noise got the best of me, and moments that helped me realize how much I really wanted to marry Jason.

The first one was when I was trying on wedding gowns. I had flashes of fear and panic and anxiety that day, but when I found the one, the whole adventure began to feel even more real. I knew it was the dress when I tried it on—I started to turn into a bride, and I could suddenly visualize it all happening, owning it. Not running.

When we had our joint bachelor-bachelorette party with friends in Atlantic City, I decided to bring up the subject: How sure were my friends before they got married that they were with the right person? This question was the subject of an entire episode. What percentage of certainty did they have, going into this lifetime commitment? Were they 100 percent sure? 75 percent? Everybody had a different answer. I felt it was very important to assess how confident I really was—my doubts weren't about Jason, but about myself and my own ability to get down that aisle.

I told Jason about the conversation we'd all had and I said, somewhat jokingly, that in my mind I was 88 percent sure I was doing the right thing. As soon as I said it, I could tell how much it hurt his feelings. The look on his face said it all—he was 100 percent sure, and that's what reminded me in the best possible way that my truth noise was messing with my head again.

The idea of getting married was so overwhelming, so difficult for me to believe, that it took a minute for me to process: Was it really happening? Could I really have it all? Was this amazing man in front of me really going to be my partner for life? Maybe I hadn't fully believed that it would happen up until that moment, but when I saw that look on Jason's face, I knew. I was 100 percent sure, and I had been all along. It's just that I hadn't let myself really believe. Jason wrapped his arms around me, and he's held me up ever since.

Another time when it all came together was when we talked to the officiant before we got married. She asked me what family members I would have present at the wedding. I said none—and then I started to cry. Jason asked her to excuse us, and he said the words that I would never forget: "We're going to start our *own* family."

Remembering that moment, I had no doubts left. They all dissolved into love. There have been many other moments, too, private moments, but what they all came down to was: this couldn't be anyone else. Nobody else would ever see me as clearly as he does. He has everything I need. It had to be him.

Owning it doesn't mean you always have to be 100 percent sure about everything you do. It just means you have to stand behind your decisions and, when the time comes, trust that you know how to do what is necessary.

The Wedding

True love stories never have endings.

—Richard Bach, author

I didn't run. Of course, it was the best day. My wedding was everything I had dreamed and hoped it would be—the gorgeous Four Seasons Restaurant decorated in white with red flowers, candles, a beautiful cake. It was perfect. When I first arrived to get ready, wearing my "bride" sweatpants with my hair in rollers, there were paparazzi outside the hotel, and I have to admit, I was thrilled. It was fun! I was a pregnant bride in sweats, and I wanted the world to know how happy I was. I felt as if the whole world had showed up to celebrate with me.

As we were all getting ready, none of it felt quite real. I was nervous but also in a floating kind of mental state where I couldn't quite get my feet on the ground or wrap my head around what was about to happen. When I was finally in my gown, my hair and makeup done, waiting to enter the Pool Room of the Four Seasons, and the doors opened, I became hyperconscious. A friend had told me to taste the moment, because life whips by so quickly. It's so important to really experience moments like these. That idea came into mind as the world seemed to slow down.

I kept reminding myself: *Remember this. Be here. Be here.* It was truly a gift to be able to enjoy this time the way I did. Too often, our special moments slip by and we look back trying to piece together the memories. Obviously, not every moment in life is as momentous as a wedding, but you have to allow yourself to enjoy it, whatever it is. Life doesn't serve up a wedding celebration every day.

I felt hopeful and proud of myself for arriving here and sticking with the decision to marry Jason and have his child. As I walked to him, I felt like the baby and I were walking forward together, joining him to complete our family. I stood there in my beautiful wedding dress, in a room filled only with people who were truly happy for us, I was overjoyed to realize that I didn't have even the slightest desire to run. I felt so grateful and sentimental. I couldn't stop smiling.

People ask me if the television cameras were intrusive. Truly, they weren't. A lot of people film their weddings. It didn't matter to me that it would end up later on television. It wasn't live. Somehow, the cameras and photographers and even the paparazzi made the whole event feel more fun and more grandiose. This was my *wedding*. It wasn't like a television wedding. It was a *real* wedding. Maybe some of you reading this feel as if you couldn't enjoy this kind of attention, but it's something that I'm comfortable with. I think it even helped me to own every moment. Knowing that I was surrounded by some of the dearest people in my life was all that mattered.

And Then There Were Three

Birth is not only about making babies. Birth is about making mothers—strong, competent, capable mothers who trust themselves and know their inner strength.

—Barbara Katz Rothman,
author and sociology professor

We didn't expect Bryn to come five weeks early, but I guess she likes to be early, just like her mother. I had done some preparation—I went to an infant care class, but it only gave me anxiety because it made me realize how much I didn't know. Jason and I were basically completely clueless. We didn't take a birthing class, and we didn't have any idea how to handle a baby. Neither of us had ever changed a diaper before.

I had no idea what was coming.

When my water broke, we were both enveloped by a strange sense of calm panic. Jason started calling family members and I was like, "Hello, can you call the doctor first? Maybe we should go to the hospital? Nothing has happened yet, are you telling them we've given birth to a puddle of water?"

Believe it or not, I loved every second of giving birth, even the painful parts. Being in the hospital with Jason for six days was like living in a safe little cocoon. The pain of labor was difficult and exhausting, and I thought having a C-section would be scary and painful, but it wasn't. Jason was there for me from the moment we arrived at 6 a.m. on a Friday to Wednesday afternoon when we left with our new baby. It was an emotional time. Baby Bryn was so small that she had to be in the NICU (the Neonatal Intensive Care Unit). We were worried about her, but she was doing so well and she was so beautiful that we were completely absorbed in our idyllic reality.

The hospital, Lenox Hill Hospital in Manhattan, was sheltering and warm and the nurses and doctors took care of our basic needs, so we could just be there together, snuggling and helping each other and transitioning from being a new family of two to a new family of three. It all felt so secure. We both knew that as soon as we left that hospital, life would never be the same, so we weren't eager to leave. We really needed that time, to get physically and emotionally ready to face the world—all three of us were getting stronger.

And so we brought Bryn home, and life hasn't been the same since. It's been better, so much better. I can't believe I'm the same person I was before getting married and giving birth to Bryn. It's a whole new universe. I just feel different in my skin. Life means more now. Every moment is precious. And my future is so full of hope, anticipation, and excitement.

We're raising a little girl!

My next challenge is to find balance. Three days after I returned home from the hospital, I was back to work. So much for maternity leave. Even though my life is crazy, I feel so lucky. I work at home so I can snuggle with Bryn all day, whenever I need a break.

My show is already filming a second season, and the house is so full of love. All Jason and I say to each other these days is, "I love my husband!" "I love my wife!" "We love our peanut, our burrito, our chickpea!" "We love our *family!*" It's love, love, and more love.

I never really took maternity leave—or, I took it in bits and pieces, whenever I could get a few days away to be alone with Jason and Bryn. When we took our first family "vacation" (coinciding with some work I had to do) and flew to Los Angeles, the trip was great. Traveling takes on a whole new dimension when you do it with your family. Every new experience in my new role all felt so right, as if family life is what I was meant to be doing all along.

I still have to get up and get dressed and go out and be seen, but I feel quieter inside. I'm in a calmer, happier place. I have something to come home to now, something that really matters. When a decision must be made, I don't have to make it alone. We have a team meeting. I've taken some nasty knocks along the way for owning what I've done, but it's now clearer to me than ever that whatever happens along the way, there will be rewards if you own it and stay true to yourself.

I'm still moving forward. Now that I'm used to experiencing every possible emotion in my life on television, I think about when we might step away from it for a while. As Jason says, someday our lives will have to become private again. It's just a question of when. When the moment is right to move on to the next stage, we'll know. I've shared some of the most incredible high points of my life with you—my wedding, my trip to St. Bart's, giving birth to my daughter. No matter what comes next in my life and career I will continue to share my life with you in new and better ways.

Now, I need to work on coming together and nurturing my family. I'm open to whatever happens. Whatever it is, I'll create what happens next. It's not random. I'm driving. And I'll own it, because now I know I can—and that I never have to do anything alone again.

Come Together
My Life Now

Coming together is a beginning. Keeping together is progress. Working together is success.

—Henry Ford, founder of Ford Motor Company

After two companies merge, there's often a transitional team that comes in and helps with the restructuring. Each part of the new company has to figure out how its individual methods and systems can work best within the newly created team. Following a successful merger, the whole system renews, changes, and strengthens. It's bigger and better.

But, unlike in corporate America, when you come together with other people, in family there is no team to help you integrate and transition. You *are* the transition team. And that's when you need rule #9: *Come together.*

So much of this book has been about being true to yourself, but you don't exist in a vacuum. Whether it's a love relationship, a family relationship, or a business relationship, we live in a social world and we have to learn how to get along with other people.

This rule comes at the end of the book, even though you have to deal with other people probably most days of your life. The reason is that although rule #9 is a necessity in life, it's even more important to get the other rules under your belt first. To come together successfully with others, you first have to know who you are.

When you've got the other rules down, you will have a lot more success in all your relationships because you'll be able to come together with something to offer. Coming together is not a rule dictating that you have to find someone to marry or someone who will commit to you. I learned a long time ago that this goal cannot—must not—be the focus of your personal achievement. As much as we'd all like a "you complete me" moment, I'm not talking about finding your personal Jerry McGuire or some copycat version of yourself so you can mutually admire each other.

Coming together is the opposite of a codependency. When you seek to come together, what matters is your wholeness. When you become someone in your own right and are no longer dependent on the labels and opinions of others, you can get a grip on the kind of lasting contentment that carries you for a long time. Together, the two wholes become greater than the sum of their parts. You are complete, and so is your partner, and together, you become something even more amazing.

This can only happen when you've got yourself figured out, because then you won't be grasping at others for something you are missing. You won't be missing anything. You *aren't* missing anything you don't already have inside yourself. Once you realize that, you can get down to the business of coming together.

But working through these stages and growing a little at a time into the person who could do what I'm doing now was all part of the process for me. Whether it was Jason #1 or BethennyBakes or a career in event planning that wasn't my ultimate goal, I had to log each one of those experiences and learn something valuable from each before I could let myself off the hook a little bit and really open up to being happy.

First find yourself, your path, your mission, your passion, and your direction—pour all your energy into *that*. Don't be afraid to set off in that direction, even if it's uncharted territory. Soon enough you'll find yourself following your own map in a place that's much more familiar and comfortable, because you *made* it familiar by going there and making yourself at home. Learn to live in your own skin—there's nothing like that feeling, and it's the most important thing you can ever do for yourself.

Then, if you are lucky enough to find someone else going in the same direction as you, and if that someone's life begins to merge with yours, then and only then will you be ready for a truly fulfilling relationship and for rule #9, *come together*. Give yourself anything less, and you'll spend your life searching for someone or something else to make you feel whole. A big house, a fancy car, a prestigious job, or a picture-perfect spouse won't make you happy. If you've learned anything from these rules, I hope you've learned that this approach to life and love simply doesn't work.

But rule #9 isn't just about your love life. When you focus on coming together as a goal for all aspects of your life, think about improving how you work with others, in any situation, whether it's your job or friends or family. Like it or not (and I don't always like it, in my antisocial moments), we can't make it on our own. Coming together with others is just a fact of life. It has to be done; sometimes it's a joy and sometimes it's a pain in the ass. However, an effective partnership of any kind is not about compromising yourself or playing trust games at your corporate retreat. Instead, take yourself out into the world and find a rhythm that works with the people around you.

When I was rehearsing for *Skating with the Stars,* I experienced this every day. In the past, I've often had difficulties working with other people, but when you are doing couples skating, you absolutely have to depend on your partner. I had to trust that my partner wasn't going to let me fall, and he had to trust that I would do everything right, too. Back when I was trying to be an actress, I always had trouble listening to the other person's lines and responding to them authentically. Being on ice skates taught me how far I've come since then. When I was able to get out of my own head and look at what my partner was doing, suddenly I could see, with so much more clarity, how to respond to him. I wasn't skating. *We* were skating.

This is why I called him my ice husband—it was a perfect metaphor for marriage, or any coming together that is necessary in your life. When you come together and work together in a mutual give-and-take way, rather than simply working side by side, then everything changes. You make each other better, you are stronger, and when you are really doing it right, you'll discover the true meaning of the word "relationship." I never thought I would be able to work so well with someone else. I also never really thought I could be truly, deeply, happily married to someone. I've finally learned the essence of rule #9.

This also applies to my career. In the past, I've often tried to do everything myself, but I'm getting better at working with others, and even having business partners. I'm still not the type who likes to have people around all the time. My essential nature hasn't changed. But I've learned that there are benefits to cooperating and letting others take over the parts I can't do. For example, in my negotiations to sell the Skinnygirl Cocktail line, I recognized that the right allies with the right qualities, people who actually understand the brand and will grow it in a way that is true to its origins, can actually expand the cocktail line more effectively and efficiently than I could do on my own.

I can work on my book on my own, but sometimes I have to come together with editors and publishers and hash things out. On my show, I'm not always crazy about having a TV crew in my house (that's an understatement), but if I want to have my show, that's part of the reality. Sometimes I don't want to get out of bed, but I have to, because we're filming and I have to work closely with the crew and the network and I have to fulfill my responsibilities to other people. Sometimes Cookie wants to bite people and it's stressful. She's acting out what I'm feeling, but she is not allowed to bite people, and neither am I. (Although, I have to admit, we do it anyway, on occasion.)

Coming together in my personal life has been even more difficult for me. I didn't have a role model for family togetherness, so I could never imagine what it would be like to be at the helm of a family, or to have everyone get along and exist in happy harmony. And yet, I find myself right in the middle of one—and the four of us (including Cookie) are creating our own family dynamic, day by day.

The key to making it work has been to look back over all those other rules, including rule #1 (break the chain) and remember that coming together, right here, right now, has nothing to do with what anyone did before, or what anyone else thinks we should do. Every family is unique, so there is no right way to be a family. You don't *need* a role model, you just need love. Here at the Frankel-Hoppy household, we come together the way it works for each individual in our family. It's the only way. We forget about "normal" and we simply are who we are—you know by now I could never be quite "normal" (whatever that means), even if I wanted to. It's not me and I'm not trying to push "normal" on you, either.

Normal Noise

The way a team plays as a whole determines its success. You may have the greatest bunch of individual stars in the world, but if they don't play together, the club won't be worth a dime.

—Babe Ruth, Major League baseball player

A lot of different kinds of noise can interfere when you are working to come together, even when you've got a pretty good sense of who you are and are following the other rules. Money noise, childhood noise, truth noise, relationship noise can all interfere, but one type of noise we haven't talked about yet is particularly insidious as you are trying to build and maintain successful relationships, whether in work, family, or love. I call it *normal noise*.

Normal noise tells you that the other person is doing something that isn't normal, and therefore they are wrong, and you are right. It also has a flip side: This is the noise that makes you believe it when someone else tells you that *you* are normal. Normal noise eats away at a couple's or family's or group's efforts to be unique and make things work. If you are always throwing "normal" into the conversation, you'll miss out on what's special about your situation. It can eventually destroy any relationship. Normal noise happens when your husband says you aren't normal because your family is crazy and you are just like your mother, or you tell your husband he's not normal because his parents don't show their feelings and neither does he. It hovers over all those kinds of comments: "What's wrong with your sister?" "Doesn't your father know how to behave?" "Why don't you sleep/eat/talk/look/act like a *normal person?*" Comments like these make it nearly impossible to come together because they are divisive.

This can be particularly obvious during the holidays. Last holiday season, I received thousands of tweets and Facebook messages from people who were thrown together with family they wouldn't necessarily have chosen. You know what they say: You can choose your friends but not your family. During the holidays, you are forced to come together with people you may automatically assume aren't "normal," and then normal noise becomes deafening. How many holidays have you spent with people you have deemed "crazy," whether they are your own family or in-laws or the families of friends? So your mother-in-law is a chain-smoker, your sister won't shut up, your aunt is a horrible cook, and you are a nervous wreck. This is one reason why many people gorge on comfort food and/or drink too much during holiday gatherings. This is why holidays are so stressful. Sure, there are great parts—a baby opening her toys, good food, high points where everyone is laughing and having fun— but there are also those times when people yell, argue, bring up all the old issues, storm out, cry. That's because during the holidays, you have to come together—you have to eat, drink, and be merry— with people that aren't normal to you.

But that's the key—maybe they aren't normal *to you*, but they are perfectly normal to themselves. And you may not seem at all normal to them. The entire point of rule #9 is to attempt and learn and get better at understanding others, rather than criticizing them. Here's an announcement: No one is guiltier of this than I am. But I work on it every day, and God knows I'm no poster child for "normal." Tolerance is the key. You may not understand why your brother married someone of a different race or religion, why your husband's uncle is gay, why your little sister can't seem to hold down a job, or why anybody is different than you are in any way. But you don't have to understand it. You just have to respect that everyone has their own normal, and the only "normal" you have to worry about is your own. What's right for you? What's true? When you're okay with who you are, you won't have to criticize others. That's when you can finally come together.

The truth is that there is no objective normal. You have to find your own normal. It's like "finding your truth," but for a couple or a group. Your normal won't be the same as anyone else's normal, and throwing someone else's normal (including society's) in their face is a betrayal.

For Jason's mother, normal is going to church almost every day. That's who she is. For Jason, normal is going to church once a week. That's who he is. For me, normal is not going to church at all. For Jason and Bryn and Cookie and me, what we have, no matter how anyone would describe it, is perfectly, beautifully *normal,* because it's *us.* For our family, right now, being on television is normal, no matter how abnormal it might be for someone else. For our family, right now, putting one another first is normal, and as much as I might tell myself that this *should* be normal for every family, it isn't, and that's not my business.

In fact, the word *should* is your first clue that you've got normal noise. Here are some examples: *You should clean the house. You should get married. You should want to have children. You should go to bed earlier. You should be healthier. You should eat better. You should make more money. You should love me.*

If you have to say *should,* then you are probably trying to control who someone else is, and that never works. Instead, look at yourself. Do *you* want to clean the house, get married, have children, go to bed earlier, be healthier, eat better, make more money, love someone else or yourself? Those are issues you can actually do something about.

Jason and I often have normal noise. He says it's not normal that I don't want to spend all my time with his family and friends. I say it's not normal that he wants other people around all the time. To me, Jason's upbringing is unfamiliar, and sometimes I translate that to mean "not normal." It doesn't seem normal to me that Jason has never been on a ski trip, or that he never tried sushi or rode on an airplane until he was in his twenties. To him, it's not normal that I grew up in an adult world of high rollers and was practically raised on the racetrack. My parents divorced. His didn't. I grew up in the city. He grew up in a small town. He eats cereal for breakfast. I like a spoonful of frosting. Who's normal? Who's not normal?

Who cares?

When Jason and I moved in together, he didn't want to hire a mover. He is used to doing things himself. To him, that's normal. To me, however, a mover makes sense because they have all the right equipment and covers for the furniture and are professionals. To me, time is money, and I don't know how to move furniture, so hiring a mover seems normal. However, what we first thought was a battle of "who's normal?" eventually became a simple question of "what makes sense?" Jason picked up one table and cracked the corner. Let's just say we'll be using movers from now on. It was the "I-told-you-so" moment of the century.

But that didn't mean my way was normal and his wasn't. Instead of making it personal, we realized that we could make it practical. (I just happened to be right. Jason says I always have to have the last word—I guess that's my "normal," too!)

The question isn't "Is he normal?" or "Are you normal?" but "What is normal for *us?*" When one person in a relationship is always trying to convince the other person they are not normal, it can cause immense damage, especially if one person had a dysfunctional childhood like I did, and begins to believe they really aren't normal. Just because one person talks more or yells louder doesn't mean they are right. Just because one person tries to avoid conflict doesn't mean they are wrong. Don't fall into the trap of telling yourself (as I tend to do), "Oh, I was raised by lunatics, so I'm not normal, he must be right."

The fact is, if you chose to marry someone, or be with someone, or be friends with someone, or even work for a certain company, you can't then turn around and tell them that they aren't normal. People are just different. You chose that person, so now you've got to work with the person and situation in front of you. If you merge two companies, you did it for a reason—because each company had strengths that the other needed. But every company, not to mention every person on the planet, also has weaknesses, so you have to come to the table understanding that. You don't merge with a company that's exactly like yours. What would be the point? You don't just force one company, one partner, to be exactly like the other one. You make it work.

I chose Jason because he's a family person, so I'm not going to be brainwashed by my normal noise and start punishing him for exactly the qualities I love so much. But I also have to preserve what's unique about me.

When you come together, there will be conflict. It's inevitable, and you can't run away from it. Normal noise can also make you fear what you don't understand, or shut down in the face of an argument and agree to anything. It can make you bigoted or prejudiced or it can make you conform to your own detriment. Instead, you have to learn how to manage the conflict by shutting down your normal noise. Be who you are, let other people be who they are, and then come together and find the common ground. If you need to walk away and come back during an argument, then do that, but end on a happy note. Jason and I always try to do this when we fight. It's our version of never going to bed angry. Never go to bed with normal noise.

Choose, accept, adapt. That's coming together. I chose Jason, I accept him (most of the time), and I'm trying to adapt. Hey, it's a process. I didn't claim to be perfect!

(I do have to add a quick disclaimer here: Coming together means working with the person you chose, but that doesn't apply when you are in a relationship that isn't right. Whether it's abusive or just makes you unhappy, there is a line between causing problems for yourself in a relationship that works, and recognizing when you need to move on from a relationship that isn't going to work no matter what you do. This applies to love relationships and family, too. If it hurts you, you don't need to come together. You need to do what's right for you, and that may mean starting over. Come together applies only when you've chosen someone who is good for you. Only then, accepting and adapting will make you a better person.)

For Jason and me, fighting is natural but we also believe that you can't allow too many cracks in your foundation. If you don't deal with your differences in the beginning, those cracks will grow until your house crumbles. Come together and face what's happening, and you'll repair any crack when it's still small and easy to fix.

Coming together often applies to a couple, but it also applies to a group, whether it's a family or a work environment.

Whenever you build a family, a group of friends, or a company, you have to understand the group dynamic as much as, if not more than, the individual personalities. However, no matter what kind of group you find yourself a part of, you will probably always be influenced, consciously or not, by your preconceived, learned notions of how groups are supposed to work.

This mentality can be a problem when you bring any group of people together with individuals who have a lot of differences, no matter what they are—cultural, religious, political, or emotional. Your fixed ideas might happen to clash with the preconceptions of others, and then you've got conflict.

Patterns established by your own family are inevitable, but you aren't destined to repeat them. If you grew up in an environment where it was "normal" to interrupt, yell, be disrespectful, criticize, hate, or just say mean things, then normal noise can cause you to behave inappropriately in a work environment or with friends. Your actions might tear down the group, or you might accept bad behavior in others just because your normal noise say it's okay.

Cultural or societal expectations can generate normal noise, too, whether it's basic ideas about the roles of men and women (do you respect your male bosses more than your female bosses?), wealth, race, religion, or something subtler, like respecting a workaholic more than someone who may have a more balanced sense of work, fun, and personal time but doesn't make much money. No matter the group, you may have to take a few steps back when things aren't working. Chances are, normal noise is at fault, so root it out, look at it, and then decide to see instead what's normal for your situation, specifically.

Now that I'm married, coming together has become the rule at the forefront of my consciousness, so I'd like share with you some specific ways it's working for me now, and how I'm dealing with coming together in so many wonderful ways. I hope that these thoughts will inspire you to come together in your life, too.

On Being a Newlywed

I am a member of a team, and I rely on the team, I defer to it and sacrifice for it, because the team, not the individual, is the ultimate champion.

—Mia Hamm, professional soccer player

So here I am, a newlywed at forty, and it's actually working.

The success of my marriage with Jason is no coincidence. Marrying someone who is here for me, someone I can talk to, someone I trust, and someone who can handle things when I'm working has turned out to be exactly what I needed. For me, coming from a place of yes meant choosing a man who was truly a good person, who pushed me to be better, who makes me better. *Coming together* allowed me to open up, be vulnerable, and build a bond with him. Jason has helped me to uncover a Bethenny who had long been buried under disillusionment.

Fill your life with people who are good under pressure, not just during the easy times. I believe you should marry someone who would be decent if you ever got divorced (not that I have any such intentions!)—someone who, no matter the situation, will be a good person. Deal with people you respect and whom you would want as friends.

I still have noise and I still have my independent side. I'm still me, and that's as it should be. I certainly wouldn't say that I've conquered all my issues—for me, it's all about the baby steps. Sometimes I get so focused on what I'm doing that I forget about what Jason needs, but I'm learning to make a conscious effort to be kinder and more aware, instead of just rolling over Jason and doing what I want to do. Sometimes I still have to remind myself that I'm part of a wonderful little family now and it's not just me anymore.

I have never wanted to admit that I need anyone, but I can finally say that I need Jason. That's a huge confession for me. Seeing the words, I'm amazed that I can even admit this to *myself*, let alone to you. But it's true. When I travel, he and Bryn travel with me, and Jason does most of the heavy lifting with our baby. He'll come to L.A. with me, fly on the red-eye, and come to every photo shoot, just to keep our family together. I know it can be excruciating for him, but he does it because he understands what it means to be in a relationship, to have a family, and to be a good husband and father. This is marriage.

So how I can get irritated when he wants to go to the gym every day, or hit golf balls for a few hours, or have his parents come for a visit? I am learning to say *yes* to him as much as he says it to me. By suggesting that he invite his parents for the weekend, by being in a good mood, I can make those little gestures that acknowledge his place of yes. This is marriage, too.

Being a newlywed is both challenging and incredible. Jason and I had to work out the issues any people have when they first move in together. Add to that the pressure of a wedding and having a baby and my crazy career, all with a camera crew in tow. It all happened at once, and it's a lot to handle. It was quite a year.

I could focus on all the little, yet annoying, things Jason (or anyone) does. Those are just excuses to find a way out. Where once upon a time I might have locked in on them and hammered away at my partner, I realize now that in the scheme of things, those little annoyances are nothing. The good so far outweighs the bad that I hardly see these potentially irritating things anymore. Coming from a place of yes means focusing instead on the things that I love about Jason, and that make us such a good team.

I joke that Jason is a "civilian," not being in the entertainment business, but he's far from ordinary. He's extraordinary. He's a kind, generous, normal guy with a normal salary, from a kind, generous, normal family. Frankly, he's remarkable in being so secure and so supportive of me, and in the calm way he deals with the whirlwind I've subjected him to. He also understands in a way I don't think many people do how to really reach out and be there for someone else. He's exactly what I needed to bring balance to my extreme existence. And I balance him, too. I feel very, very lucky.

Marriage is a whole new ball game, and I'm loving the rules I thought would terrify me. When you take the risk and step through that dark door you fear, that's where the gifts are. I'm now more successful in every area of my life because of my husband. He makes me a better person.

My reality, when I looked beyond "normal," turned out to be the opposite of what my noise had been telling me all those years. Our marriage is the secure structure we've built around ourselves, and it's something we can depend on now, as we navigate these first few years, with Bryn in tow. Marriage isn't for everyone—I've seen enough bad marriages to know that's true, but just as many people who aren't married are also in incredible relationships. If you're doing it all on your own and loving life, then that's how it should be for you, and I congratulate you. However, I do believe that *connection* is for everyone, one way or another, even if it's with your dearest friends or family or even your work, and not with a so-called "life partner."

I know the emptiness of being famous, just for being famous, so to have this connection with someone means the world to me now—I can truly appreciate how important it is to come together. For Jason and me, that came in the form of marriage—it was the right thing at the right time for us. It was *our* "normal," but I would never say it should be yours.

Marriage cemented the idea for both of us that from now on, whatever we do, we do as a team. We make decisions together, based on what's in the best interest of the family unit. What will benefit and strengthen our family?

Now, to go even further, Jason and I are seriously considering working together in my business; he is great with the parts I don't want to do, like reading contracts and doing the taxes, so in some ways it's a no-brainer. It just makes sense. We think that working together on separate aspects of the business will strengthen our relationship even more. Jason is protective and loyal, and he actually cares about the business because it's so much a part of his life, too. He has already begun to tackle some of these tasks in a big way, and I'm already recognizing how valuable he is in this capacity. He, in turn, is more involved in what I do, which helps him better understand and be supportive of my crazy schedule and the nuances of what I do.

When Jason is involved at this level, I don't have to go insane trying to explain what I'm going through or how I need help, because he's already up to speed. I can talk to him about every aspect of what I'm doing and he can help me solve problems and make decisions. We already talk about everything, but this kind of a partnership helps us communicate on an even more meaningful level. Because my work is so important to me, I need to be able to talk about it with someone who understands. And now, he does. I see so many couples who don't discuss their work or their passions with each other. Many people have no idea what their partners really do for a living. I believe that if something is truly meaningful to you, you must be able to talk about it with your partner. This is one of the ways you forge a stronger bond.

It's funny and ironic that I find myself being such a strong proponent of marriage after I finally reached the point where I decided it was unnecessary. But here I am. I say it because it's true for me. I've finally found my connection. Jason was the one who softened my hardest edges and opened me up to recognizing what my soul really needed.

Marriage has changed me in some interesting ways. I still surprise myself. I've become so conscious of the importance of taking care of Jason, letting it be about him, giving him what he needs, because I'm more conscious of how much he gives to me. I like to tell him how good-looking he is, how smart he is. I often hear people ripping down their husbands, but that will deteriorate your relationship. Your kids are watching. I definitely still have an occasional impulse to do this, but now that I've recognized that tendency, I'm able to work on it. So can you—come from a place of yes. Whatever your relationship is, and whatever stage you find yourself, whether it's the very beginning or the middle of the long haul, build each other up. There is always a way to choose to see the good, and then the bad doesn't seem quite so terrible anymore.

When our little family came back on the red-eye from Los Angeles after recent television appearances, I confessed to Jason that I felt guilty because so much of what we do every day, so much of our time and energy, is about me. He took my hand and he looked me in the eye and said, "Look. This is your time. Very few people get to do what they love. You're lucky. You have to go for it."

That's what kind of man he is, but we are also making this our time now. I am embarking on a motivational speaking tour, and all four of us will travel together on a tour bus—Jason, Bryn, Cookie, and I. We have decided that this isn't just about me. It's about us. It's our trip. In this way, everything truly becomes my business, and I can make my business into everything. It's all one. It's all coming together. But I never could have done it without Jason, so no matter how hard it is, no matter what issues I might have, how could I have done anything but come together with this amazing person, the father of my baby, the love of my life? He's been a miracle.

So that's my latest report from the Jason Hoppy Admiration Society, and I hope you'll bear with me. After all, I'm a newlywed. Maybe as time wears on, it won't all feel so magical, but somehow, I think it will just get better.

If someone loves you, it's so important to love them, and make time for them, and give them what they need, and let them love you back. Coming together is a give-and-take of equal proportion. There will also be ebb and flow—times in your life when one of you gives more, or takes more. But in a relationship of equals, of two whole people, it all evens out in the end. So give all your love and don't be stingy. Don't hold any in reserve. If you've held it inside for too long, it begins to decay. Let it go. It will all come back to you, and you'll find a whole new level of meaning in your life. The more you give, the more you have to give . . . and the more you get.

It sounds like such a cliché that it makes me laugh sometimes, but it's true: it's about love, in the end, the ultimate message at the end of the journey to yourself.

On Being a Mother

Motherhood has a very humanizing effect. Everything gets reduced to essentials.

—*Meryl Streep, actress*

Bryn has been the second miracle in my life. It's hard for me to put into words how I feel about her and how much having a baby has changed me. I can't believe I almost didn't do this. She inspires love in me that I didn't know I was capable of feeling. The first moment I held her in my arms, even before I really understood or could wrap my mind around the idea that I was a mother, this wave of feeling washed over me and I *was* a mother. It was chemical, biological, emotional, and spiritual, all at once.

I'm still in wonderment at it all. Now I more clearly understand the fierce protective nature of the mother. I can't stand to hear Bryn cry because I don't ever want her to have to feel fear or pain. I can't fathom ever speaking ill of your own child. I admit I'm obsessed with shielding her from the world so she can stay pure and joyful for as long as possible. Sometimes I joke that I don't care if she ever learns her ABCs or colors or numbers—I just want to love on her every second of every day. I never want her to have noise about money or weight or relationships or love. I want to give her everything I didn't have as a child, and more. Every day, I feel so inspired to make her feel completely and utterly loved.

I keep thinking about all the babies who aren't loved or are living without the advantages we have, and it makes me feel sad. Everybody in this life should be able to be loved as much as they possibly can!

Sometimes, I still have family noise, but mostly it makes me feel melancholy—my mother must have felt this kind of love for me when I was born. I worry about how to make sure that what happened between my mother and me never happens between me and Bryn. I can't imagine being jealous of her or leaving her for months at a time. Having a child is an absolute gift, and anybody who doesn't appreciate it doesn't know how much they are missing.

Every day I come to a new realization about being a mother: I am not my mother, nor am I bound by anything she did. I will not repeat what I perceive as her mistakes. My slate is clean. I'm sure I'll make different mistakes, but I will do my best to be what Bryn needs.

And Bryn is not me, either, even though I consider her to be mine. She is her own beautiful little person, and I get to be her mother, and that's the ultimate job title and honor. She inspires me to do better: to have higher intentions, to clean up my act, to clean up my *mouth* (this will be a hard one!), to be a worthy mother. One of my biggest conflicts with motherhood is finding the balance between family and career. I don't think I could ever give up working, even though there are mornings when I can't stand the thought of leaving Bryn and going off to give an interview. I know I can be a role model for Bryn and let her see that I followed my dreams so she can learn how to follow hers.

At the same time, I never want her to doubt for a second that she is my highest priority. Being my own person is part of showing her that, and so is taking care of her. Our family has become about taking care of one another. When you have children, family dynamics change—not that Jason and I had much time to settle into routines as a duo before we became a trio. I know that many new moms struggle to do it all and give everybody what they need. It can be exhausting. I still struggle with that, too, but there are a few things I've figured out so far, that I highly recommend for any new mother struggling to keep it all together:

1. Sleep when the baby sleeps. Sleep is *essential*. You already know it, but you actually have to *live it*. This remains one of my greatest crosses to bear. Lack of sleep will add to your anxiety and stress, and it can make you look old. Turn off the TV and read until you get tired, or take a bath. On the plane, stop paying attention to the movie and close your eyes. If you've shorted yourself on sleep all week, don't make plans on Friday. Go home. Go to bed. Forget that idea that you can sleep when you're dead. If you don't sleep, you'll go through life *as if* you were dead.

I'm still working on this, and as I write this, I have dark circles under my eyes because I have trouble sleeping. When I don't sleep, everything is harder, takes longer, and feels more like torture. When I've had enough sleep, I can be a human being again, I feel good and healthy and I feel as if I can handle everything. I still find it challenging to balance my schedule with downtime, but I'm working hard on this because I strongly believe that sleep can cure almost any ill.

Sleep noise is a big problem for some people. It's maddening for me. You think you just don't have time to sleep, but that's like saying you don't have time to breathe. If you have the over-whelming urge in the afternoon to put your head down on your desk and slip away into sweet dark oblivion for *just a minute,* you are not getting enough sleep. Sleep should always be your priority, ahead of anything else that isn't absolutely necessary, including exercise. But don't let it stress you, either. If you lose a night and feel horrible, make up for it the next night. Your body will catch up.

I am not always good at exercising and sometimes I didn't go to yoga for weeks. But that's fine. It's an ebb and flow. You do what you can, when you can, and only after you've had enough sleep. If your mind is racing, just lie there and relax. Sometimes you simply have to stop moving your body and your brain for a while. Both sleep and exercise are gifts to yourself. Give them whenever you can. I've realized how important it is for mothers to be good to themselves.

2. Prioritize. Prioritizing means that sometimes you have to say no in order to come from a place of yes. I'm working on this with my therapist because it's difficult for me. Sometimes you have to say no, even if it means people will be upset with you. You have to prioritize your time when you are a new mom, because all of a sudden you don't have nearly as much as you used to. Sometimes I feel guilty that I can't give everything to everyone. I've recently missed events that were very important to some of my friends—a wedding, an art opening—but the fact is that I'm just trying to hold it all together, and I can't possibly do it all. Some things have to go. Just remember that at different times in your life, you'll have more or less time, and you'll be able to do other things later. Nothing is forever, so prioritize what matters *today,* and worry about tomorrow tomorrow. It's not selfish, it's *survival.*

Especially prioritize family time. When the baby wakes up, make yourself get out of bed. The baby will make you smile.

Put away your BlackBerry or your iPhone and focus on your family. Giggle, dance, tickle, sing, do all of that. Children know when you're not focused on them. Bryn can already tell when I'm looking at my phone and not her. When I'm focused on her, she giggles and coos and smiles, and when I focus on work, she begins to fuss and looks uncomfortable—and that makes me so sad, to think about how many children grow up without anyone really paying attention to them. They deserve your attention! Let work time be work time, and family time be family time. Also prioritize what's important to you, whether that means making time for your hobby or exercise or cooking or friends, or whatever fulfills you. You have to have something to run on. The more I prioritize family time, the happier I become. It fuels me, and helps me to focus when it's work time.

The fact is that most of us take on too much, we try to do and be everything and that's a killer. I am certainly guilty of this, and then I get to the breaking point. Just remind yourself every day about what's *really* important.

3. Let yourself be happy. Many women beat themselves up all the time, myself included, making ourselves miserable about sleep, body image, men, dieting, or whatever it is. You have to give yourself a break. You can't come together with anyone else if you can't even get yourself together.

Sometimes your sanity is the most important thing and if channel-surfing for two hours will help preserve it, then that is your priority. Regular exercise can make you feel happier, but if you just don't have time, let it go. You'll get back to it soon enough. Sometimes all you need are a few deep stretches and cleansing breaths.

If you can stay calm, play your own game, and appreciate yourself, then you will find time to enjoy the little things in your life. Work when you have to work, then let yourself play. Go to a movie. Go on a date with your husband. Take an afternoon off and hang out with your kids. Bryn and I have "Mommy Mondays" whenever we can.

I'm not always the best at letting myself be happy, and I'm not ecstatic every moment of every day, but I've recognized how much joy there is in the little things, like being there when my daughter wakes up each morning and starts her day with a big smile. Little things like this make me very happy. Embrace them. Let yourself feel them. Do it for you. Everyone who loves you will be happy about it, too, and those little things might just be what get you through the day.

On Breast-feeding

Breastfeeding is a mother's gift to herself, her baby, and the earth.

—Pamela K. Wiggins, author

I'm compelled to say this: Breast-feeding is not the only possible option, and if it's not for you, that is completely fine.

I want to talk about breast-feeding—a nurturing way mother and baby can come together—because I have never felt more tested in my resolve to come from a place of yes. I think many people struggle with breast-feeding, and are afraid to talk about it because so many others are militant about how it's the only possible option. Those people can give the struggling mother terrible *normal noise*.

I do believe it's a good thing to do, if you can. I do believe in its benefits from the perspective of both nutrition and bonding. Ultimately, breast-feeding was right for Bryn and me, but it took some time to get there, and it certainly wasn't easy for either one of us.

Coming together can be difficult, and you have to find a way to do it that works for you. Maybe it won't be breast-feeding. Ultimately, my place of yes was to find a happy medium—*not* to be militant about it, but to do it when I could in whatever way that I could.

That said, I could only sustain it for four months. I would have loved to have gone longer, and I beat myself up about this. I felt guilt and remorse, but realistically, it was all I could do, so that was right for me. You might breast-feed for a year or more, or for just a few months or weeks or not at all. Whatever happens is what's right for you.

Some people feel awkward breast-feeding. It doesn't express their love in a way that makes them comfortable. I believe you shouldn't do things that don't feel right to you. You have to follow your instincts, and maybe choosing not to breast-feed is your place of yes. If that's you, then you and your baby will come together in other ways that can be just as meaningful. There are many, many ways to love your baby and to be a good mother. You have to choose the ones that work in your life—find *your* "normal."

I get annoyed with women who say how easy it is, how effortless, how natural, how it's the only way to feed a baby, even how it should be illegal not to do it! I've been told I shouldn't tell other people that it's hard.

Give me a break. Maybe nobody else wants to say it, but I'll say it, and I'll say it again: breast-feeding *is hard.* It might be natural, but it's definitely not easy for everyone who tries it. Maybe some mothers and babies take to it right away, but most mothers I've asked say that it was a struggle at first, and sometimes a serious struggle. For some new moms, it just doesn't work and there can be any number of reasons that have nothing to do with a mother's desire to do it or commitment to her baby. So we're going to make those poor new moms feel guilty, too, on top of everything else they are going through? Let's not do that.

Babies don't come out automatically knowing how to do it, either. It's something you both figure out, and thank god for the breastfeeding consultant at the hospital who finally grabs your nipple and shoves it all the way into the baby's mouth. That's when you go: *Ohhhh,* so *that's* how it's supposed to feel.

I'm glad I didn't give up. I almost did, but I pushed through it and we found our rhythm. I strongly suggest doing this, if you can, but don't make yourself crazy, either. Breast-feeding is a very emotional process, full of ups and downs. You can feel guilt, joy, rejection, or connection—sometimes all in one day. In the beginning, I breast-fed Bryn pretty much exclusively, so she could get all the antibodies and nutrients that were made for her. Then our breast-feeding time became all about our connection and alone-time together. I feel we developed our relationship during this time and in a really primal way understand each other better because of it—it was how we came together. I think mothers and babies establish an unspoken language through breast-feeding, but it can happen in plenty of other ways.

I know I did the best I could. I came from a place of yes and did it in a way that I felt was right for us. It was my journey. If and when I have another child, it might be the same, or it might be completely different.

Breast-feeding, if you can do it, helps to form a bond and a connection, and you will never get that opportunity back again. It's a very intimate, special time, and you'll remember it forever. When it's over, you'll be glad you did it, but do it your way. Make it work for you. Make it your own. And never let anybody else torture you about it, whether you do it or don't. Nobody else knows what's best for you and your family.

On Being New Parents

Being a father is the most wonderful feeling in the world. If I'm half as good a father to Bryn as my father has been to me, I'll be in pretty good shape. I finally understand what unconditional love really means.

—*Jason Hoppy*

Jason and I learn more every day about how to be parents together, and one of the things I cherish the most about this experience right now is that neither of us has been through it before. We are learning together, day by day. Parenting is not something I do over here and he does over there. It's truly a coming together, a joint effort of bringing up our baby, and every step is a discovery for both of us.

And we love it. We've developed our own silly language at home. We talk about "morning times" and "batheez" and how Cookie is Bryn's "furry big sister." I know, we are so corny, but we don't care. My favorite is when Jason says, "Bryn loves her mommy!" That makes me so happy. It's all very positive. I tell Bryn, "You have the best daddy in the whole world." Talking like this makes everybody feel good. It brings more love into the house, so we don't care how silly it sounds.

We're also learning to be calm, not neurotic, about our baby. She's not made of glass and I don't need to douse everything she touches with antibacterial rinse. When she cries and screams, she's going to be okay, and so am I. I constantly tell Jason, "She's going to live!" I am also reminding myself.

I know now that when we leave town and forget the baby wipes or the baby detergent and we have to wash her clothes in regular detergent, she'll be fine. At first, when I accidentally scratched her with my fingernail, I panicked that I had injured her, but she's strong. She has a survival instinct. In the hospital, they whip those babies around like ducks hanging in a grocery in Chinatown, and you know what? They are all just fine.

Jason and I have also experienced how people feel compelled to give new parents advice. Perfect strangers can get crazy about your business, and sometimes (ahem) in-laws and well-meaning friends will inflict their passive-aggressive opinions about how you are doing it all wrong. Forget about what Pattie Miss Perfect down the street with her three perfectly matching children thinks you should be doing with your baby, as you're wearing your pajamas and slippers and trying to get your kids to school on time.

You should see me on planes when I'm traveling with Bryn. My pants are falling off, my underwear is showing, my hair is flying every which way, and the baby is dangling from my belt loop. I'm Pigpen with a stroller. A walking garage sale. I stare at these women with their perfectly organized strollers and neat little babies sitting upright and shiny, and I honestly have no idea how they do it.

If Bryn's slightly uncomfortable for a few minutes, that's not a crime. We aren't going to leave her in the sun and roast her like a turkey. We aren't going to forget to put warm clothes on her when the weather gets cold, and we're not going to leave her in a cab. We may not always know what we're doing, but we have some instincts and we want to let our baby be herself, too. Other people don't always know best, even the ones who will tell you they raised thirteen perfect children, so new mothers take all that advice with a grain of salt!

My biggest piece of advice about parenting is to worry less and have more fun. We sing a lot at home. We sing Katy Perry's "California Gurls" and joke about dressing Bryn in Daisy Dukes and a bikini top. We make up fantasy parties and tell Bryn that Jay-Z and Beyoncé will come, how even Cookie is invited. It's stupid, I know, but it's delightful to us.

There's a rhythm to being together and to helping an infant find her way in the world. We each need to try and tap into that rhythm so that we are not fighting it but moving in synch with it. It's your family and your home—only you know what will work. If you're having trouble with something, sure, get some advice from someone who knows, but don't be so quick to dismiss your instincts, either.

For instance, recently my doctor told us exactly the way to introduce solid food into Bryn's diet. He said start with rice cereal, but my gut instinct said to start with sweet potatoes and avocados. I'm a natural foods chef, I studied nutrition, and I believe brightly colored foods like sweet potatoes and avocados are a better choice than rice cereal. You should listen to professionals, but you should also trust yourself. If your baby is sick, certainly take her to a doctor, but I'm going to feed my baby in the way that I believe is healthiest. Besides, in my admittedly limited experience, babies tell you what they want. Recently, I was eating guacamole in a restaurant, and Bryn started tapping my arm like she wanted some. I asked for them to bring her a plain mashed avocado, and she ate almost the whole thing. Another time, she wouldn't stop staring at me as I ate butternut squash soup. She wanted some! So I fed it to her and she loved it. So now I know she loves avocado and butternut squash, just like I do. Keep your eyes open and look for the signs. Your baby is communicating with you.

Jason and I have worked out our parenting rhythm, taking turns changing diapers, giving Bryn her bottles, and when it's time for "batheez," I get in the bath with Bryn and Jason sits beside the tub and washes her. We pick up each other's slack, depending on who has to be somewhere or do something. It's our unspoken rule that whoever can—will.

I love how much Jason loves to take care of Bryn. He's the most involved daddy I've ever seen. I couldn't have asked for a better man to be a father to my daughter. She's Daddy's Little Girl and he'll do anything for her. When I see him holding that little peanut against his chest, it makes me want to cry. If Jason had married someone who took over all the parenting and left him out of it, he would have been miserable. I've seen relationships where this happens, where it's all about the mother and the baby, and the father might as well just move out for a couple of years. It's really important for us to do this as a team. It's our place of yes—we're a family and we do it all together.

On Relationship Sex

Sex is emotion in motion.

—*Mae West, actress*

Sex has a whole new dynamic now. When you're thinking about the baby or listening for her cry, it's hard to focus on sex. Having baby-on-the-brain isn't exactly an aphrodisiac. However, sex is crucial. The physical contact between you and your partner helps you feel close and trusting and affectionate. It's a necessary part of any healthy relationship. Even when you don't necessarily feel like it, the bond it establishes is essential. It's one of the things you do for each other, even when you'd rather watch reality TV.

We're working this out. Let's just say that the mandatory post-childbirth celibacy period was pretty rough on Jason, but he's feeling much more content these days. The way he's talking about having another baby, it couldn't have been *that* rough. I'm just saying.

I like to use surfing metaphors, and these days, I think of relationship sex like surfing. Surfing is a schlep, the water is freezing, and you're not always in the mood to paddle out there. You might not have your mind completely on what you're doing—maybe you're thinking about who is doing the carpool next, or wondering whether you turned off the coffee machine, or, in my case, thinking about what to name your next Skinnygirl cocktail. But when you catch the wave, you know why you paddled out there. That long-awaited orgasm will remind you why you came from a place of yes, so try to be present for each other and let go.

On In-laws

The responsibility of married couples to each other involves a total commitment. This means literally "forsaking all others." This not only includes in-laws and parents, but friends, fishing companions, tennis cronies, and so on, for the sake of the marriage.

—Norman Wright, author

I love my in-laws. They are wonderful, good people. I love that Jason comes from such a strongly bonded family, that they have an intact relationship, and that they love me and are thrilled to be grandparents. It's all great . . . except when it isn't.

I can love my in-laws and still like my alone time. Jason's mother loves to chat and hover, and of course Bryn is their first grandchild, so how can they help it? I don't blame them one bit. It's just difficult for me because that kind of attention is not what I'm used to. I have normal noise when it comes to family, but truthfully, I think I'm getting better. Still, I'm not always in the mood to put on a big smile.

The Hoppy family has endured its own tragedies, and I'm sure that taking me on isn't always a picnic for them. I don't always act the way they probably think a daughter-in-law should—at my baby shower, I was going on and on about how Jason was an animal, trying to control himself until the doctor said we could have sex again. Of course, his mother was sitting right there. Oops.

They would probably appreciate someone simpler who lived closer to them and wasn't quite so brash, or someone who lived a quieter life, rather than my crazy, surreal one. Sometimes I say things that might shock them, and they probably wonder what the heck I'm doing half the time, but making peace with your in-laws is definitely part of rule #9 if you are married. Coming from a place of yes means welcoming them, and keeping them both near and just far enough away that our little family unit remains the central core.

Every new family will have these elements—maybe you are best friends with your mother and your husband finds it annoying, or you can't tolerate your mother so it bugs you when your husband is nice to her. Maybe it's his father that's the problem, or yours, or maybe you all get along great but you never get to see them, and that's the problem.

The bottom line is that extended families always pose some difficulties, no matter how wonderful they are. Of course they do—they aren't your family, but now they are, and that's odd in itself, and an adjustment. I've seen plenty of couples who have had a wedge driven between them by in-laws, even well-meaning ones. I'm lucky in the in-laws department—mine couldn't have better, sweeter, with more loving intentions. At the same time, Jason belonged to them for so many years that I'm sure it's hard for them to let him go to a new family. But he's mine now.

You have to come together to make it work. You can do it. It won't happen overnight. It's a process of adjustment. Just stay centered and calm and patient with yourself. It's not wrong that you need your alone time, too. (Maybe I'm talking to myself.) There are always layers and levels to every relationship, and you can't pretend the rest of the world isn't there. Relationships don't exist in a vacuum, and I think it's important to understand and believe that this is *good*.

On Finally Having My Own Family

The house does not rest upon the ground, but upon a woman.

—*Mexican proverb*

I know I'm just at the beginning of this lifelong adventure, but so far I've found that having a family has been bittersweet. It's a coming together, but something I've also realized is that, like it or not, the family dynamic centers around and rests on the woman. She sets the tone, and her energy becomes the family's energy.

It's still strange for me to recognize that this is now my role, and I still play it with some surprise and not complete recognition. Sometimes I look at myself in the mirror and I just have to laugh. Who am I?

I am woman. We do it all, and it's inspiring to see other women do it, and it feels so empowering when I see myself doing it. When I make it work, it works. When I come from a place of yes, the whole family comes from a place of yes. If you are a mother, or even if you *have* a mother, you know what I mean. Sometimes I still feel like it's too much about me—it's my office, my mood, my plans, my cooking, my schedule, my decision about what Bryn should wear, my my my my my.

But, as Jason said, this is my time, and I see that the family revolves around me in a way that makes me feel strong and important and also grateful. My mother's dysfunction was, in many ways, the reason why our family fell apart all those years ago.

The mother can't be afraid. Like it or not, she has to be the strong one. It's not what little girls are necessarily raised to believe, but it's the truth. I see that now. I have to stand up if I want my family to stay together. I'm giving it everything I've got.

In some ways, it's an overwhelming responsibility, but the best part about coming together is that I don't have to do it alone. When

I can't quite muster the strength or the place of yes, for the first time in my life I can truly trust that someone will be there to hold me up and help me and say yes for me. I have to be stronger than ever now, but at the same time, I can be more vulnerable than ever, too. It's a strange but wonderful feeling.

I think that I have more at stake in making a family work than people who take their own happy memories for granted. If this family doesn't make it, then I'm out of luck. It's the only one I've got. I can't pack my bags and go home. I would never want to live without them, and I was totally wrong thinking my career would be enough. Now I realize that *this* is what's important. *This* is what matters. Coming together is being whole. *I needed a family.* I can't curl up at night with my career.

That's why every moment of this life is now precious to me. Every moment with my husband, my baby, my dog—every moment means the world to me. I'm discovering a whole new universe of love that I'd always heard about but never totally believed was out there for me.

So in this way, I've come full circle—from the child of an absent father to the wife of a husband who is present for me in every way, from the daughter of a troubled mother to the mother of a beautiful daughter—and as a mother, I finally feel remarkably free of trouble, myself.

That's why it's so important to me to maintain an unbroken life and an unbroken source of love, security, and routine for my own daughter. All my life, I've resolved to do things differently than my parents did. Now I've got the chance. And I think I can pass this test. I've studied hard. My whole life has been an all-nighter to get this right, even when I didn't know what I was studying for.

On Balance

At times I experience hardship in trying to find the proper point of balance between traditional things and my own personality.

—Crown Princess Masako, Imperial House of Japan

One of the biggest challenges for me in my new life has been to balance it all: family, friends, work. Who needs me most at any given moment? How do I spread the love equally among everyone who deserves it? Balancing is a huge challenge after a major life change—and I've just leapfrogged through a few of them. You might feel like you're white-knuckling it just to keep up with everything, even as you marvel at what you have.

When everything happens at once, when all the planets align like an eclipse and you feel like the whole world has gone dark with the novelty and rarity of what you're experiencing, you have to be very careful. This is the moment when you risk sabotaging yourself. Having it all come crashing down on you in a wonderful, terrible tidal wave is the blessing and the curse of getting what you've always wanted.

Balance is crucial. You need to find a new sense of balance, like learning to walk with a book on your head. It's not just a matter of shifting your schedule around or paying attention to where you are going for the first few steps, then losing your path. It's a matter of shifting your whole *mind* around.

Three days after I came home from the hospital with Bryn, I was working. I had the delusional idea that I would go home and rest, take some time off, take it easy. Ha! What a joke. I went right back to work, because my business demanded it. There was nobody else to do the things I had to do, so I had no choice.

But while I was trying to get back to work, everything was turned upside-down. Cookie and I barely knew what hit us. I had to find time to be a good wife to Jason. I had to find time to be a good mother to Bryn, to breast-feed and bathe and take care of her. I had to find time for Cookie. I had to find time to locate my missing brain. I want everyone in my family to be happy, to give them what they need, to help them be strong and confident and share in my success.

On top of all that, my career was undergoing a major shift, and that required my attention, too. I've transitioned to a new place that requires energy and momentum and maintenance. I'm running several businesses here, and it's not easy.

This is my next big challenge, my next great adventure, and my path into the future: mastering the balance. I can admit I take on too much, and sometimes I teeter on the brink. I've been wearing myself down trying to do it all. I would love to spend all my time giving Bryn and Jason all the love and kisses and hugs they deserve and rubbing Cookie's belly—you never get those moments back, any of them, so don't let them slip away.

Yet, I've also got to keep working, and sometimes that means making things even harder for myself than they could be. I try to live my life as an example for the people who watch my show and read my books. I live by the credo that anything I do, you can do. If I can eat well under pressure, so can you. If I can be moderate and healthy about exercise, so can you. After I had the baby, I didn't hire a personal trainer because I wanted to prove to you that you can stay healthy without one. I did it myself—and so can you.

If I can come from a place of yes in my crazy-busy life, then so can you.

Just as I come together with Jason, and Bryn, and Cookie, and my in-laws, and my television crew, and everyone else in my life, I also come together with *you*. Even if I've never met you, I come together with you as part of my mission. It's who I am. We are all greater than the sum of our parts when we come together.

I'm not being hippy-dippy about it. (You probably won't ever see me wearing hippie sandals and a daisy chain, although I do love my

Uggs.) I'm not perfect—I'm still probably going to throw out the occasional snarky comment in my life, and sometimes, it's bound to be caught on camera. Coming from a place of yes is not about being zip-a-dee-doo-dah, and I'll probably never be someone who wants people around all the time. I'm still me, but I have come to believe in my heart in the power of coming together, because when we stand together, as human beings, we're all stronger than when we stand alone.

Rule #9 will change your life, when you're ready for it. Coming together gives all your striving the meaning you were looking for. It's the culmination of the things you thought you weren't going to be able to do—and then realized you could do after all.

This is the ultimate yes. Find yourself, your own yes, and then come together to find a bigger yes—and you'll find what you've been searching for all this time.

Rule 10

······················

Celebrate!
The Business of Being Happy

Celebrate what you want to see more of.

—Thomas J. Peters

I just turned forty.

I've never liked birthdays. I don't remember most of mine, other than a vague feeling of disappointment. There were a few happy ones I remember, thanks to my stepfather, but I also remember often getting sick on my birthday. My father never called me on my birthday, and I have the same birthday as my mother, so my birthday comes with a lot of baggage. Every year, it comes and goes and no matter how great it is, it always feels like a let-down. My life is so full of ta-da moments, but I never liked "birthday attention." Yet, without it, I always feel like I missed out on something. This conflict has always made me dread my birthday.

However, now Jason says that I have to break that chain, so as I begin to tell you about rule #10, I have to circle back myself and remember rule #1. I have to leave all that birthday darkness behind me because now I have a daughter, and she will get excited about her mommy's birthday, and I don't want to unload my birthday negativity on her.

So I'll start over: I just turned forty!

For me, forty is just a number, but I have to admit that forty is also a moment, a milestone. In some ways, it feels sad to me because I realize that when my own daughter turns forty, I'll be eighty. I don't like thinking about that, but it's my reality.

On the other hand, that's not coming from a place of yes, either. So it's time for me to pull out the final rule of this book, the rule that brings sweetness to life, the rule that can help you come from a place of yes on any occasion, big or small, whether it's your birthday or just any other day in your life. Rule #10: *Celebrate!*

Celebrate!

The more you praise and celebrate your life, the more there is in life to celebrate.

—Oprah Winfrey, actress and host

Milestones have a way of freaking people out. Whatever your milestone, you can choose to get anxious about it, or you can choose to come from a place of yes and celebrate it. Milestones present you with good reasons to breathe and reassess your life. Will you focus on aging—the dark circles, the fine lines, the stress they cause that makes them worse? Will you look in the mirror and feel like a hag as your husband sleeps like a baby because he has no anxiety about getting older?

Or will you celebrate how far you've come, how much you've gained, all the good things you have? Maybe it sounds like a cliché, but if you can make celebrating a real, honest part of your life, then every gain, all your work, will be worthwhile. You can celebrate as much or as little as you want. Make it yours. You decide.

I was fretting to my agent recently about all the things I'm doing and which choices I should make for my business, and he said to me, "Bethenny, this is the time of your life. If you aren't enjoying it, then what's the point?"

He's right. And that's my goal now—the next great challenge of my life: to practice rule #10.

The art of being happy is a tricky, complex, difficult art I have yet to completely master, but I'm committed to it. The truth is, I've never been happier. I'm surrounded every day by my amazing family. Now I just need to learn how to be nicer to myself, and to relax.

I've allowed myself to be loved. Now I have to allow myself to appreciate what I have, to slow down and enjoy it. That is my wish for my birthday and my goal for next year: to learn how to relax and appreciate the wonderful parts of my life. Because what's the point of having everything you ever dreamed of, if you can't slow down long enough to relish it? This past New Year's Eve, we celebrated simply, with a few friends, and there was something so comforting and calm about it. Jason and I remembered so many unpleasant New Year's Eve celebrations from our past, when we were lonely or angry or lost, and we both felt so grateful to be together—it was peaceful and tranquil. It was our way of celebrating.

The business of being happy requires making a conscious choice. People think being happy will just happen to them someday, if only they do this or that right. But it doesn't—you have to choose it. You choose happiness, you don't wait for it to choose you.

You have to choose to celebrate.

Whatever your milestone is, whatever great or terrible things are happening to you or about to happen to you, you always have a choice. You can have anxiety about it, or you can come from a place of yes, and focus on the goodness in the situation, and all the things you've learned and gained and achieved.

Now that I'm in my forties, I can't help but be overcome by waves of gratitude. I feel so lucky to have gotten this far and to be surrounded by my amazing family, work I love, people who care about me.

It's taken me a long time to get here, and if I chose to, I could spend my days worrying about Bryn, worrying about my career, wondering if my marriage will last, stressing about Cookie, and killing myself over every little thing that goes wrong—and there are plenty of little things that go wrong. I still do this sometimes—I'm certainly not cured—but I'm getting so much better.

Instead, I choose to intervene in my own noise and purposefully engage in the business of being happy.

Worry Noise

I'd never worry about age if I knew I could go on being loved and having the possibility to love.

—Audrey Hepburn, actress

If I could change one thing about my younger self it would be this: worry less. Worry is just noise, and it can wreck the best celebration. Yet I still find myself doing it. I worry about whether we should have another child, whether I'm too old, whether it will be too difficult, whether our family is complete or not. I worry about work— will I finish my book on time, can I keep all the stores stocked with Skinnygirl products, can I get to all my rehearsals and appearances, am I overscheduled, am I underscheduled, am I over- or underexposed in the media? What's my next move?

It's all worry noise.

No matter where you are right now, no matter how far along you are on your own path, don't wait to "have it all" to celebrate. You're never going to figure it all out. Make being happy your business, all along the way. Life can't be one long, tough haul, with a little party at the end. What good is that? Life should be punctuated with celebrations and you have to build them into your time because being happy isn't easy. In fact, it's impossible without gratitude and perspective.

If happiness were easy, everybody would feel it all the time, and it wouldn't seem like such an elusive prize. At the same time, it's almost absurd what lengths we go to *avoid* being happy. If good things happen, we may think the big bad thing must be right around the corner, or that we don't deserve the good thing.

I've spoken recently to successful professional women like Rachael Ray and Ellen Degeneres, and they tell me that I really have to learn to be more loosey-goosey about things, and that the key is to make everything simpler.

Happiness takes work, and celebrations don't just happen all on their own, but you can do it.

As you know from sharing my journey up to this point, it took me decades to get to this spot, and there were plenty of times when if you told me where I'd be today, I would never have believed it. It's hard, but like anything else great, it's worth every second of the work to get there. But remember, this should be *fun* work. Make happiness your business. Be silly and sweet and open, and make laughter a priority. Choose to celebrate.

Celebration is life's frosting: isn't frosting the very best part of the cake?

I hope you'll take my advice and follow this rule to the best of your ability, so that you don't waste any time slogging through your days without relief—even if I'm still struggling to follow my own good advice. I know from those moments when I get it right that when you make it your business to be happy, everything takes on a new glow. Everything gets lighter. Rule #10 becomes an item on your to-do list—make it a priority item. When you schedule it like you would any commitment—like your workout or yoga class or healthful dinner—other things begin to fall into place. You tap into your creativity. You feel inspired. You smile more. You worry less.

Make Fun Happen

If you obey all the rules, you miss all the fun.

—Katharine Hepburn, actress

Life isn't always fun, but rule #10 can always make it more fun than it would have been. Whatever it is that doesn't thrill you, find ways to make it fun. Recently, Jason and I were talking about jargon, and how every industry has its own language. In fashion, everything is "chic." In TV, "it's a wrap." Jason works in a very corporate environment, and we began to make a list of corporate jargon: *Circle back, speak off-line, hard stop, run it up the flagpole, I'm out-of-pocket for the rest of the day, 30,000-foot view, where the rubber meets the road, knock it out of the park, shoot me an email, copy me on that, take the minutes of the meeting* . . . by the time we were done, we were laughing so hard we were crying and I was peeing in my pants. We laughed about it for two days.

I posted what we were doing on Twitter, and tons of people twittered more hilarious business jargon. Then they started posting jargon from other industries. One person said they got all of their best jargon from the guy who fixes the copy machine. The next day, Jason couldn't wait to get to work and get on a conference call so he could listen for more jargon to add to our list. It helped Jason to conquer the Monday blues.

And what about holidays? What a perfect excuse to celebrate.

It's become so important to our family to celebrate every little thing. We make a big deal about holidays, and every chance we get we celebrate. I used to ignore victories because I was too busy moving on to the next thing, but even if it means ordering a glass of champagne at lunch to celebrate finishing a book or some other business success, Jason and I have vowed to make space in our lives for that.

When I was on *The Ellen Degeneres Show* while doing *Skating with the Stars* last year, Ellen gave Bryn an adorable little skating dress and ice skates, so we decided to build our Christmas card around it. We went to the costume department and Jason put on my partner's skating outfit, I put on one of my outfits, Bryn wore the outfit from Ellen, and we even smuggled Cookie in (no dogs are allowed in the building), because we can't possibly have a Christmas card without Cookie. We draped her in sequins, and that was our Christmas card. We loved it. It was *us*.

Make the most of every moment. Get excited about every little thing. Why not? Why not have your wonderful moment of excited anticipation? Why not be happy *now*? This is my greatest challenge, but something I'm pouring my heart into: learning how to enjoy what I have, right here, right now. Every moment is precious and although sometimes I struggle to see it, I see it more and more every day.

On a recent trip to Montreal, Jason and I were shopping in a Christmas Wonderland store. Jason asked why I was buying a snow globe. He said, "You're forty years old, what do you want with that?" I've always wanted one, so why not buy a beautiful snow globe? Every day I look at it, and it makes me happy.

Last year we had what we hope will be the first of many hideous ugly Christmas sweater parties.

Celebrate the way you want to celebrate. The night before my fortieth birthday, I had a birthday party—and a meltdown. It wasn't the way I wanted to celebrate. So I wanted to spend the next day quietly with Jason, getting massages and having lunch, taking a bath and having a romantic dinner and going to bed early, so that's what we did. It was wonderful. At night, we even made the bath into a pool party. We put on our bathing suits, and brought Bryn and even Cookie into the bubble bath. It was so much fun. Do what's right for you, but whatever way is right, do it—celebrate your life. You deserve it.

Last Halloween, we all dressed up like a family of pandas. I've always loved Halloween, and I always made a big deal about what my costume would be. For the first time this year, it wasn't just about me. It was a family decision. What would *we* be?

So we went with pandas, and it was definitely a challenge. We had to wear these big giant panda heads. Jason said I should be a "hot" panda, so I put on a belt and high-heeled boots, but as we went out to trick-or-treat, the heels started buckling and my pants started falling down. I was doing the panda walk of shame, I was a hooker panda. Poor Bryn was getting hot and she had black fake panda fur all over her, and she was getting fussy in her panda suit, because of course she had no idea that we were out trick-or-treating. And although we even put Cookie in a panda suit, I'm not sure she was particularly happy about it.

But this is all part of celebrating. Despite all the trouble, I think we looked so cute, and it was worth the effort and the pictures. We are committed to the celebration, to making the most of these moments in our lives. It doesn't have to be a holiday—you can celebrate anything.

I used to be someone who couldn't wait for the next thing to happen. I would count the days until the next big event, whatever it was, ignoring the now. Lately I never count the days, because each day is so full and precious. That's one way I've truly changed.

Sometimes a celebration is just about a simple thing—about staying home and baking cookies and snuggling. Sometimes the simplest things are the purest and truest and most real. A good sound sleep, a great meal, and a quiet evening with family can equal the best day ever. Spend your time on what really matters to you. Keep your word. Take risks, but take responsibility. Don't waste your time, money, or words. Do happy things. And *celebrate*, all the way through the ten rules in this book.

With this in mind, here's a recap for you, so you can keep the ten rules for coming from a place of yes in your mind and in your heart as you move forward and on with your life from here:

1. Break the chain. Your past happened, and it's part of you, but you don't have to carry forward the bad habits, bad feelings, and ideas about who you are from that part of your life. Break the chain and celebrate coming into your own as an adult who is in control of your own life. What happens from here on out is entirely up to you.

2. Find your truth. Only you can know who you want to be, what you want out of life, and what the right path for you could be. Investigate yourself, your true desires, what feels right to you. Listen to your gut and celebrate who you really are, apart from anyone else's expectations. Knowing your truth will make every decision in your life easier.

3. Act on it. *You* make things happen. Don't wait for someone else to make them happen for you. Act on your beliefs and instincts and the things you know about yourself. Don't just sit there—*do something*. Forward is always the right direction, even if you aren't sure where you are going, as long as you act with integrity from a place of yes.

4. Everything's your business. You never know what could become your next big break. Do everything to the best of your ability, give every job your all, and treat everything like it's your business. Respect others, play fair, do what feels right, and always keep both eyes open for what might be your next great path. That way, you won't miss an opportunity.

5. All roads lead to Rome. You won't always know what's over the horizon, but you will get somewhere good if you stay focused on what you want. Even when something bad happens, you're likely to see why it happened later. Everything you do leads to something else, and in the end, if you stay on your path, you'll get to the place you wanted to be—even if it isn't what you expected. It's probably going to be even better.

6. Go for yours. You have to get what you want before you can have the inner resources to give to others. Clarify your goals and then go for them. It has to be about you first. It's not selfish. It's common sense. It's the only way to be whole.

7. Separate from the pack. To find your calling or succeed in the path you've chosen, sometimes you have to step out of the crowd and remember who you are. You'll distinguish yourself, and you'll have a much better view of where you are going. When the way gets crowded or obscured, stand up, step forward, and move away from the masses.

8. Own it. Keep your word, act on your beliefs, and whether you regret something or not, always own up to it. You did it. Admit it, even when it's hard. It's the only way to maintain and build your integrity, not to mention your good reputation. You'll never have to regret that you didn't cop to the truth, and owning it always turns out for the better in the long run.

9. Come together. When all is said and done, life is about connection. Come together with others. They may be work colleagues or family or the partner you've chosen to share your life. No matter who they are, get yourself right first and then you'll be able to come together to do something even greater together.

10. Celebrate! Life is precious. Love is precious. Celebrate the many good things you have instead of focusing on the worries, and you'll find success, inner calm, and happiness at last.

Live Happily Ever After

Promise me you'll always remember: You are braver than you believe, stronger than you seem, and smarter than you think.

—Christopher Robin,
to Winnie-the-Pooh (A. A. Milne)

I feel like I have license to quote Winnie-the-Pooh now that I'm a mother, and the above quote is exactly what I want Bryn to grow up *knowing*, not just believing. This is what it's all about: driving your own life, even when you have to floor it, speeding in the opposite direction from where you started out. You can choose to be successful, you can choose to be great, you can choose to be happy. You can choose love.

It's all up to you. You are in charge. It's your life. Don't hand the wheel over to anybody else. Take responsibility for *you*, and the rest will fall into place.

Even if it doesn't happen until you're forty. Or fifty. Or any age at all.

On my birthday, I choose to make happiness my business. I choose to celebrate—when the cameras are on, and also when they are off. I choose to be a wife, a mother, a businesswoman, an ice skater. I choose to love where I am right now. I choose to dance with Jason and with Bryn and even with Cookie. I'm older and wiser and better because of the path I've traveled, and I choose to be grateful for that. I have a family now, and that makes every day a day to remember. I choose to remember.

So take what you want to take from this book. I hope it has helped guide your path. You have been an inspiration to me, and I hope I have returned the favor.

To come from a place of yes is everything this book is about—it's the jewel in the crown. I hope you'll remember all the rules in this book, but they are all arrows pointing to this one pinnacle concept. Come from a place of yes, and someday, maybe sooner than you expect, what you really wanted all along will come rolling into your life.

If you watch my show, you know by now that it is no longer called *Bethenny Getting Married?* All the question marks in my life have fallen away. Now it's called *Bethenny Ever After*, because that's how I'm finally living.

Because of a place of yes.

You come, too. We can all live there—happily ever after.

Acknowledgments

Thank you my faithful and loyal fans. For you, I never gave up on this book and dug to the depths of my soul to share with you my experiences. Without your support, I wouldn't know that any dream you can dream is possible. Thank you for accepting and embracing me for exactly who I am. It has made me strong enough to tell my story. This book is my heart. This book is my soul. This book is my life.

Thank you to Julie Plake, my tireless warrior of an assistant. The word assistant doesn't come close to describing what you do and how important you are and have been. You've kept me sane (or attempted to) and personify coming from "a place of yes."

Brian Dow, thank you for supporting me, understanding me, obsessing with me, and sharing my vision. You are a unique individual and for that I am grateful.

I would like to thank Zachary Schisgal, Stacy Lasner, and Marcia Burch for your endless efforts to make this and all of my books a success. And everyone at Touchstone, thank you for your incredible support throughout my entire writing career. You gave me independence and autonomy and allowed me to be me and tell my story my way. There is no greater gift you can give to a writer.

Thank you to Maggie Gallant. You and your team define coming from "A Place of Yes" and have helped me to get here in so many ways. There is no I in team.

Eve, my dedicated writing partner. Without your patience, your calm nature and ability to write at one hundred miles an hour, we wouldn't be where we are today. I've enjoyed making this journey together. Thank you for trusting me throughout.

Cookie: you are my first baby, Bryn's furry sister and my best friend. You were my family when I had no one and no idea who would take care of me. Thanks for sitting by my feet during every moment of my life.

Bryn, my bumble bee: you are my beautiful gift, the little girl I knew in my heart that I wanted and needed. You showed me what it meant to really love someone more than you could ever dream of loving yourself. You showed me how to break the chain. You are my heart.

Jason: you changed every aspect of my life forever. You showed me that true love and being taken care of is emotional and not material. You taught me how to share and be a partner. You taught me how to love. You have fulfilled the dream I never imagined possible by giving me the family I have always wanted, a family of my own. Thank you for supporting me every second of every minute of every day. I could never be where I am today without you. All of my dreams began to come true when you entered my life. I love you with every ounce of my being and I am finally home.